EDMUND HUSSERL
AND THE PHENOMENOLOGICAL
TRADITION

STUDIES IN PHILOSOPHY
AND THE HISTORY OF PHILOSOPHY

General Editor: Jude P. Dougherty

Studies in Philosophy
and the History of Philosophy   Volume 18

Edmund Husserl and the Phenomenological Tradition

Essays in Phenomenology

edited by Robert Sokolowski

THE CATHOLIC UNIVERSITY OF AMERICA PRESS
Washington, D.C.

LIBRARY OF CONGRESS CATALOGING-IN-PUBLICATION DATA
Edmund Husserl and the phenomenological tradition : essays in
    phenomenology / edited by Robert Sokolowski.
        p.   cm. — (Studies in philosophy and the history of
    philosophy ; v. 18)
    Includes index.
    ISBN 978-0-8132-3080-1
    1. Husserl, Edmund, 1859–1938.   2. Phenomenology.
    I. Sokolowski, Robert.   II. Series.
    B21.S78 vol. 18
    [B3279.H94]
    100 s—dc19
    [142'.7]   87-38181

Gratitude is expressed to
THE EXXON EDUCATION FOUNDATION
for its support of the series
which made this volume possible

Contents

Introduction

Edmund Husserl's first published work, *Philosophy of Arithmetic,* appeared in 1891, almost one hundred years ago. We are therefore approaching the end of the first century of the philosophical movement that he originated and called by the name of phenomenology. Husserl himself flourished during the first fifty years of that century, Heidegger's star predominated from the late 1920s to the middle 1970s—also a period of some fifty years—and the more recent decades have seen this philosophical style and doctrine taken up by many diverse thinkers and commentators and applied to ever new fields of thought.

The movement inaugurated by Husserl has been philosophically and culturally fruitful. Much significant work was done under the rubric of phenomenology itself, and subsequently the forms of thinking called existentialism, personalism, hermeneutics, structuralism, linguistic formalism, and more recently deconstructionism grew up within the horizon set by phenomenology; now the relations between phenomenology and both cognitive science and artificial intelligence are being investigated.

The essays in this collection are meant to illustrate the richness of Husserl's own work and the variety in the tradition he began. All but two of the papers were originally given in a lecture series at The Catholic University of America in the Fall of 1985, sponsored by the School of Philosophy and directed by Dean Jude P. Dougherty. The essays represent commentaries on Husserl's own work, studies of other figures in the phenomenological tradition, comparisons between Husserl and writers from other philosophical periods, and applications of Husserl's methods and doctrines to new areas in philosophy, science, and art.

Thus the essay by Rudolf Bernet, "Husserl's Theory of Signs Revisited," explores Husserl's understanding of signs as it is presented in *Logical Investigations* and as it is modified in some manuscripts from 1914; all this is done in the light of questions raised by Jacques Derrida concerning Husserl's idea of signs. John Barnett Brough, in "Art and Artworld: Some Ideas for a Husserlian Aesthetic," makes use of

Husserl's theory of life-world to clarify what makes an object to be an art object; he joins Husserl's ideas to current interpretations of the nature of a work of art. Richard Cobb-Stevens's essay, "Hobbes and Husserl on Reason and Its Limits," engages the current distinction between two ways of taking reason, as calculative and as presentational; Hobbes reduced reason to reckoning but Husserl is able to restore a power of intuition to reason. His restoration of reason as intuitive can be considered a critique of the empiricist tradition of Hobbes and Hume. Steven Galt Crowell, in "Husserl, Lask, and the Idea of Transcendental Logic," interprets both Lask and Husserl as reacting in different ways to Kant; they each develop transcendental logic as a theory of the conditions of possibility of knowledge, but Husserl is able to give a better account of the role of subjectivity and of the special point of view from which philosophy carries out its investigations.

John Drummond's paper, "Realism *Versus* Anti-Realism: A Husserlian Contribution," analyzes many logical and epistemological themes in Husserl, in the light of issues raised by Frege and his followers. The essay by Dagfinn Føllesdal, "Husserl on Evidence and Justification," draws comparisons between Husserl and Nelson Goodman, John Rawls, and Willard Van Orman Quine, it makes some comments about Husserl's thoughts concerning ethics, and it argues against an interpretation that would make Husserl a "foundationalist" philosopher. "Truth and Freedom," by Karsten Harries, is an interesting revision of the common interpretation of Heidegger's concept of truth; Harries shows that Heidegger, in his later thinking, restored a measure of correspondence as essential to the understanding of truth, and did not remain with unconcealment as the single and primary sense of truth. Patrick A. Heelan compares Husserl and Hilbert on their understanding of science in "Husserl, Hilbert, and the Critique of Galilean Science"; his paper is significant not only as a contribution to the philosophy of science, but as a contribution also to the history of science and philosophy during the first half of this century.

The essay by J. N. Mohanty, "Husserlian Transcendental Phenomenology: Some Aspects," discusses ways in which Husserl's philosophy can come to terms with relativism: not by resorting to dogmatic counter-assertions, but by showing how various points of view can come to mutual understanding, and by bringing out dimensions in the activity of knowing that must be shared by all points of view. Maurice Natanson's "The Strangeness *In* the Strangeness: Phenomenology and the Mundane," makes use of Husserl's technical analysis and of Henry James's story "The Beast in The Jungle" to clarify the difference between a look and a stare, to clarify what it is to perceive and what it is to be a self who carries out perception. Thomas Prufer, in "Heidegger, Early and Late, and Aquinas," reflects on themes in Heidegger and criticizes three of Heidegger's interpretations: his reading of Plato and his restriction of Plato to the doctrine of forms; his reading of medieval notions of creation, essence, and existence; his reading of Husserl's doctrines of the self, temporality, and the interplay of presence and absence. In "Husserl's *Ideas* and the Natural Concept of the World," John Scanlon discusses the special character of phenomenological reflection and examines the world as seen from the two perspectives of the natural attitude and the phenomenological attitude. He also provides a historical study of Richard Avenarius, whose concept of the world served as a foil for Husserl's thoughts on these issues. The paper by Robert Sokolowski, "Moral Thinking," attempts to describe the categorial form and the identity-synthesis appropriate for moral action. It makes use of Husserl's concepts of intentionality and categoriality. The contribution of Elisabeth Ströker, "Phenomenology as First Philosophy: Reflections on Husserl," discusses the various senses in which Husserl claims that his phenomenology is "absolute" knowledge and a "foundational" science, and how it can be called "first philosophy," questions which are of special interest for the current debate about "foundationalist" aspects of philosophy; this essay deals with themes that are also treated, from another point of view, in the paper by Føllesdal.

I am grateful to Steven Galt Crowell and John Drummond for contributing essays to this volume. I also wish to express my thanks to Jude P. Dougherty for his work in organizing the lecture series on which this book is based, and for his help and encouragement in bringing this volume to print. My thanks are also due to Daniel J. McInerny for helping prepare the index.

R.S.

1   Husserl's Theory of Signs Revisited

RUDOLF BERNET

Husserl's theory of signs is best known under the form it was given in the First *Logical Investigation,* which is entitled "Expression and Meaning." A renewed interest in this early text of Husserl was created by the publication of Derrida's *Speech and Phenomena.*[1] In this careful and yet impetuous interpretation of Husserl's First Investigation, Derrida is especially attentive to the hidden presuppositions and problematic consequences belonging to Husserl's phenomenological approach to the sign. The determination of the sign in the First Investigation is made a test case against which to measure the philosophical ambition, method and anticipatory decisions guiding Husserl's entire phenomenological enterprise.[2] Such an interpretation seems somewhat arbitrary so long as one does not prove: (1) that the First Investigation actually offers Husserl's most typical and most systematic account of the sign; and (2) that the sign must be understood as a condition of phenomenality allowing phenomena to show themselves rather than as a particular phenomenon.

These two questions also indicate what is at stake in the present essay. On the one hand I want to show how a few years after the publication of the First Investigation Husserl criticized and thoroughly modified the analysis of the sign he had offered in his earlier text. On the other hand it will be shown that this important progress in the description of the sign is due principally to a progress achieved elsewhere, that is to say in the phenomenological understanding of inter-subjective empathy, of the ideality of linguistic meaning, of intentional acts of will, desire, tendency, etc., and eventually also in the

---

1. J. Derrida, *Speech and Phenomena. And Other Essays on Husserl's Theory of Signs.* David B. Allison, trans. (Evanston, 1973).

2. Cf. R. Bernet, "Differenz und Anwesenheit. Derridas und Husserls Phänomenologie der Sprache, der Zeit, der Geschichte, der wissenschaftlichen Rationalität," *Studien zur neueren französischen Philosophie. Phänomenologische Forschungen,* vol. 18 (1986), pp. 51–112.

understanding of the phenomenological reduction and of its relation
to acts of phantasy. The sign thus appears to be a non-independent
object of phenomenological investigation; it gathers many other phenomena and it therefore can possibly be taken as revealing phenomena and their phenomenological apprehension rather than as being a
particular phenomenon itself. This dependency on the phenomenological analysis of other phenomena and this disclosure of the foundations of phenomenology itself is something the sign has in common
with temporality.[3] With regard to Derrida's critical interpretation of
the First Investigation, we must examine not only whether Husserl's
new theory of signs meets the critique Derrida has addressed to the
former theory, but also whether this improved account of the sign is
due to any radical change in the understanding of the phenomenological method and of the primary object of phenomenological endeavor.

Husserl's new theory of signs was developed in the year 1913 and
even more fully in 1914, shortly after the publication of Book I of the
Ideas. The best of Husserl's work in this period was devoted to a revision of the *Logical Investigations.* This led to the publication, in 1913,
of a second edition of Parts I and II/1 of the *Investigations.* The revision of Part II/2, which contains the Sixth Investigation, quickly
grew out of proportion and led both to a thorough correction of the
original text and to the writing of four new and independent texts.
These four texts are entitled: (1) "Expression and Sign" (*Ausdruck und
Zeichen*), (2) "Modification of Emptiness" (*Leermodifikation*), (3) "Possibility and Consciousness of Possibility" (*Möglichkeit und Möglichkeitsbe-
wusstsein*), (4) "Evidence and Truth" (*Evidenz und Wahrheit*). While the
second edition of the Sixth Investigation appeared in 1921, the four
separate texts just mentioned remained unpublished.

These four texts, together with complementary unpublished materials from the same period, are expected to be published shortly in
Volume XX of the *Husserliana,* entitled *Logische Untersuchungen: Ent-
würfe zur Umarbeitung der VI Untersuchung. Texte aus dem Nachlass, 1911–
17.* The volume will be edited by Felix Belussi. Text (1), "Expression
and Sign," grew out of a revision of the first sections in Chapter One
of the Sixth Investigation. It develops a new theory of the sign, often
in the form of a direct criticism of the doctrine of the First Investigation. This new theory of the sign is worked out also in a more thorough and yet more fragmentary way in many of the complementary
texts to be published in Volume XX of *Husserliana.* My presentation of

3. Cf. R. Bernet, "Einleitung," in E. Husserl, *Texte zur Phänomenologie des inneren Zeit-
bewusstseins (1893–1917),* R. Bernet, editor (Hamburg, 1985), esp. pp. XIV–XVI.

Husserl's new theory of signs is based mainly on these complementary texts and, to some extent, also on text (1), "Expression and Sign." Both series of texts will be referred to as "Texts of 1914."

My presentation of these "Texts of 1914" is by no means complete and my discussion of their philosophical contribution is often inspired by questions which are foreign to Husserl's own preoccupations. My wish is to awaken the reader's interest in these very important texts rather than to present him with a close commentary and interpretation of texts which, unfortunately, are not yet available to the public. The fact that I want to confront the "Texts of 1914" with the First Investigation, published in 1901, and with Derrida's discussion thereof has imposed further limitations on my research. I hardly pay any attention to the fact, for example, that in Husserl's mind the phenomenological investigation of the sign belongs to the larger context of the intentional reference to an object or state of affairs, and also to the context of doxic modalities and degrees of intuitive fulfillment of this intentional reference. My interest therefore focuses more on the relation between the sensuous sign and its meaning rather than on the truth-value of a meaningful sign.

However, such an analysis of the meaningful sign understood as relation between (sensuous) signifier and (spiritual) signified bears highly rewarding results and is already more than one can reasonably expect to treat in an article. Husserl looks at this relation between the sensuous sign and its spiritual meaning from different perspectives: he investigates the difference between genuine signs and mere indications, between lingual and non-lingual genuine signs, between a communicative and a solitary use of lingual signs; he also describes how the apprehension of a sensuous sign leads to the apprehension of its meaning in virtue of a passively undergone tendency and of a pregiven familiarity with a linguistic code; and he eventually examines the appearance of the sensuous sign-phenomenon or sign-token, its real or fictional presence, its givenness together with an ideal sign-pattern or sign-type. My own contribution to all this consists mainly in repeatedly and untiringly questioning the standpoint from which, and the light in which, Husserl looks into all these phenomena.

1. WHAT IS A SIGN?

Surprisingly enough, Husserl's First Investigation does not approach in direct fashion the question concerning the nature of the sign as such. Husserl rather begins his investigation by contrasting two sorts of signs with one another: *expressions* (*Ausdrücke*) and *indica-*

tions (*Anzeichen*). In *Speech and Phenomena* Derrida takes both the incapacity to directly approach the nature of the sign as such and the decision to start from a dual opposition between two sorts of signs to be inspired by metaphysical presuppositions. According to Derrida the sign is a "trace" of other signs, a substitute for a presence out of reach, and it therefore irremediably eludes the appropriation by a Metaphysics of Presence. Quite to the contrary, Husserl's distinction between two sorts of signs and his worshipping of expressions are said to fit into a strategy which takes signs to be faithfully mirroring representatives of the inner presence of the meaning and of the outer presence of the intentional referent. This network of Derrida's interpretation is rather wide-meshed but I think that it does catch some of the hidden metaphysical presuppositions in the way the First Investigation understands the nature of the sign (and mainly of the linguistic sign). To find out whether the new theory of the sign elaborated in the "Texts of 1914" still falls prey to such a deconstructive interpretation is one of the tasks I pursue in the following investigation. The main task, however, remains to account in detail for the refinements of Husserl's theory of the sign without making it all a matter of presence and absence alone.

A careful reading that is not a mere hunt for so-called metaphysical, dual oppositions discovers that not only the "Texts of 1914" but already the *Logical Investigations* actually distinguish at least three sorts of signs: (1) *natural signs* such as "fossil vertebrae indicating the existence of prediluvian animals"; (2) *non-lingual artificial signs* such as "marks" (e.g. "a flag," "a brand") and "memorial signs" (e.g. "the much used knot in the handkerchief"); (3) *lingual artificial signs* which are called "expressions." Non-lingual artificial signs (=2) and lingual artificial signs (=3) have in common the capacity to signify (*Bezeichnen*). Natural signs (=1) do not signify and therefore are not to be taken as "genuine signs." The *Investigations* say that only those signs signify which are "deliberately brought about" and this remark still guides Husserl's further investigation into the function of signifying in 1914. The texts of 1901 and 1914 also agree on calling natural signs (=1) "indications" and lingual artificial signs (=3) "expressions." Basically, they agree about the determination of how both, indications and expressions, work, although the texts written in 1914 are much more explicit in explaining this.

The only fundamental disagreement concerns the non-lingual artificial signs (=2) such as signals, marks, memorial signs, etc. The *Logical Investigations* call them "indications," just like the natural signs (=1) and furthermore pretend that both sorts of signs are related in the same way to what they stand for. The "Texts of 1914," on the contrary, call these non-lingual artificial signs (=2) "genuine signs," just like the lingual "expressions" (=3), and furthermore explain that both have a common (although differentiated) way to "signify," that is, to "point to" (*Hinweisen*) the signified, to what they mean. This disagreement seems to be due mainly to the fact that the *Logical Investigations*, out of epistemological and metaphysical prejudices, consider only lingual expressions (=3) to function as genuine signs. In 1914, the non-lingual artificial signs (=2), far from being taken as indications, function as paradigmatic cases for all genuine signs including the lingual expressions (=3). Both texts, however, basically agree about the functional characteristics of indications and genuine signs and about their difference. This is what I want to begin with.

The First Investigation gives a precise definition of the relation between the *indicative sign* and what it indicates: ". . . Certain objects or states of affairs of whose reality someone has actual knowledge indicate to him the reality of certain other objects or states of affairs, in the sense that his belief in the reality of the one is experienced (though not at all evidently) as motivating a belief or surmise in the reality of the other" (§2). In indication, the sign and the signified are *naturally* tied together, whether for physical reasons (when the smoke indicates fire) or for psychological reasons (when, to take an example from Nabokov, through habitual association the perception of a particular person's face always makes me think of a cow's udder). The *Logical Investigations* mainly stress the element of *motivation* which leads from the perception of an empirical thing (taken as an indicative sign) to the *belief* in the *existence* of another empirical thing or state of affairs. This motivation of a belief is said not to be based on evidence; that is, it is based on no cognitive evidence, on no logical inference or necessary relation (§3). In the most common cases the motivation leading from an indicative sign to what it indicates is based on physical causation (perception of smoke leading to belief in the existence of fire) or on an underlying physical identity (perception of fossil vertebrae leading to the belief in the existence of prediluvian animals).

In 1914 Husserl mainly stresses that in indication one is led *directly* from the sign to the signified, i.e. not *via* a meaning-intention. One immediately sees or notices B when seeing A (*Daran-ersehen, daran-merken*). Natural signs (=1) are the best examples of such indications and if "natural" means that a sign refers without any deliberate meaning-intention, then all indications can be said to be natural signs. In this sense the "expression" of a face can also be said to be a natural sign (i.e. an indication), and even a sign that is artificially brought about can become a natural sign when its meaning vanishes. Contemporary linguists usually are not willing to take natural signs to be signs, because in a sign the signifier and the signified are interdependent in a strong, necessary way, while in a natural sign the signifier is an object of its own and consequently it can be grasped independently of what it signifies (e.g. the smoke without the fire). Natural signs cannot be taken to be genuine signs because the signifier and the signified are in a relation that is physically too close (natural interdependence) and significatively too loose (significative independence). It is for similar reasons that Husserl too, both in 1901 and in 1914, consistently refuses to consider natural signs (indications) to be authentic signs, because their referring does not have the form of a meaningful signifying.

What is this "meaningful signifying" proper to all genuine signs? It first means, negatively, that genuine signs do not signify or significatively refer in virtue of any natural, physical, or psychological link between the sign and its referent. They signify, as one text from 1914 states, without any material basis (*ohne jede sachliche Unterlage*) or, as we could also say, without any *fundamentum in re*. In the case of indications, quite to the contrary, the relation between the indicative sign and its referent has such a *fundamentum in re*, and the indicating is materially founded (*sachlich begründet*).

Genuine signs—and this is their second, positive determination—signify (*bezeichnen*) on the basis of a deliberate decision, on the basis of a will. This will, which is responsible for the signifying proper to genuine signs, actually encloses two decisions. The first decision amounts to a deliberate reference to something, whether in the form of a thought, a memory, or a phantasy. Genuine signs refer to their objects in virtue of an intentional act which Husserl calls their meaning-intention or "significative intention." The second decision consists in deliberately making a sensuous object function as a meaningful sign. Genuine signs, in virtue of an arbitrary personal will or on the basis of a commonly shared conviction or code refer to their meaning. Husserl says that genuine signs refer or "point" (*hinweisen, hinzeigen*) to their meaning in virtue of a "signitive intention" and refer to their intentional object in virtue of a "significative intention." Genuine signs emerge from the combination of both decisions; they "significatively" refer to their intentional referent by means of a "signitive" "pointing" to their meaning. This twofold intention, this indirect referring is common to all genuine signs. Besides lingual signs, the texts from 1914 list many other sorts of genuine signs: (a) *memorial signs* (e.g. the knot in the handkerchief which I use to remember—as one of Husserl's examples runs—that I want to be a better man); (b) *marks* (e.g. a scarf that helps people to recognize each other as supporters of the same soccer team); (c) *signals* (e.g. a rotating yellow light on the shore of a lake which tells me that a storm is imminent and that I should return to the harbor with my boat).

All these examples of genuine signs have in common the intentional reference to a state of affairs *via* a meaning and only in virtue of a meaning. This meaning, in its turn, being the meaning of a genuine sign, intentionally refers *via* a sign. Husserl regards the meaning as the decisive component of a genuine sign and therefore usually presents the sign as a medium or as an instrument through which the intentional referring of a meaning is accomplished. Thus a handkerchief helps to keep present my former decision that I should remember to become a better man. However, since a sign signifies only in virtue of its meaning, one can also consider the meaning as a medium through which a sign intentionally refers to what it signifies. To put it more precisely, one must say: (1) that in all signs the sign refers *via* the meaning and the meaning refers *via* the sign; (2) that "referring *via*" has a different sense in both expressions: when a sign refers *via* a meaning, then the meaning provides the sign with an intentional reference; when a meaning refers *via* a sign, then the sign provides the meaning with a sensuously recognizable presence. According to Husserl this is made possible because the sensuous presence of the sign points (*hinweisen*) to the meaning ("signitive intention") and the meaning intentionally refers to the object signified ("significative intention"). I shall not enter further into Husserl's phenomenological analysis of the intentional reference and the truth value belonging to this meaning.[4] In the following I shall rather confine myself to a study of the relation between the sensuous sign and its meaning under two correlative aspects: (1) the bestowing of meaning upon a sensuous object which thereby becomes a sign; (2) the experience of a sign and of its pointing to the meaning. Both aspects are given a new and rich development in the texts from 1914, and the following considerations are based mainly on these texts.

To bestow a meaning upon a sensuously given object or, to put it otherwise, to create or to use a meaningful sign is the result of a *voluntary decision*. This was already emphasized in the *Logical Investigations*

---

4. I have dealt with both problems in two earlier articles: R. Bernet, "Bedeutung und intentionales Bewusstsein. Husserls Begriff des Bedeutungsphänomens," *Studien zur Sprachphänomenologie. Phänomenologische Forschungen*, vol. 8 (1979), pp. 31–64; and R. Bernet, "Logik und Phänomenologie in Husserls Lehre von der Wahrheit," *Tijdschrift voor Filosofie*, vol. 43 (1981), pp. 35–89.

within the limits of the treatment of lingual signs or "expressions." In his interpretation of the First Investigation in *Speech and Phenomena,* Derrida underlines this voluntary character of the meaning-intention which gives birth to a meaningful expression. He therefore suggests calling the meaning-intention a "will to say" (*vouloir-dire*). With the extension of the class of genuine signs to memorial signs, marks and signals—an extension proper to the texts from 1914—we can say also that memorial signs have their origin in a will to remember, that marks have their origin in a will to make something recognizable as such and such, that signals have their origin in a will to draw attention to something and to make people behave accordingly. This will is responsible both for bringing about a sign and for this sign's pointing in a definite fashion to its meaning. The arbitrary or conventional nature of the genuine sign and its signifying function are both rooted in the same creative will.

In the revised version, from 1914, of the first chapter of the Sixth Investigation, Husserl goes so far as to understand this will in analogy with the kinesthetic "I can." A speech act or an act of writing is just another form of a voluntary bodily movement, an action proceeding from an inner decision and carried out in the outer world. To call the lingual sign the expressive body of a meaning is thus more than just a metaphor for Husserl. Husserl moves here on grounds that Merleau-Ponty has made familiar to us, but seemingly without quite giving up the underlying metaphysical dualism between the spiritual meaning and the physical sign. The expressive will, however, builds a "bridge" between them; it both bestows meaning upon a sign and makes the sign point to its meaning. For Husserl to deliberately create or use a meaningful sign is equivalent to making the sign point to its meaning. He says that to the will (*Wollen*) to make a sensuous object signify corresponds necessarily the obligation (*Sollen*) to turn from the sign to its meaning. This will is usually a will belonging to a person or to a community of persons. Following the pointing from the sensuous sign to its meaning goes along with the awareness to obey a request or a demand (*Zumutung*). We shall see later, however, that especially for lingual signs this will can become an impersonal, anonymous one, and the ensuing obligation may become "unconscious," obeyed in the form of a "blind, habitual tendency."

The experience of a meaningful sign, like the expressive will bringing about a meaningful sign, has both a sensuous and a spiritual aspect which are closely tied together. The spiritual aspect is what both the First Investigation (§10) and the texts from 1914 call the *pointing* (*Hinzeigen, Hinweisen*) of the sensuous appearance to the meaning.

The texts from 1901 and 1914 also agree about the fact that, in virtue of the dominance of this pointing, a sensuous object is not experienced any longer as an autonomous object when it becomes a sign. Husserl's notion of the sign seems almost to coincide with the function of signifying (*Bezeichnen*) and as a consequence he usually prefers to call the sensuous object a "sign-phenomenon" (*Zeichenerscheinung*) rather than a sign. This sensuous sign-phenomenon has the property of catching one's interest, not for its own sake, but for the sake of the meaning to which it points. The experience of the sensuous sign-phenomenon is a "medium," an "instrument" which opens access to the meaning. When the First Investigation states that the word "excites" (*erregt*) a meaning-conferring act (§10), it means something which is directly opposed to the Lockean meaning of this vocabulary. Far from being caused by the material occurrence of the word, the meaning-conferring act is an independent spiritual entity which finds in the experience of the "word-presentation" (*Wortvorstellung*) merely a sensuous "support" (*Stütze, Anhalt*).

This conception of the relation between meaning-intention and sensuous sign leads to a progressive dematerialization of the sign. The First Investigation already hesitates as to whether the sensuous sign is the object of a genuine act of intuitive presentation or not. On the one hand, this seems to be the case, since the meaning-intention is said to be an act founded on another act in which the sensuous sign is experienced (§23). On the other hand, one also finds the following remark: "The word remains intuitively present . . . but we no longer intend it, it no longer properly is the object of our 'mental activity'" (§10). The latter conception is the one which the texts from 1914 consistently develop. These texts insist that the sign is a mere medium experienced not in an objective presentation that terminates in it, but rather in a "medium-intention" (*Intention als Mittel*). What counts is the preservation of this function as a medium and not the physical existence of the sensuous sign. In the later course of our investigation we shall come across another instance of Husserl's dematerialization of the sensuous sign, namely the contention that in certain cases the *phantasy* of a word suffices to accomplish the act of speech or of verbally articulated thought. Husserl's dematerialization of the sign has the consequence that the determination of a meaning through the way different signifiers "horizontally" refer to each other in a "chain of signifiers" or in a con-text is not taken into account. This dematerialization of the sign and the ensuing blindness toward a contextual form of meaning-production are due to a strong *logical* and *psychological* interest which makes Husserl practically reduce the sign to the function of signifying, and to reduce this function itself to an indirect intentional act of consciousness. In contrast, Heidegger's *ontological* approach to the sign in §17 of *Being and Time*, even if it remains a mere outline without any special consideration of lingual signs, does not miss the phenomenon of contextuality.

Husserl emphasizes that the marginal or transient awareness of the sensuous sign is intimately linked with its "pointing" to the meaning. In 1913 this pointing is also called the "significance" (*Bedeutsamkeit*, not to be confused with the *Bedeutung*) of the sign. It is basically what makes the sign "signify" (*bezeichnen*). Again, Husserl stresses that this pointing of the sensuous sign to the meaning is not an independent intentional act but rather a mere tendency or an "intention of transition" (*Übergangsintention*). As such it is dependent on both sides (*zweiseitig unselbständing*): on the experience of the sensuous sign-phenomenon and on the performing of a meaning-intention. Through its pointing the sign-phenomenon leads to the meaning, but without making it present in the form of an object. Thus, the pointing is not properly an intentional act, not even a non-thematic intentional awareness of a horizon. But how then must this pointing, this "combination-form" (*Verbindungsform*), this "intentional layer" (*intentionale Schicht*) be determined? Husserl says that this pointing to the meaning is a "tension" (*Spannung*) one undergoes when experiencing a sign-phenomenon. This tension results in a "tendency" to turn to the meaning and it is "released" (*entspannt*) when the meaning of the sensuous sign is attained.

The experience of a sensuous sign is thus linked with the experience of a "demand" (*Zumutung*). Here, Husserl comes very close to the doctrine of the contemporary French linguist Todorov, who describes a signified which is referred to by the signifier in the experience of a "lack" (*manque*) which awakens a tendency.[5] As it is well known, Lacan takes this lack of and search for meaningful objects to be proper not only to the experience of lingual signifiers but also to the working and articulation of unconscious desires. What differentiates Husserl from both Todorov and Lacan is, however, that he pretends that this experience of a lack or of a demand has its origin in a subjective *will*. A sensuous sign is deliberately bestowed with a meaning in such a way that the experience of the sensuous sign demands its meaning-complement. In Husserl's own terminology: To the "will" (*Wollen*) to express a meaning in a sensuous sign corresponds the ob-

5. T. Todorov, "Signe," in D. Ducrot and T. Todorov, *Dictionnaire encyclopédique des sciences du langage* (Paris, 1972), pp. 131–38.

ligation that this sensuous sign should (*Sollen*) point to its meaning. Put in another way, the pointing of a sign derives from a meaning-intention which goes together with a "will to say." Such a way of deriving the "significance" of a sign from a former voluntary decision to express a thought by means of a sensuous sign is certainly problematic in the case of the lingual sign. We shall see later, however, that Husserl's position is more subtle and that, in the case of lingual signs, he distinguishes between different ways in which one can undergo and satisfy a demand in the sensuous experience of a word.

This analysis of the different elements entering into the experience of a genuine sign, as it is carried out in the text from 1914, often uses *memorial signs* as typical examples. This is not surprising at all because memorial signs illustrate nicely indeed how a genuine sign (e.g. a knot in the handkerchief) is brought about by a will (to remember such and such) and consequently leads to the recognition of this particular will whenever it is experienced. In memorial signs just as in the understanding of all other genuine signs we have a "significative intention" (intentionally referring to an object or state of affairs) intertwined with a "signitive intention" (pointing to the meaning of the sign-phenomenon) and we have also an arbitrary sign, deliberately brought about, which functions as a medium allowing this meaning-intention to be expressed or understood. What is surprising rather is that the First Investigation considers memorial signs, signals, and the like to be indications instead of genuine signs.

It is true, as Husserl convincingly observes in 1914, that genuine signs are used as mere indications when their meaning-force vanishes. We are all familiar with traffic signals which through repeated use become directly referring indications, and we all fall prey to labels which are not meant to provide any information about a particular sort of product but just indicate directly a consumer's paradise. But this is not what Husserl has in mind when he regards memorial signs, signals, marks, etc. as indications. The reason for this must be sought in the fact that the *Logical Investigations* consider to be an indication whatever is not a (lingual) expression. In such lingual expressions the sensuous sign and the meaning belonging to it are much more intimately linked than in the case of memorial signs and the like. According to *Logical Investigations* there is a strict parallelism between the articulation of lingual signs and meaning, between grammatical forms and forms or categories of thought. This parallelism almost amounts to a fusion when the First Investigation says that there is only one lingual sign (or rather one combination of signs) which can adequately express a meaning: ". . . It is the one, uniquely adequate way of expressing . . . its meaning" (§11). No knot in a handkerchief can ever dream of serving its meaning so well and thus making itself absolutely irreplaceable!

2. LINGUAL SIGNS

The texts written in 1914 are remarkably attentive to the distinction and difference between non-lingual genuine signs and lingual genuine signs. This difference is occasionally given a terminological fixation in the form of the distinction between the (non-lingual) "signum" and the (lingual) "verbum." The *Logical Investigations,* quite to the contrary, neglect this difference and thus also the specificity of lingual signs, because they blankly identify genuine, i.e. meaningful, signs with lingual expressions. "Expressions," according to the First Investigation, result from the *will* to sensuously *express* and communicate a *thought* about something primarily by means of speech (§5). Such lingually expressive, sensuous signs not only signify in virtue of a meaning, they also form an intimate unity with their meaning. Husserl says that in this case the sign and its meaning are "phenomenally one" (§5) and I would add that they are also formally and even logically one. "*Phenomenal* unity" means that meaning and sensuous word are given together and experienced as forming a unity which is not fortuitous but necessary. Husserl is, of course, aware of exceptional cases where we have a word and are still searching for its meaning. Such cases, however, do not harm his thesis that the unitary joined presence of word and meaning forms a minimal condition for all meaningful speech. Such an understanding of the meaningful sign presupposes a strict correspondence between the inner presence of meaning and its outer re-presentation by the word.

It becomes particularly questionable whether such a correspondence can be found in language when one moves from words to larger fragments of discourse or text. According to Derrida's analysis, such a correspondence is typical of a "Metaphysics of Presence" insofar as it starts from a metaphysical opposition between inner and outer reality and understands this distinction in terms of different modes of presence. Husserl actually goes beyond this *phenomenal* unity and states that there is a formal or *logical* unity between word and meaning. Such a thesis is at work in Husserl's contention that elementary logical forms of meaning (e.g. the subject of a predicative sentence) are mirrored in elementary grammatical forms of lingual signs and that all combinations and modifications on the grammatical level must have their correlate (and even their foundation) in the logical forms of thought or meaning. Such a strictly isomorphic correspondence between meaning and lingual sign can be taken as faulted where lingual signs allow for a further analysis into more elementary particles than does the corresponding meaning. To phonemes for example there correspond no correlative meaning-elements; but this does not imply that they are meaningless, as Husserl, by virtue of his thesis, is forced to conclude.

This parallelism or isomorphic correspondence between meaning and word can be shown to rest on metaphysical grounds when it is related to the even more basic thesis concerning a pretended parallelism between the logical forms (or categories) of thought and the ontological forms of actually existing objects. Real objects owe their formal-ontological articulations to the formal-logical categories of the thought which intentionally refers to them. In language this intentional referring is accomplished by means of lingual signs, and these lingual signs therefore must faithfully mirror the logical forms of the meaning which makes them refer to real objects. In such an "ideal language" the isomorphic correspondence between the lingual signs and the real object to which it refers rests on the primacy of the logical forms which are mirrored by both, the ontological forms and the lingual forms.[6]

Distinguishing between "signum" and "verbum," between non-lingual and lingual genuine signs, the "Texts from 1914" also devote more attention to what distinguishes lingual expressions from other sorts of genuine signs. This further determination of lingual signs does not, however, change much with regard to Husserl's notion of an ideal language as it was at work already in the *Logical Investigations*. In the later texts, the main emphasis lies on the development of the insight that all lingual signs are "categorially formed." This insight can be understood, on the one hand, as a further explication of what the *Logical Investigations* state about an isomorphic correspondence between expressive signs and their meaning. On the other hand, this insight is developed also in the framework of Husserl's new analysis of the nature of genuine signs. In the first approach of the properly lingual sign one is led to a new investigation concerning the formal correspondence between the expressive sign and the object expressed, especially in the case of perceptual judgments (*Wahrnehmungsurteil*). This new analysis of the categorial articulation of both the lingual sign and the signified objective referent is carried out together with a new

6. For a further analysis of this system of correspondences underlying Husserl's understanding of language, cf. R. Bernet, "Logik und Phänomenologie in Husserls Lehre von der Wahrheit," pp. 72–89.

⌐ description of the synthesis of fulfillment. This is not particularly surprising, since lingual signifying is said to attain its full "realization"
only in intuitive fulfillment. We cannot develop this point any further
in the context of this paper,[7] because we have deliberately excluded
the examination of intentional reference and its possible intuitive
fulfillment from our scope.

What we can easily do, however, is to develop the second approach
where the specificity of the lingual sign is brought out in contrast to
other forms of genuine signs. In all genuine signs the experience of
the sensuously given sign comprehends two elements that are inseparably linked: the awareness of the sign-phenomenon and the awareness of its pointing to the intentional meaning. The specificity of *lingual* genuine signs manifests itself in both elements: (1) Already the
sensuous sign-phenomenon bears the trace of a categorial formation.
This categorial articulation is visible from the fact that a word is always noticed in function of other words. Punctuation for example
seems to me to be such a categorial form proper to the lingual sign-
phenomenon. (2) The pointing of a lingual sign-phenomenon also
and even more obviously comprises categorial forms. In my opinion
this is to say, for example, that a lingual sign-phenomenon points both
to "its" meaning and beyond it to other meanings yet to be expressed.
The pointing proper to a lingual sign-phenomenon has an associative
and discursive form and it bears, more than in the case of other signs,
the trace of an awareness of a lack in all presentations of meaning,
and consequently also the trace of a desire to go on writing, reading,
listening, speaking. . . .

Husserl says that instead of pointing directly, as other genuine signs
do, the lingual sign-phenomenon points in a categorially articulated
mode. If pointing is an "intention of transition," it follows that the categorial formation of pointing is dependent on the categorial forms of
both the sensuous lingual sign-phenomenon and the spiritual meaning. Lingual pointing or signifying must be categorially formed, because a lingual meaning-intention refers to an object in a determinate
or qualified way. Lingual statements never simply denote an intentional referent; they always present objects *as* being such and such. It
is obvious, however, that Husserl understands this categorial articulation of the object expressed by a lingual expression in terms of a logical rather than of a lingual articulation. It is the meaning-intention

7. These questions have been carefully investigated in R. Parpan, *Zeichen und Bedeutung. Eine Untersuchung zu Edmund Husserls Theorie der Sprachzeichens.* Unpublished
doctoral dissertation (Heidelberg, 1984). The author of the present article owes many
valuable insights to Parpan's work.

which logically articulates the intentional referent and which thereby allows for categorially formed lingual expressions about this object. The categorially formed pointing of a lingual sign-phenomenon derives from the categorially formed "will to say" and from the logical articulation of what one wants to say.

Another difference between the treatment of lingual signs in the *Logical Investigations* and in the texts from 1914 is that the later texts explicitly distinguish between an "active" and a "passive" signifying, for example, between writing and reading. Surprisingly enough, these texts also stress that passive signifying, instead of being just a consequence of active signifying, is rather a necessary moment in the constitution of a lingual sign. "*Active signifying*" (*aktives Bezeichnen*) can mean both: the originary creation or institution (*Stiftung*) of a meaningful lingual sign and the deliberate production or use (*Erzeugung*) of such a sign in order to express and communicate a thought, a wish, etc. What the *Logical Investigations* call an "expression" originates in such active signifying. In 1914 Husserl still maintains that in this case meaning or at least the "practical intention" to produce a meaningful sign precedes the lingual expression. This chronological *and* logical anteriority of meaning concretely has the form either of a thought still in search of an adequate expression or of a vague meaning-intention which finds its fully distinct articulation only in a subsequent verbal expression.

Turning now to "*passive signifying*," one can, in a way, take it to be just the consequence of active signifying. This is the case in lingual exchange or communication where something needs to be said or written before one can understand it. In understanding or passive signifying the attention of the listener or the reader first goes to the sensuous sign which serves as a medium allowing for the grasp of the meaning. In personal communication this pointing or turning from the sensuous sign to the meaning is the result of a "practical demand": the speaker wants to be understood and therefore asks the listener to take the sensuously experienced sign in such and such a way, as bearer of such and such a meaning. In the texts from 1914, Husserl, however, insists that despite this priority of active signifying in actual communication, one can also speak, on a more fundamental level, of a priority of passive signifying or, as he sometimes calls it, "reading taken in a large sense." It remains true that, in the last resort, all signifying has its "origin" in an active institution of a meaningful sign, but it is also true that without the passive understanding of the meaning of this sign, the constitution of the sign remains incomplete. I think that with this remark Husserl acknowledges that genuine signifying must allow for both recognition and intersubjective communication. Only a sensuous sign with a meaning that can be understood, recognized and communicated functions properly as a genuine, i.e. a meaningful, sign. A meaningful sign needs to be the same in active and passive signifying, and this sameness or identity of the meaningful sign is first constituted when the (active) institution of the sign is followed by its (passive) understanding. This entails a priority of passive signifying insofar as every active signifying which has the form of speech or writing presupposes that one already understands the meaningful sign one uses. The facticity of language precedes and allows for all lingual acts. Thus Husserl holds: The intention to speak presupposes a reproductive consciousness of a signifying, and this reproductive consciousness refers backward to an originary consciousness of signifying which is a *passive* understanding of the sign and not an active signifying or speaking.

Coming from Husserl, this is indeed a remarkable claim. Neither the *Logical Investigations* nor most of what has been written about Husserl's philosophy of language ever since has prepared us for what looks like a hermeneutical turn in Husserl's work. I do not think, however, that what is introduced here should be taken as the outlines of a new phenomenology of language which would contradict the analysis of the *Logical Investigations*. It seems rather to me that Husserl here investigates for the first time the background which allows for what the *Logical Investigations* state about the subjective will to speak and its expression or realization in language. Husserl does not turn away from his understanding of speech acts as voluntary acts and even as actions with a practical purpose or "demand." He rather states that such a deliberate lingual action comes out of an underlying, passive familiarity with language. Nor does Husserl turn away from his understanding of speech acts as acts originating from a subject. He rather suggests that the subject making a statement always already is part of a social community sharing the same lingual signs. Finally, Husserl does not even give up the idea that there must be such a thing as an origin of language. However, he carefully distinguishes between creating lingual signs and using them according to their original meaning in order to produce a statement. To speak meaningfully one must understand what one says, one must correctly use a pre-given language instead of arbitrarily shaping a new, private one. To speak (*sprechen*) is always to repeat another's words (*nach-sprechen*) for one's own sake. For Husserl it is always a subject which speaks, but it speaks and realizes the goal it pursues when speaking by making language speak through itself or even in its place.

In a way, Husserl thus shows himself to be prepared to accept Heidegger's statement that it is language itself which speaks (*Die Sprache spricht*). This is the case when, as Husserl says, it is not a person but the sensuous lingual sign which demands of itself that one turn to its meaning (*das Zeichen mutet mir rein von sich aus zu*). This demand of the lingual sign, however, still addresses itself to a person or at least to a subject which can understand it. Husserl also insists that this anonymous demand by a sign must not be taken to be the most fundamental way in which lingual signs signify. Far from revealing the true nature of language, this case rather derives from the more basic case where, in active signifying, the sensuous sign-phenomenon is made to point to its meaning by a speaking or writing subject. In such a case understanding, the turning from the sensuous sign to its meaning goes together with the awareness that one does so and must do so in order to meet the speaker's will expressed by means of this sensuous sign.

This happens in those forms of lingual communication in which one person actually addresses another person with the practical demand to pay attention to what one wants to say. More common, however, is the case of lingual communication in which one understands a statement, that is, in which one turns from the sensuous sign to its meaning, without being explicitly asked to do so by the author of the statement. The turning from the sensuous sign to the meaning has here the form of a "blind tendency" which seems to be based on the familiarity one has with the correct use of a system of meaningful lingual signs. According to Husserl this blind tendency, however, goes together with and derives from the implicit awareness of a somewhat personal demand. Husserl says that this is shown first by the fact that this tendency is not a mere being-carried-away by the sign (*blosses Fortgezogensein*), since it includes also the implicit awareness of an obligation that does not originate in the sensuous sign itself. Husserl's second argument in favor of the implicitly personal character of the demand made by the sensuous lingual sign is that whenever one understands a spoken or written statement, the understanding goes together with an implicit and possibly entirely indeterminate reference to its author.

I think there is little to object to in Husserl's first argument if the argument is taken to emphasize that a lingual sign is a sign with meaning. It is true, indeed, that the signifying and intentional referring of a lingual sign is not a matter of associative contiguity or resemblance. A sign which leads directly to the signified without any understanding of what it means is an indication rather than a genuine sign. The problem with the first and especially with the second argument is whether, in order to understand the meaningful signifying of a sensuous word, sentence, or text, an implicit awareness of the author is required. I do not doubt, of course, that there is no spoken word where there is no speaker, and that there is no text where there is no author. I think, however, that the interest in the speaker or author, as implicit as it may be, is a matter of the causal origin of the spoken word or of the text rather than a matter of understanding its meaning. Husserl's position presupposes that there are no other forms of active signifying than those originating in a personal demand.

I would say, to the contrary, that in most cases active signifying—and also most understanding thereof—is impersonal. Our ordinary way of speaking and listening, writing and reading, is often just a matter of giving in to the requirements of a linguistic code, of a literary genus, of a habitual chain of words. In these cases lingual signs are used meaningfully, but we are spoken by language rather than speaking it. One could object that what Husserl had in mind was not chatter but scientific speech, in which one is personally responsible for what one says and understands. But if "science" means "objective science," then, as Husserl has also taught us, it is impersonal. In science it is nobody rather than somebody, it is science rather than the scientist who speaks. In objective science, statements are said to be true in virtue of the objective states of affairs they refer to rather than in virtue of the personal credit the speaker enjoys. Only the language of transcendental phenomenology, "transcendentalese," as Thomas Prufer and Robert Sokolowski call it, is a form of language which both is scientific and originates in subjective responsibility and thus in a subjective mode of actively and passively signifying.

The insight that most speech acts are impersonal does not, of course, exclude the existence of *personal* speech acts as well. Likewise the insight that many forms of communication are impersonal does not exclude the existence of *personal* communication. *Personal communication* relies on the exchange of personal speech acts, more precisely, on an exchange between active and passive personal signifying. In this case too, the texts from 1914 improve remarkably on the analysis proposed in *Logical Investigations*. The First Investigation takes personal communication to be the normal function of lingual expressions (§7). Such lingual communication is more than a speaker showing the correct use of a lingual sign to the listener, or a listener showing the speaker that they both share the same linguistic code. In lingual communication the speaker also intends more than just bringing about a modification in the behavior of the listener or calling into existence a new state of affairs. He strives to be understood by the listener in what he says and expects an agreement or disagreement concerning whether what he says is correct or not. Lingual communication presupposes both the will to make oneself understood and the readiness to understand what the other wants to say. The sensuous lingual sign is not given in exactly the same way to the speaker and the listener (Husserl says that in the listener the grasp of the sign precedes the grasp of the meaning and that in the speaker the grasp of the sign follows the grasp of the meaning), but it must be actually and materially present to both of them. It is by means of physical signs that lingual communication is made possible, that the speaker's active signifying and the listener's passive signifying can be made to share the same meaning.

So far the First Investigation and the texts from 1914 agree in their description of personal, lingual communication. Their disagreement concerns the analysis of how the sensuous experience of a physical lingual sign allows the listener to understand what the speaker wants to say. According to the First Investigation, this sign serves the speaker to "intimate" (*Kundgabe*) what he has in mind and allows the listener to grasp what is thus intimated (*Kundnahme*) (§7). What is problematic in this analysis is mainly Husserl's contention that in such an intimation the lingual sign functions in the manner not of a genuine sign but of an indication. It is obvious, however, that the speaker's words neither make the addressee notice directly what they refer to nor do they make him believe, by way of causal inference, in the existence of some mental process going on in the speaker's mind. It is obvious also that if this happened, it would not count as an understanding of the speaker's statement by the listener. Instead of proving this obviously strange analysis to be wrong, one needs rather to come to understand how Husserl could ever take it into consideration. I think that the reason for this is that according to the *Logical Investigations* a lingual sign, which cannot signify without being present physically, and whose significance does not proceed from a directly accessible will to speak, must be an indication rather than an expression. This is the case in verbal communication, where the physical presence of the sign is required to grant access to the speaker's mental states. For the listener, the perception of the physical lingual sign and the grasp of the meaning-intention from which it proceeds are not "phenomenally one," and this is to say, according to the *Logical Investigations*, that their conjunction appears to the listener in the form of an indication rather than of an expression.

The strange analysis of personal lingual communication in the *Logi-*

cal Investigations is the consequence of a lack of means to do better. The "Texts from 1914" are more faithful to the phenomena, because Husserl now employs better means. The new means are: (1) a clearer distinction between indications and genuine signs, and (2) a new phenomenological account of how we become aware of other subjects' mental states. Signs which are not "expressions" in the sense of the *Logical Investigations* can still be genuine signs and even genuine lingual signs, according to the texts from 1914. Passive signifying is as good as active signifying, and in lingual communication it even enjoys some priority: in order to address someone meaningfully, one must be familiar with the language one uses, one must be a member of a group sharing the same lingual idiom, and one must also care about how one is to be understood. In passive signifying the sensuous sign is given prior to its meaning, and in passive signifying occurring in the context of personal communication, the sign must be given physically, that is, in an act of perception. In this case, the perceived sensuous sign-phenomenon points to a meaning-intention and this meaning-intention is understood both as to its ideal meaning and as to its origin in someone else's life.

The second form of understanding, the awareness of another subject's mental states, is what the texts from 1914 call "empathic understanding" (*einfühlendes Verstehen*). The physical sign allows the listener to receive the intimation (*Kundnehmen*) of the speaker's meaning-intentions, but this reception is a form of "empathy" (*Einfühlung*) rather than a form of indicating or natural motivation of belief. A physical sign which must exist (in order to allow for communication) must not therefore directly motivate the belief in the existence of what it refers to; it must not become an indicative sign. The physically existing genuine sign remains a genuine sign, that is, a sign with a meaning. In intersubjective communication the understanding of this meaning goes together with the empathy into or "appresentative representation" of (*vergegenwärtigende Appräsentation*) somebody else's meaning-intentions. Here Husserl puts to work his new analysis of how we understand our fellow-subject's mental processes, an analysis first developed in a course given in 1910–11 (see *Husserliana* XIII, No. 6). Personal lingual communication of meaning or, more precisely, understanding someone else's meaning-intentions, is made a particular case of "empathic re-presentation" (*einfühlende Vergegenwärtigung*).

This new account of lingual communication was made possible by the new insight that a lingual sign continues to genuinely signify even when its physical existence is required. However, this does not mean that *the physical existence of the sensuous sign* is always necessarily required to allow for its genuine signifying. Genuine signifying is not a property of a really existing object, it is a "functional character" referring from the sensuous sign or signifier to the signified. According to the texts from 1914, this functional character realizes itself in a twofold mental process: The actual signifying of a genuine sign requires an actual awareness of a sensuous sign-phenomenon and also of its pointing to the meaning and to the meaningfully intended object. Such an actual signifying can take place even where the sensuous sign does not really exist, i.e. where it is not given in the form of a perceptual object (and also where the intentional object significatively referred to does not exist). For a signifying actually to take place, it is enough that a sensuous sign be intuitively given, regardless of whether it is in perception or phantasy. There is no actual signifying left, however, when not only the sensuous sign but also the meaning-intention which makes it signify is a product of phantasy.

The difference becomes clear at once when one considers the following examples: I can mutely speak to myself or silently think in lingual terms. When I do so, I produce words without uttering any sound or writing any letter. Husserl says that in such a case signifying is actually taking place, but that the lingual signs which are made to signify by the silent speaker have no physical existence. Since, however, they have to be present somehow, these signs are said to be present in phantasy. This is to say that I actually speak or think by means of lingual signs which do not really exist. I work with phantasied words, or rather with sound-patterns and letters whose sensuous appearance I just imagine. It makes quite a difference when I do not actually speak to myself but rather just imagine that I speak to myself or to someone else. In this case, I work with phantasied words too, but just in imagination, without putting them to work in an actual signifying. Soliloquy consists in actually speaking to oneself by means of actually phantasied words and not at all in phantasying that one speaks to oneself.

The analysis of soliloquy offered in the First Investigation is utterly confusing, because it neglects this distinction and presents soliloquy as a form of signifying in which "one merely conceives of himself as speaking and communicating" (§8). A second reason for discomfort with the way soliloquy is presented in the *Logical Investigations* is, of course, that soliloquy is made a privileged or "pure" form of lingual expression. This is obviously a consequence of the fact that the *Logical Investigations* consider lingual communication to include an indicative use of lingual genuine signs. Husserl says we have purely expressive signs only in soliloquy, where lingual signs are given in phantasy instead of existing materially. With the new analysis of the lingual sign and of communication developed in 1914, there is no reason any longer to give priority to phantasied signs over really existing lingual signs or to soliloquy over lingual communication. On the contrary, so-liloquy, just as all other forms of active signifying, presupposes that one belongs to a social group communicating by means of a com-monly shared lingual idiom. With this new analysis of the lingual sign, of communication, and of soliloquy, it also does not make much sense any longer to prove, as Derrida does in his critical interpretation of the *Logical Investigations,* that in soliloquy just as in allocution expres-sive and indicative signs remain "entangled" (*verflochten*). Soliloquy and allocution both work exclusively with meaningful lingual signs (i.e. "expressions") and these cannot be taken to be "indications" with-out losing their meaning altogether. It is true, however, that Husserl does not give enough credit to the material presence of the lingual sign (e.g. in a con-text) and to its capacity to produce a meaning which does not derive from a personal will.

According to Husserl's analysis, a phantasied sensuous sign and a really existing sensuous sign are equally well prepared to function as a support (*Anhalt, Stütze*) for an actual meaningful signifying to take place. Signifying as a function realized in a mental state, the sign as possibly a product of phantasy—is this not to say that Husserl's new theory of the lingual sign falls prey to plain psychologism? The an-swer to this question must clearly be negative. It is easy to show that just as logical psychologism was crushed by Husserl's analysis of the ideality of meaning, lingual or semiotic psychologism is overcome by what Husserl calls the *"irreality" or even the "ideality" of the sensuous lin-gual sign.* The First Investigation already emphasizes the ideality of the sensuous expression, without, however, making clear how some-thing can at the same time be both sensuously given and ideal (§11). The ideality of meaning and the ideality of the sensuous lingual sign both refer to their capacity to be identically recognized in different circumstances and by different persons. "Ideality" is an epistemologi-cal rather than a metaphysical category; it means identity recognized in different circumstances rather than a mode of being which is sepa-rated from real being. Sensuous signs are "ideal" or "irreal" if they always function in the same way and are recognized or assumed to do so. Sensuous signs must be "ideal" or "irreal" in order to point to the same meaning in different circumstances and for different persons. There arises, however, a difficulty in understanding how a sensuous sign, at the same time and in the same respect, can be both ideal-iden-tical and factually individuated, irreal and empirically existing. This is why contemporary linguistics distinguishes between the sign as a "type" and the sign as "token." Different empirical signs or "tokens" can be recognized as pointing to the same meaning insofar as they are recognized to be the same; that is to say, recognized as instances of the same ideal sign or "type."

The "Texts from 1914" deal with this ideality of the sensuous sign much more carefully than do the *Logical Investigations*. They differentiate clearly between the logical ideality of meaning and the properly lingual ideality of the sensuous lingual signs. They also distinguish different levels in the ideality of the lingual sign. The invariance of a sensuous pattern is a first form of ideality and it can best be illustrated by the case of a phoneme whose identity remains unaffected by the variance of the pitch, force, etc. of the physical sound. Another form of ideality is reached when a word is taken to be the same whether it is given in oral or in written form. With regard to the ideality of the lingual sign the most difficult question however concerns the relation between the sensuous sign *qua* empirical "token" and *qua* ideal "type." On this question too, the texts from 1914 shed new light. In opposition to the *Logical Investigations,* the relation between "type" and "token" is no longer understood to have the form of a relation between an essence and its individual instance. Husserl now argues that just as no abstract universalization is required to grasp an ideal meaning,[8] so the sensuous type too is reached without submitting manifold sensuous "tokens" to a process of eidetic variation. The ideal "type" of a sensuous word does not exist in itself, independently of an empirically given, individual "token." Rather, it is grasped at once whenever a concrete sensuous sign is experienced. The ideality of the sensuous sign thus appears as a minimal requirement for the meaningful signifying of lingual signs rather than as the consequence of a metaphysical approach to language. Metaphysical presuppositions do play a decisive role, however, in Husserl's account of the isomorphic correspondence between the categorial articulation of the sensuous lingual sign and of the intentionally referring meaning. But this is a matter which concerns ideal language and not the ideality of lingual signs.

Again and again, the anticipation of ideal language, and the understanding of logical thought it presupposes, have appeared to guide Husserl's approach to the phenomenon of the sign. Despite the substantial progress accomplished by the "Texts of 1914," these texts share and even develop further the hidden presuppositions of the

---

8. The position of the *Logical Investigations,* in which the identity of a meaning is assimilated to the logical form of a species as essence, is criticized by Husserl himself as early as 1908; cf. R. Bernet, "Bedeutung und intentionales Bewusstsein," pp. 48–58.

First Investigation. Thus, even though the "Texts of 1914" deprive
Derrida of some of his arguments, his main charge is given new evidence. Signs continue to function as an extension of self-present, voluntary thought. The refinement of Husserl's analysis of the sign para-
doxically makes it more and more difficult to understand the positive
contribution made by the sign: if the materiality of the sensuous sign
is reduced to its phenomenological appearance, if this appearance of
the sensuous sign is understood as a mere support of its pointing to
the meaning, if this pointing to the meaning is said to depend on the
structure of the meaning-intention, and if this meaning-intention is
understood as an act of intentional and possibly also categorial representation of an object, then the sign cannot present intentional thought
with anything original. It can at best help to preserve and transmit
thought, but it does not, as Kant said of the symbol, give rise to thought.
It is a mere instrument in the hands of self-centered thought.

When he tries to get hold of the origin of language and when he
locates this origin in logical thought, Husserl abandons the grounds
of a properly phenomenological approach to language. Despite the
many valuable and lasting results to be found in Husserl's analysis of
the signitive relation between the signifier and the signified, the manifold modes of appearing of the sign are neglected in favor of a construction of the logical function and the mental use of the sign. Husserl's account of the sign both opens and closes a phenomenological
interrogation of the logos pertaining to the phenomenon of language
and of the way in which language discloses other phenomena.

2	Art and Artworld: Some Ideas for a Husserlian Aesthetic

JOHN BARNETT BROUGH

A few years ago, Edward Cone, a composer and Professor of Music at Princeton, suggested that a moratorium be declared on the use of the terms "art," "artist," and "work of art."[1] The contemporary art scene, he argued, is just too muddled and anarchic to permit meaningful application of the terms. In 1929, at the age of twelve, Professor Cone saw for the first time Matisse's "Blue Nude" in his Aunt Claribel Cone's apartment in Baltimore, and experienced a different kind of bewilderment.[2] He knew that Matisse's painting was a work of art; he just did not know how to appreciate it. Later he learned. But what is one to make of certain phenomena in the contemporary artworld? Is a person gnawing on himself in front of a television camera a work of art? Do written instructions for drawing a geometrical figure on a wall make a work of art? Is the building of a fence, running 24.5 miles across Sonoma and Marin counties in California, and then straight into the Pacific Ocean, a work of art? Nor do such questions apply only to recent *avant garde* art: it is just as reasonable to ask them about some of the seminal creations of the early twentieth century. The "readymades" of Marcel Duchamp would be a case in point. Duchamp's readymades, the art historians tell us, were immensely influential in shaping the aspects of the contemporary artworld that Professor Cone finds so disturbing. The readymades are artifacts such as a bottle dryer, a bicycle wheel, a snow shovel or, most notoriously, a urinal, plucked from the context of ordinary practical life and set down on the "planet of aesthetics"[3]—placed, for example, in an

1. Edward T. Cone, "One Hundred Metronomes," *The American Scholar* (Autumn, 1977), p. 453.
2. Edward T. Cone, "Aunt Claribel's *Blue Nude*," *Art News*, Vol. 79, No. 7 (September, 1980), pp. 162–163.
3. *Marcel Duchamp*, edited by Anne d'Harnoncourt and Kynaston McShine (New York: St. Martin's Press, 1977), pp. 196–197.

exhibition of conventional objects of art, and given new titles: the snow shovel called "In Advance of a Broken Arm" (1915), the urinal titled "Fountain" (1917), and so on. But are these readymades works of art, and if they are, why?

Professor Cone suggests that we decline to answer such questions directly. Better, he says, to call these items or activities just what they are, and refuse the title "artist" to their producers, instigators, or perpetrators, instead naming them after the activities they have undertaken: thus Vito Acconci would be a "self-masticator," Sol Lewitt a geometer, Christo a fence-builder, and Marcel Duchamp someone who signs his name to, and dates, useful artifacts made by others.

What is interesting about Professor Cone's proposal is not its content but what it suggests about the contemporary state of the philosophy of art. If the world of artists and works of art is complex, confused, and perplexing, so too is the philosophical world which is supposed to understand it. Professor Cone implies that philosophy cannot do what it has traditionally sought to do: find and formulate in a definition the essence common to all works of art. The failure, it must be added, concerns not simply the marginal *avant garde* works such as Duchamp's readymades, but all works, even the most conventional. "Work of art" on this reading is not even what W. B. Gallie has called an "essentially contested" concept—a single concept which we use, but for which we cannot specify necessary and sufficient conditions. What Professor Cone is saying, in effect, is that when we use the term "work of art" *different* concepts are at stake. In this kind of conceptual situation, as Gallie puts it, there is no "real ground for maintaining that . . . [the concept] has a *single* meaning, that *could* be contested. . . ."[4]

Must we therefore despair at ever achieving what the tradition has for so long been attempting? Is there any philosophical way to handle at once the complexity of the artworld and the confusion in aesthetics?

1. TRADITIONAL AESTHETIC THEORY, THE INSTITUTIONAL THEORY OF ART, AND PHENOMENOLOGY

I want to suggest in this essay that a phenomenological philosophy of art, the outlines of which derive from Husserl's *The Crisis of the European Sciences and Transcendental Phenomenology*, might furnish a way

4. W. B. Gallie, "Essentially Contested Concepts," *Proceedings of the Aristotelian Society*, 56 (1956), p. 175.

of bringing order into the chaos of aesthetics, and of shedding light on what has become for many the obscure world of art. This attempt will operate under several restrictions. First, I will offer *suggestions* for a Husserlian aesthetic, not a final and certainly not a complete phenomenological philosophy of art. Second, the attempt will be made from the perspective of the phenomenology of Husserl, with emphasis on certain themes in the *Crisis*. I am working on the assumption that, while there have been efforts to formulate an aesthetic theory in what can broadly be called the tradition of "*existential* phenomenology," attempts to develop a *Husserlian* aesthetic have been much more rare. Indeed, Roman Ingarden may be alone in undertaking a full-scale aesthetic investigation under mainly Husserlian auspices. Ingarden's work is rich and suggestive, but suffers from its relative neglect of the communal, cultural, and historical themes which figure so prominently in the *Crisis*—the very themes which, I believe, will prove most useful in developing the kind of aesthetic theory our contemporary situation demands. In saying that, I am not agreeing with those who see in the *Crisis* a radical shift in Husserl's thought.[5] On the contrary, I find the *Crisis* to be continuous and consistent with Husserl's earlier works, enriching the original sense of transcendental phenomenology without in any sense abandoning it. Third, although Husserl himself never developed an aesthetic theory, the *Crisis* is rich in the analysis of cultural worlds, and particularly of science as a cultural formation, and much of what Husserl says in these respects offers fertile soil for a phenomenology of art. Thus when I put themes and passages from the *Crisis* to work in the service of aesthetics, the reader is asked to keep in mind that they are being applied in an area in which Husserl never applied them himself. I hope that I have remained faithful to the spirit of Husserl's thought throughout, however. Finally, this attempt to sketch the outlines of a Husserlian aesthetic owes much to a theory which, at first glance, might appear to be altogether at odds with the spirit of Husserl's thought: the "institutional theory of art." The institutional theory is a conscious attempt to overcome the impasse that traditional approaches have reached by taking up a fundamentally new way of doing the philosophy of art. In its new approach, the institutional theory does not intend to surrender the traditional quest for a satisfactory definition of "art" and "work of art." George Dickie originally advanced the institutional theory on the basis of cer-

---

5. A recent claim that Husserl's thought changes fundamentally with the *Crisis* may be found in Richard Gier, *Wittgenstein and Phenomenology* (Albany: State University of New York Press, 1981), p. 118.

tain suggestions in contemporary aesthetic literature, particularly in
the writings of Arthur Danto. The theory intends to account for all
works of art, including those of the sort that presented such difficulties
to Professor Cone. In his most recent version of the theory, Professor
Dickie characterizes it as follows: "By an institutional approach I mean
the idea that works of art are art as a result of the position they occupy
within an institutional framework or context. The institutional theory
is, then, a kind of *contextual* theory" [D7].[6] Despite appearances, the
theory is not, or at least does not have to be, one of thoroughgoing
relativism. It is also not a phenomenological theory in any kind of
"official" Husserlian sense, but it does possess a number of features
which would be fundamental to any phenomenological aesthetic
rooted in the *Crisis*, and therefore furnishes clues for the shape such
an aesthetic might assume. Husserl always showed great respect for
clues, and we can do no less in this essay.

a. The Traditional Approach in Aesthetic Theory

Dickie claims that his theory is not traditional, and that it can respond to the protean quality of the artworld precisely because it is not
traditional. What, then, has been the flaw in traditional aesthetics?
Dickie traces it to a Platonic search for a timeless essence which is usually identified with some prominent feature of the art of a particular
period. The idea that art is the imitation of sensuous appearances
would be a case in point. More recent examples would be the theories
that art is essentially the expression of emotion (as in Collingwood), or
the communication of feeling (as in Tolstoy), or intuition (as in Croce),
or significant form (as in Bell and Fry), or symbolic form (as in Langer).

Such theories have the virtue of neatness, but Dickie observes that
all of them suffer from the same failings. First, they claim to have
found art's essence "in some highly visible property which is of some
obvious value" [D110]. The theorist inspects the individual work of
art closely and hopes to find the essence there, like a pearl in an
oyster, in some easily noted property. Second, while each of these
properties may be found in some works of art, no one of them characterizes every work of art [D110]. Some works obviously do "imitate"
nature, for example, while others just as obviously do not.

The failings of traditional theory have a number of unfortunate con-

---

6. George Dickie, *The Art Circle: A Theory of Art* (New York: Haven Publications,
1984). Page references to Dickie's book will immediately follow each citation and will be
placed in brackets with a "D" preceding the page number: for example, "[D7]." An earlier version of the institutional theory is presented in George Dickie, *Art and the Aesthetic: An Institutional Analysis* (Ithaca and London: Cornell University Press, 1974).

sequences. On the one hand, the philosopher, convinced that he has found the essence of art in some property or other, will be tempted to use his discovery as a principle of inclusion and exclusion, thereby dictating to the artist and threatening the freedom that is at least as essential to art as any property it may be said to have. On the other hand, acknowledging that no one property seems to characterize every work of art, the philosopher may surrender his search and declare that art has no essence at all, is at best an "open" or "essentially contested" concept in the sense noted earlier, that is, not "'closed' by necessary and sufficient conditions" [D30]. This may, of course, be the case, but before saying that it is, the philosopher owes it to himself to determine whether a different approach might have a more fruitful result. The stress must be on the difference in *approach;* it will do no good to try to discover one more property in the traditional sense that then might be used to still once and for all the clamor among the fractious aestheticians.

b. The Phenomenological Approach

George Dickie offers the institutional theory as an alternative to traditional aesthetics. I believe that the value of this alternative can best be realized if it is situated within a phenomenological setting.

Dickie himself asserts that "the institutional theory completely rejects the platonic example and purports to discover the defining conditions of art in not-so-easily-noted properties of art" [D110]. From the phenomenological perspective, the difference between the traditional approach and a new one would not consist in the difference between the *properties* sought—in this case between easily noted and not-so-easily-noted properties—but in a fundamental difference in *attitude.*

In Husserlian terms, traditional aesthetics has been carried on in the natural attitude. A phenomenological philosophy of art would be undertaken in the transcendental attitude. Art itself is created by artists, displayed by collectors and curators, appreciated by the public, studied by art historians, and criticized by critics, all in the realm of the natural attitude. Husserl does not hold this realm to be inferior to the realm of the transcendental attitude. On the contrary, the transcendental attitude, reflective in the phenomenological sense, exists solely to make possible the understanding of the subjectivity that functions anonymously in the natural attitude, presenting a world. The natural attitude is the attitude in which we live, always and everywhere, insofar as we are not doing philosophy; the comprehension of the natural attitude and its world is the reason why we do philosophy.

This means that the natural attitude, while always the theme of philosophy, can never itself be genuinely philosophical. Authentic philosophical reflection for Husserl is inseparable from the turn to the subject, while the natural attitude is firmly entrenched in "the naiveté of speaking of 'objectivity' without considering subjectivity" [99;96].[7] The subject in question is transcendental in Husserl's sense: it is the subject that intends or presents the world. The Husserlian turn to the subject is therefore not a turn away from the object into a solipsistic self, nor is it a turn to a self which creates its object out of whole cloth; it is rather a taking up of the object in its relation to the subject, the "dative of manifestation," as Thomas Prufer so aptly puts it, to which the object presents itself. Phenomenology takes the world "as the world of the subjectivity which functions for it, the world insofar as it is subject-related" [305;326].

The move across the threshold separating the natural from the transcendental attitude is accomplished through the reduction or epoche. Under the full epoche, the phenomenologist detaches himself from the plane of ordinary life in the world, and, so to speak, rises with his reflective eye to a transcendental perch above the universal "correlation between the world itself and world-consciousness" [154; 151]. Thus situated, the phenomenologist investigates, on the one hand, the subjective accomplishments through which we have a world and objects in it [163;160], and, on the other hand, the objects intended—not, however, "straightforwardly but rather as objects in respect to their 'how,'" [147;144], that is, the "how" of their manners of givenness, their "manners of appearing and being conceived" [311; 332]. As Robert Sokolowski says, phenomenology "is not an analysis of meanings. It explains how things present themselves, among which meanings are included."[8] In the epoche, then, the phenomenologist is no longer focused on the work of art as an object "in itself," but on *how* the work of art presents itself *as* a work of art in experience (as opposed, say, to something that presents itself as a perceptual object only, or as an object within the realm of physical science).

Thus understood, Husserlian phenomenology is a turn away from

7. Edmund Husserl, *Die Krisis der Europaischen Wissenschaften und die Transzendentale Phänomenologie*, 2. Auflage, Husserliana VI, herausgegeben von Walter Biemel (The Hague: Nijhoff, 1962). The English translation is by David Carr: *The Crisis of European Sciences and Transcendental Phenomenology* (Evanston: Northwestern University Press, 1970). Page references to the *Krisis* will immediately follow each citation and will be placed in brackets with the page of the Husserliana edition preceding the page of the English translation: for example, "[99;96]."

8. Robert Sokolowski, *Presence and Absence* (Bloomington: Indiana University Press, 1978), p. 180.

objectivism. Objectivism is philosophy attempted from the standpoint of the natural attitude. The natural attitude is properly the home of all of our activities with the sole exception of philosophy, which can understand the natural attitude only by leaving it. The intending subjectivity towards which phenomenology turns is already there in the natural attitude, but hidden, latent, taken for granted. Philosophy undertaken in the natural attitude will fail to uncover the intending subject because it will be absorbed in the object—not in the "how" of the object's appearance but in some quality or property it possesses. And when such objectivistic philosophy does turn towards the subject, it will treat it too as if it were an object, even a natural object, for particularly in the modern era objectivism has fused with naturalism, the tendency to reduce everything to the status of nature as understood in physical science.

Traditional theories of art have proven unsatisfactory precisely because they have moved within the natural attitude. They are instances of objectivism and naturalism. Their focus has been on the individual object—the work of art or the artist taken as an object—and their effort has been directed towards isolating some defining property belonging to that object. Their endless disputes arise because no property or properties can be found which belong to all works of art without exception, and none can be found which might not also be shared by things which are not works of art. The failure, again, is not that the "right" property has yet to be discovered, but that philosophers have taken up the work of art in the wrong *way*. What Husserl says of scientific constructs in the *Crisis* may equally be said of works of art: they are "not things in the life-world like stones, houses, or trees" [132; 130]. Or as George Dickie writes, traditional theories fail because they do not take into account "the fact that works of art are cultural objects which are created within complex artworld practices. They . . . treat works of art as if they were natural objects such as orange trees and sunsets" [D98].

And when objectivistic philosophies turn to the artist, they do not uncover a subject intending a world in a unique way, but a kind of Cartesian self within whose monadic confines a creative process is supposed to run its private course. Reality is still viewed naturalistically, only its *locus* has been changed: from external work to internal self. The real work of art is then said to be in the mind of the artist and is identified, for example, with an "intuition." The external work, the actual painting or sculpture, is superfluous, a public effluvium of the real artistic event, which is locked away within the artist's self.

A Husserlian aesthetic offers a plausible way out of the crisis of tra-

ditional aesthetic theory. It does so because it embraces the fullness
and complexity of art, but also because it takes up art as an achievement of subjectivity and never loses sight of either the accomplishing
subject or what it accomplishes. To be sure, the phenomenologist will
look for the "essence" of art, but not for a timeless essence in the sense
of the property of a thing. The essence will rather be "the invariant
essential structure" [363; 350] of a whole world, the "artworld,"[9] constituted through transcendental subjectivity. The phenomenologist
seeks to describe this essential structure with full respect for the phenomena whose essence it is supposed to be. The phenomenologist
goes to the "things themselves," takes them up as they are and takes
them up *whole*, not in the light of this or that property which may be in
vogue at the time. The essence he claims to discover will not be offered
as a weapon that a philosophical dictator might wield against this or
that suspect citizen of the artworld. Indeed, the phenomenologist
himself is not part of the artworld. He does not compete with the artist, the critic, the art historian, or the public, all of whom carry out
their vital functions within the natural attitude. The phenomenologist
simply wants to understand what they constitute in their complex intentional lives. His method is descriptive, but the description is intended to culminate in a grasp of what George Dickie calls "the *essential* framework of art" [D111].

Now what indications can we give about the nature of this framework?

2. THE WORK OF ART AS ARTIFACT

Under the aegis of the transcendental turn, we will consider the
work of art, in the language of the *Crisis*, as the product of human
praxis, that is, as the accomplishment of a unique mode of intending
subjectivity. Methodologically, we will take up the work just as it presents itself in our experience.

However else it may appear, the work of art presents itself as something that has been made, an artifact. The Aristotelian distinctions between *praxis* and *poesis*, and art and nature, assert themselves in the
experience of the work of art, although the non-philosopher will just
assume the differences without thematizing them. George Dickie
understands "artifactuality" to be an essential feature, in the sense of a

9. Arthur Danto, "The Artworld," *Journal of Philosophy*, 61 (1964). I follow throughout the essay Danto's spelling of "artworld."

necessary (although not sufficient) condition, of the work of art [D46]. He also observes that aestheticians have traditionally held this view.

Artifactuality is not so much a *property* as a *status* of the work. As Dickie observes, it is a status that must be achieved by a particular kind of human activity and cannot be conferred [D44]. Artifactuality, in other words, is not simply a matter of convention and context. It is rather a matter of *making*, and of making *something* through the creative use of a sensible medium, such as pigment, stone, sound, or human movement.

The condition of artifactuality may seem to be such an obvious feature of what we call art that it needs to be mentioned only in passing. The situation is not quite so simple, however, as the following complications suggest.

First, do we not sometimes call things which are not artifacts—sunsets, pieces of driftwood—"works of art"? We do, but this is a metaphorical use of the term. The philosopher of art, Dickie argues, attempts to isolate the "classificatory" [D8] sense of the concepts of art and work of art—in phenomenological terms, the essential presentational features of what comes before us as art in our experience. These are the features that distinguish what appears to us as art from what does not appear to us as art. Now these features are not in themselves of an *evaluative* character. We do, of course, evaluate works of art: we say that some are good and some bad, that some succeed while others fail. This evaluation, however, is not the same thing as the classification of the object *as* a work of art. When we call a piece of driftwood "a work of art," we are not *classifying* it as a work in the sense of Michelangelo's "David" or Bartok's "Concerto for Orchestra." We are calling it a work of art because it has certain aesthetic qualities, usually ones we admire such as good form or harmony, which resemble in some way qualities possessed by some real works of art, that is, by *artifacts* which are works of art.[10] "Work of art" is here used metaphorically and honorifically. The sunset and the driftwood do not present themselves as artifacts, which is the way in which objects we classify as works of art do present themselves. Sunsets and pieces of driftwood are therefore not literally works of art because they do not display themselves as having been made by a human being working in a sensible medium. Many people who have encountered Duane Hanson's "photorealist" sculptures have had this difference in presentation

10. Dickie discusses these themes in Chapter VI of *The Art Circle* ("The Aesthetic Object").

brought home quite dramatically. Hanson's sculptures often appear at first glance as real people, even when they have been placed in the gallery of a museum. On closer inspection, they suddenly present themselves as not at all real, but as made. At that point, and not before, they are on their way towards being appropriately named works of art. This example also tells us something important about artifactuality: it is something presented, but not always in an obvious or immediate way. An artist may well make something that at first or even second glance does not appear to be an artifact, and therefore does not appear to be a work of art. But eventually, and perhaps after considerable effort on the part of the perceiver, the object will reveal itself as an artifact, and then its presentational character will alter fundamentally.

A second complicating factor concerns the breadth of what can display itself as an artifact. Professor Cone urges a return to the distinction between making and acting because he thinks the distinction is a useful weapon in fighting against the current tendency to confuse art and life. His point is that while the artifact presents itself as different from the natural thing, it also presents itself as different from human acting and doing. This does not mean, of course, that human action and the making of some product may not have an intimate connection. Aristotle, who clearly points to the distinction between making and doing, understands the tragedy, which is something made, to be the imitation of human life and action. But the tragedy, the literary work, is not itself human life and action. Now the difficulty today is that the border between making and doing in art may become obscure, with the result that the border between art and reality also becomes obscure. If Chris Burden, who claims to be an artist and who is acknowledged as one by numerous critics and other artists, intentionally has himself shot in the left arm, as he did early in his career (Shooting Piece, 1971), are we presented with an action or with an artifact? From the point of view of art, we must distinguish between the possibility that the shooting taken simply as an action is supposed to be the work of art, and the alternative possibility that the shooting is really supposed to be a kind of making, like chiseling stone, with the riddled arm as the product, that is, the work of art. The first alternative—shooting as action pure and simple—shuts the door on the possibility that what occurs could appear as art. On this view, Burden's shooting of himself no more presents itself as a work of art than did Van Gogh's shooting of himself. On the other view, we might be forced to admit that an artifact is present—not the body simply, but the body altered in a certain way through a purposeful process. There is, after

all, nothing new or surprising about a human being altering the appearance of his or her body. (What is new and surprising is that Mr.
Burden did it with a gun.) But before this "sculpted" body could be
called a work of art, it would have to present itself with still other presentational features which we have yet to discuss.

Two final comments about artifactuality are in order. First, the
work of art must not simply be made; it must be made out of sensible
materials and must be something sensible itself. One might metaphorically speak of a scientific theory as having been "made" (Husserl
sometimes calls them "constructs" [132; 129]), but scientific theories
are not works of art because they are not sensible, except incidentally.
Not everything generated by human subjectivity is an artifact. The
second comment is that not every artifact is a work of art. It may be
true that everything that presents itself as a work of art must present
itself as an artifact, but this condition of presentation is not sufficient
to make something a work of art. Television sets are artifacts, but we
do not consider them to be art. We must now turn to the further presentational features that let some artifacts appear as art.

3. THE ARTWORLD

An essential presentational dimension of works of art is artifactuality. But things other than works of art also present themselves as
artifacts. What are the presentational differences between artifacts
which present themselves as works of art and those which do not?

In Husserlian terms, the answer is that the work of art appears with
a unique horizon. In terms of Professor Dickie's institutional theory,
the answer is that the work appears within the context of a particular
institution. The horizon, or the institution, is what Arthur Danto has
called the "artworld." Dickie says this explicitly, while Husserl, of
course, does not. But Husserl does offer a general account of cultural
worlds in the *Crisis* and this account can be put to work profitably in
aesthetics, particularly under the guidance of certain aspects of the
institutional theory.

The institutional theory claims that "it is the work done in creating
an object against the background of the artworld which establishes
that object as a work of art" [D12]. In Dickie's language, the artworld
is the "background," "framework," "cultural matrix" [D55], or "context" in which alone an artifact can achieve the status of art. In Husserlian terms, the artworld would be an instance of a "self-enclosed
'world'-horizon" [459; 379], determining what will count as reality
and unreality within its sphere, and constituted through the voca-

tional pursuit of a specific goal which we and others may share. While the artworld is the "institution" from which the "institutional" theory derives its name, it is not an institution in the sense of an *organization* such as the Catholic Church or the Fiat Corporation or the United Nations. It is rather a "cultural practice" [D52], as Dickie writes, or as Husserl would call it, "a particular praxis" [132; 129]. The terms "contextual" or "horizonal" would therefore serve better than "institutional" to describe the theory. It is when an artifact is made and presented within the horizon of the artworld that it can be intended as a work of art.

But why is this cultural framework essential to something's appearing as art? In terms of Husserl's argument in the *Crisis,* a cultural object can arise and can present itself *as* a cultural object (and not simply as a natural thing) only within a particular cultural world in which those creating the object and those to whom the object is presented form a community of praxis bound by a common goal. Just as a scientific theory can appear in its proper sense only to those who are scientists or who understand science [311; 332], so works of art can appear as works of art only to those who play roles within the artworld. The artworld as the cultural horizon "within which, for the individual, possible ways of understanding this culture are present" [311; 332] serves as the necessary and sufficient condition for the presentation of artifacts as works of art.

The artworld is a specific achievement of subjectivity. When we as phenomenologists make the transcendental turn, this intending subjectivity and its correlative world reveal themselves as vocational, communal, and historical. Let us look at each of these aspects in turn.

a. The Artworld and Vocational Roles

The artworld is complex, and its complexity involves, in part, different individuals fulfilling different cultural roles [62; 51]. Thus the artworld depends at a minimum on the artist and a public to whom the artist presents his work [D72]. Other roles are played by those who facilitate the presentation of art, such as museum curators, critics, and art historians, or by those who acquire art, such as collectors.

To speak of the function of roles in the artworld, as Dickie does, is really to speak of what Husserl variously calls "life projects" [157; 154], "lifetasks" [510; 392], "vocations" [300; 321], or "habitualities" [300; 321]. The artist has a unique task or project in life, different from that of the scientist or lawyer, and that is to create art. The artist does not accidentally stumble into this activity or pursue it in ignorance of what he is doing. The artist *intends* to create art, and understands, at least in a minimal way, the vocation he has taken up. In that sense, the activity of the artist at once contributes to the constitution of the artworld and also presupposes it as a "surrounding world" [302;323], a "cultural space" [510;392] and "work-world" [459;379] in which the artist can create his works, the critic can criticize them, and the collector can acquire them, all within the community of the artworld.

b. The Artworld and Community

The individual artist is not the *sole* subjectivity constituting the artworld. To claim otherwise would be to adopt the "romantic" conception of the artist. The romantic artist would work in utter isolation, generating his own purely private "art" [D52]. But if he is to be an artist at all, he must have in view, even in his isolation, other artists and critics and the public. True, he may despise what his contemporary brothers and sisters in art are creating, he may have nothing but contempt for critics and public alike, and his whole purpose may be to overthrow the established artistic order. But try as he might, he is bound to define his solitary activity in terms of its connection with the activities of others. If he pursues the new, it is because he rejects the old which other artists have produced and which critics have accepted; if he is determined to achieve something radically different, the difference will be measured in terms of what other artists have already done. The romantic artist in the very attempt to cut himself off finds himself tied with myriad bonds to the surrounding artworld, a cultural space which is constituted, not by one artist and not even by artists alone, but by a *community* of subjects engaged in a common praxis.

Thus "the personal [the individual] life-task . . . is a partial task . . . within a communal task" [459;380]. The artworld is the correlate of transcendental *intersubjectivity*, of a nexus of individual subjects unified in a single cultural praxis. In the case of the artworld, as of any cultural world, subjectivity is what it is only as intersubjectivity. To be sure, artists create works of art, but what they make is art and not something else, and they are artists and not something else, because their individual activities are moments of a larger whole which is the accomplishing subjectivity through which we and they have this world and objects in it. The world for me as artist, or as collector, gallery visitor, or critic, is also the world for *us*.

The constitution of the artworld, then, is a total, many-levelled intentional accomplishment of intersubjectivity. Levels and strata of intentional synthesis in one subject are interwoven with those of other subjects to form a universal unity of synthesis in which the artworld as a structure of meaning is presented [170; 168]. The community thus formed does not depend simply on the roles played but also on the *mutual* understanding possessed by those who play the roles [459; 380]. Someone totally ignorant of the concept of art could not make a work of art, or be aware of something as a work of art, because he or she would not know what the role of the artist or the role of the artworld public is. "What is primary is the understanding shared by all involved that they are engaged in an established activity or practice within which there is a variety of different roles: creator roles, presenter roles, and 'consumer' roles" [D74]. The artist, for example, is aware that the making of a work of art involves creating an artifact which could be presented to an artworld public [D67]. The artist's intentionality includes not just the thing made but the public to whom it is or might be presented. The thing made becomes a work of art only in the light of that reference. The sculptor who makes a workbench for his tools has made an artifact but not a work of art because, in Professor Dickie's formulation, the workbench is not "an artifact of a kind created to be presented to an artworld public" [D89]. But the sculpture he has made *is* an artifact of that kind, even if it is never in fact presented to the public, and so it is a work of art. The public, on its side, must also be aware that what is presented to it is art—an artifact made by an artist for presentation. Artist and public, curator and collector, are all co-subjects of a common praxis [300; 321]. They form an internally communalized conscious life through the understanding of their respective roles. The intentional correlate of this conscious life is the common horizon of the artworld.

c. The Artworld and History

To this point we have considered what might be called the "vertical" aspect of the artworld's constituting community—the overlapping intentionalities of those who, at any given moment, play key roles in the constitution of the artworld. But the artworld community also possesses a "horizontal" dimension—the dimension of history. The present communal life of the artworld retains "the communal life of the past" [300; 321]. Its synthetic formation involves not just the present practitioners of art but successive generations whose achievements are sedimented in the present and preserved through generative memory. In Husserl's terms, the artworld is a "'social-historical' world" [308; 329], and the attitude correlated with it—what we might call the "art attitude"—is "essentially historical" [310; 331].

Temporality, then, is the form of the artworld, but the time in question is neither the internal time of the individual consciousness nor the

"objective" time of nature. It is rather "a relative time, essentially belonging to a particular communally living and existing civilization, with
all its past periods and open future. . . ." [311; 332]. The artworld is
historical and its time is relative because it is a cultural world, and cultural worlds exist through their particular traditions [366; 354]. Traditions are not natural things, suddenly come upon in the environment.
They arise originally "within our human space through human activity, i.e., spiritually. . . ." [366; 355]. Having arisen, they become
sedimented. But they do not accumulate like rocks in a pile, nor do
they pass in frozen form from generation to generation. They are
rather taken up and transformed again and again as they are handed
down. "History is from the start nothing other than the vital movement of coexistence and the interweaving of original formations and
sedimentations of meaning" [380; 371]. Traditions thus enjoy a "mobility": they are living and leavening forces, the temporal horizon of
our artistic practice [378; 368]. This "transcendental fact" has a number of interesting implications.

First, when history is introduced, the communalization we spoke of
earlier appears as *traditionalization*. Communalization, taken as the
mutual understanding of the many subjects which constitute the artworld, occurs in the cultural present. Each cultural present, however,
"'implies' the whole of the cultural past . . . ," a whole which is a continuity of past cultural presents [379; 371]. "This whole continuity,"
Husserl writes, "is a *unity* of traditionalization up to the present, which
is our present as [a process of] traditionalizing itself in flowing-static
generality" [380; 371].

Second, the historicity of the artworld, this unity of tradition, does
not imply artistic conservatism. There can and will be innovation, but
if it is truly innovation in *art*, it can occur only against the artworld's
horizon of history. As Pierre Schneider says in his study of Matisse,
"the work of art challenges history only by placing itself squarely in its
lap."[11] The historicity of the artworld is the condition of artistic innovation, not its obstacle. Artists, to borrow Husserl's language from *The
Origin of Geometry*, "act and create in their communalized coexistence
in the world and transform the constant cultural face of the world"
[382; 374] precisely because a face is already there to be transformed.

Finally, Husserl observes that "all new acquisitions are in turn sedimented and become working materials" [378; 369], which means that
the core activity of creating the work of art consumes history just as

11. Pierre Schneider, *Matisse*, translated by Michael Taylor and Bridget Stevens
Romer (New York: Rizzoli, 1984), p. 9.

much as it consumes pigment, stone, sound, and human movement. The artist makes his work out of the material of sedimented traditions. And far from being available simply as static raw material, history *motivates* the artist and *shapes* his activity. Even the sensible medium the artist employs is shaped by history.

4. THE ARTWORLD AND CONTENDING THEORIES OF ART

The artworld is rich and complex in the roles which constitute it and in its temporal reach. The work of art is an artifact which appears against the horizon of this unique cultural world. The philosophical understanding of this world-horizon in its communal and historical aspects helps us make sense of the plentiful contending theories or "ideologies" of art advanced by critics and artists, and also by those who philosophize from the perspective of the natural attitude.

Because the artworld is communal and historical, there can be communication among its present participants and between past and present generations. Where there can be communication there can also be contradiction and disagreement. Thus the many theories of art (art as imitation, art as expression, art as significant form, etc.) and ideologies of art (art should always have or in fact always does have a political content, art and politics do not mix; art should be connected directly with life, art should be pursued purely for its own sake, etc.) can struggle with one another in a kind of endless debate because they have a common horizon. Each presumes the understanding of some historical or contemporary view which it supports or challenges. Any one of them advanced as an exclusive claim about what art is or is supposed to achieve would certainly be false. The falsity, however, is usually a matter of a part masquerading as the whole: *some* works of art, but not *all*, do "imitate" nature, just as some but not all have a political content. The value of such theories is that they reveal something about the richness of the artworld, the fact that it can be the home for many different achievements and points of view, even for those which arrogantly claim an exclusive status. They also reveal in their one-sidedness that any theory or ideology which considers art from the perspective of the natural attitude will fail as an adequate philosophical account. Artists and critics sometimes take their theories and ideologies to be definitive philosophical positions. In fact, they are important to the artist not because they are philosophical (which they are not), but because they motivate actual artistic production. The manifestos of the Futurists are clearly inadequate as philosophies of art, yet as guides and motivators for the creation of paintings and sculptures and poems they were undoubtedly effective. This is also true of the dogmas of Surrealism, of *De Stijl*, and of various other twentieth-century movements. That they are not philosophical doctrines does not prevent them from being threads in the rich tapestry of the art-world, which from this perspective is a historical process of agreement and disagreement. By the same token, a genuine philosophy of art, that is, one undertaken in the transcendental attitude, is *not* part of the artworld. It is not one more theory or ideology to be entered into the artworld's ongoing doctrinal competition.

5. ARTWORLD AND LIFEWORLD

Pierre Schneider tells us that Matisse thought that art "speaks about that which is not art."[12] Other artists would agree that art is *about* something, but would claim that what art is about is always in some way art itself. Yet anyone who considers the full range of painting, for example, might be inclined to agree with George Dickie that some works of art do not seem to be about anything [D25], that it is just not true to say that "art must have a subject matter" [D65].

Now a tempting position to adopt in the light of Husserl's *Crisis* would be that works of art in the artworld are about things in the *life-world* (*Lebenswelt*). After all, does not Husserl claim that the life-world includes and nourishes the cultural world of science which in turn has constant reference to the life-world? [132;130]. Does he not also claim that *any* form of human praxis presupposes the life-world? [123;121]. But Husserl also speaks of a tension or "uncomfortable situation" prevailing between science and life-world. "We have two dif-ferent things: life-world and objective-scientific world, though [they are] related to each other" [133;130]. What Husserl calls "the contrast and inseparable union" [134;131] of life-world and science would seem to apply to the relation between the life-world and *any* cultural world, including the artworld.

An attempt to resolve the vexing issue of the relationship between life-world and cultural worlds would require a far more careful analy-sis than the scope of this essay will allow. I can offer a few indications concerning the specific case of the artworld, however.

First, the life-world might best be viewed as a whole with parts in founding/founded relationships. The artworld is a founded part. The fundamental founding level of the life-world is the perceptual world. Do works of art always "refer" to the perceptual world? In

12. *Ibid.*, p. 10.

some more or less remote way, yes—but reference to the life-world does not seem to be essential to the thing's being art. The fact that a human face appears in a portrait by Eakins, or a bowl and fruit in a still life by Cezanne, or a piazza in a painting by de Chirico, or a street-like grid in a work by Mondrian, is not what makes these artifacts art. The *meaning* of the particular works may be affected by such references to the life-world, but their *status* as art does not depend on those references. It is true that virtually any work of art, even a canvas painted a uniform white, will enjoy some reference to or affinity with phenomena in the life-world. But it is hard to see how that ubiquitous *reference* itself is crucial to the thing's being art.

Second, the artist *uses* the life-world in its fundamental perceptual sense in the making of his works. The life-world supplies him with sensible materials and with instruments for his creative activity. The work of art produced with media such as stone or wood will be just as perceptible as the stone and wood themselves before they were taken up into the work. But, again, the perceptibility of such cultural objects does not imply that they appear to us "in the life-world like stones, houses, or trees" [132; 130]. They *are* present against the background of the perceptible stratum of the life-world—I do *see* the marble sculpture—but they are also present against the communal and historical horizon of the artworld, and that provides them with a dimension absent in the case of the unworked marble resting in the quarry.

Third, taking the life-world as a whole, that is, as encompassing not only the perceptible world but the many worlds of human praxis founded on it, we can indeed say that the artworld is included in the life-world and that it can have multiple references to the life-world's many parts, particularly the other cultural worlds contained within it. The artworld is a discernible cultural formation, the horizon in which alone an artifact can appear as a work of art, but it is not hermetically sealed. It is open to connections with the worlds of religion, morality, politics, technology, and even of science. The "ideological" disputes mentioned earlier arise because of this openness—for example, precisely because art *can* have links with politics some would argue that it *should* remain autonomous. From the perspective of history, the conception of the strict autonomy of the artworld is a recent development. When the Abbot Suger, for example, set about rebuilding the Abbey Church of St. Denis in the twelfth century, he was very much a member, or rather a leader, of the contemporary artworld. He searched far and wide for the best artisans, and he engaged in controversies over matters of taste and substance with his contemporaries.

But his artworld blended with the formal institutions of church and state, and the meaning of the art over whose creation he presided reflects these connections. Still, it would seem to be true that for something to appear as a work of art, it is not necessary that it have clear relationships with other cultural domains. There can be art which has no obvious or intended political or religious or moral content. The only cultural horizon that art *must* have is the artworld. Should this horizon happen to overlap with others, as it did in Abbot Suger's case, the art created might well answer to more profound human and spiritual needs than the newly autonomous art we have come to know. But in either case we would be dealing with art.

Finally, Husserl observes in the *Crisis* that "the life-world [presumably meaning its perceptual stratum and not the "whole" life-world as described immediately above] is a 'structure'" but "not a 'purposeful structure'" [462 ; 382]. On the other hand, any cultural world, such as the artworld or the world of science, is a purposeful structure. A cultural world is the correlate of a "goal-directed life" [459 ; 380]. An end "'makes'" [459 ; 379] this world in the sense that a community of subjects constitutes it in the pursuit of a particular vocational goal. These particular pursuits always presuppose the life-world as "the 'domain' that *precedes* all ends" [461 ; 381].

Now if a fundamental difference between artworld and life-world is that one is a purposeful structure while the other is not, we must briefly examine what the end that shapes the art-world might be.

6. THE TELOS OF ART

What is the end of art? What is the end that motivates the formation of the artworld? More precisely, granting that a particular work of art can involve a variety of purposes (religious, political, moral, and so on), is there a single end that characterizes *everything* we call art? The temptation at this point is to select one of the alleged essential properties of art and submit it as the end of all art. Thus imitation or the expression of emotion might be taken as art's purpose. But a reply of this kind seems to be as unsatisfactory as the property analysis from which it derives.

A better answer is Dickie's: "*A work of art is an artifact of a kind to be presented to an artworld public*" [D80]. The end of art would then be the presentation of a work of art by an artist to an artworld public within the framework of an artworld system [D82]. This is helpful, but it leaves the impression that more needs to be said, as if we had proclaimed that the end of science is to present theoretical constructions to the community of scientists. True as this may be, we still feel compelled to ask *why* the presentation is made.

The answer I would suggest is that the work of art is presented for the sake of *contemplation*. Whatever form our particular response to it may take, and whatever else it may be and for whatever other purposes it may exist, the work of art is an artifact presented in order to be looked at, listened to, and so on. This explains why useful objects, objects which were clearly made for some utilitarian end such as drinking or storing things, may quite properly be taken as works of art and even be displayed in museums where they can only be contemplated. If the craftsmen who made them to be used *also* produced them to be contemplated, then the useful object is a work of art. It seems safe to say, for example, that some useful objects from antiquity were made to be contemplated as well as used, and that they were indeed contemplated and "appreciated" by the "artworld public"[13] of their own time. That we now place them in museums is no aberration but a sign of their status as artifacts presented for contemplation. If they were not so rare, we would use them too.

I have tried to suggest in this essay some ideas for a Husserlian phenomenology of art. With the *Crisis* as guide and with clues from George Dickie's institutional theory, I have argued that the work of art is a cultural object which comes to presentation within the horizon of its own social and historical world. Specifically, it appears as an artifact created against the horizon of the artworld and presented to an artworld public for its contemplation.

The essay began with the notion that there is a crisis of sorts today in art and in aesthetic theory. The phenomenological approach, with its fundamental change in attitude, is intended to help clear away the theoretical confusion without surrendering philosophy's traditional quest for art's essential structure. As for the confusion in art itself, the philosopher, as philosopher, should not set himself up as the judge of

---

13. In an earlier version of the institutional theory, Dickie held that the work of art is presented as a "candidate for appreciation," thereby implying an answer to the question about art's purpose. In his most recent version of the theory, however, he says that appreciation no longer plays a role in his definition of the work of art [D91]. Perhaps I have misunderstood Professor Dickie, but I think the basic notion of appreciation, in somewhat altered form, should be preserved, and that this is accomplished in the shift from the notion of appreciation to that of contemplation. The difficulty with "appreciation" as a term is that it may suggest too definite a response. "Contemplation," on the other hand, leaves open the precise response to the person to whom the work of art is presented.

individual works of art. But if we return to the *kinds* of cases with which we started, the kinds that so disturbed Professor Cone, I think we may venture to claim that generosity should be the order of the day and that the works involved should be recognized as citizens of the realm of art. They are in some sense artifacts created against the horizon of the artworld. We may also observe that they may be no more than marginal cases of art. Works that are marginal can be influential, of course, as Duchamp's readymades were. Their marginality rests in the fact that they may barely be artifacts (D46), or that their purpose may be mainly rhetorical, or that they may not be much *worth* contemplating. It is possible to make all three points with respect to phenomena such as Duchamp's influential "Fountain" or Chris Burden's being shot, which Harold Rosenberg described as "uninteresting"[14]—*dangerous*, to be sure, but still uninteresting. What these works let us realize is that art, as a cultural phenomenon, is an expression of human freedom—always exercised within the bounds of its surrounding world. What the artworld contains will therefore be rich in variety and profound in its capacity to surprise. But variety, the ability to astound, the fact of being art at all, are not signs that we are in the presence of *good* art. In this essay I did not address the issue of good art and bad, of art that is worth contemplating and of art that is not. I rather looked at the essential boundaries of the artworld; my concern was with the "classificatory" sense of art, with the conditions under which something succeeds in *becoming* art rather than the conditions under which something succeeds *as* art. The issue of good and bad art points to what would be the next step in the formation of a Husserlian aesthetic: a phenomenological account of the presence and absence of quality in art.

14. Harold Rosenberg, "The Art World," *The New Yorker* (Feb. 20, 1978), p. 103.

3   Hobbes and Husserl on Reason and Its Limits

RIÇHARD COBB-STEVENS

Two seemingly unrelated definitions of reason appear in Hobbes' *Leviathan*. In a chapter entitled "Of Reason and Science," Hobbes describes reason as a calculative power: "Reason . . . is nothing but *reckoning*, that is adding and subtracting of the consequences of general names agreed upon for the *marking* and *signifying* of our thoughts."[1] This passage follows upon an explicit critique of Aristotle's theory that the cognitive intellect takes on the shape, or "becomes somehow" the form of the thing that it knows. The new science requires, says Hobbes, that perception be explained by the movements of elements within a formless nature. All of the forms that we seem to perceive in things (colors, savors, etc.) are illusory impressions provoked by the body's reaction to the pressure on its organs by motions of matter: ". . . Qualities which are called *sensible,* are in the object, that causeth them but so many several motions of the matter, by which it presseth our organs diversely. Neither in us that are pressed, are they anything else but divers motions; for motion produceth nothing but motion. But their appearance to us is fancy . . . And though at some certain distance, the real and very object seem invested with the fancy it begets in us; yet the object is one thing, the image or fancy is another."[2]

Thus, the "looks" of things are appearances, not in the sense of modes of presentation, but in the sense of mere appearances. Their appearance to us is fancy. Of all of the modern thinkers Hobbes makes the most unequivocal break with the tradition. His is the most decisive rejection of the Greek and Medieval notion that reason is both intuitive and discursive, and the most unambiguous description of mind as an enclosure whose contents are devoid of intentional import. As if

---

1. Thomas Hobbes, *Leviathan, or the Matter, Form, and Power of a Commonwealth Ecclesiastical and Civil. The English Works of Thomas Hobbes*, Vol. III, ed. William Molesworth (Aalen: Scientia Verlag, 1966), p. 30.
2. *Ibid.*, pp. 2–3.

to compensate for this reduction of cognitive intuition to illusion, Hobbes inflates the power of procedural rationality by advocating the extension of mathematical method and empirical inquiry to the ethical and political domains. *Leviathan* dismisses the whole sphere of prescientific experience. Ordinary language, riddled as it is with metaphors and other imprecise expressions, and practical wisdom, irreducible as it is to discernible algorithms, are as suspect as perception. Whatever cannot be quantified is assigned to the realm of illusion.[3]

In a later chapter devoted to a study of the intellectual virtues, Hobbes offers a second definition of reason: "For the thoughts are to the desires, as scouts, and spies, to range abroad, and find the way to the things desired: all steadiness of the mind's motion, and all quickness of the same, proceeding from thence. . . ."[4] Rational ends, therefore, are reducible to biological drives and needs. There is no pure interest in the free implementation of the good. Reason is merely a strategy of desire, an adaptive power whose calculative techniques are roundabout means of attaining the goals of nature. In 1747, La Mettrie spelled out the implications of this naturalism in the clearest and crudest manner possible. His *Homme machine* depicts persons as complicated material mechanisms, and characterizes the theory of the spiritual soul as a fable.[5] Subsequent empiricist philosophers tended to retreat somewhat from this full-fledged reductionism. The notion of a non-geometrical space where the intellect registers forms survives, for example, in Locke's metaphor of the mind's "inner cabinet" and in Hume's account of an interior forum containing sense impressions, moods, images, and ideas. But this residual commitment to the traditional soul-theory was ultimately incompatible with the thesis shared by the entire empiricist tradition that mental processes and contents have the same ontological status as any other natural happenings.

It has taken three hundred years, however, for the full implications of Hobbes' revolutionary interpretation of reason to become really clear. For a long time it seemed that the new scientific method could provide what philosophy had always yearned for, i.e., access to what really is. The notion that human beings are knowers of essences was not fully abandoned at first; the power of grasping essences was merely

3. For a lucid discussion of the influence on subsequent political philosophy of this rejection of Aristotle's distinction between mathematical and ethical reasoning, see Jacques Taminiaux, "Hegel and Hobbes," in *Dialectic and Difference: Finitude in Modern Thought.* ed. and trans. Robert Crease and James T. Decker (Atlantic Highlands, NJ: Humanities Press, 1985), pp. 1–37.
4. Hobbes, *Leviathan*, pp. 61–62.
5. Julien Offray de La Mettrie, *Homme Machine. Oeuvres philosophiques* (Berlin and Paris, 1796).

transferred from cognitive intuition to calculative procedures. How else explain the positivists' confidence that the sciences could deliver objective truths? Yet Hobbes' radical nominalism had in fact undermined the link between ordinary names and the natures of things, without establishing that mathematical language is any more revelatory of essences. He dismisses Aristotle's general thesis that a word's definition is founded upon an intuitive grasp of the essential whatness of the substance represented by the word: "For considering that new names are daily made, and old ones laid aside; that diverse nations use different names, and how impossible it is either to observe similitude, or make any comparison betwixt a name and a thing, how can any man imagine that the names of things were imposed from their natures?"[6] But then he seems to make an exception for the definition of the Aristotelian term '*materia prima*', noting that this name "is not of vain use; for it signifies a conception of body without the consideration of any form or other accident except only magnitude or extension, and aptness to receive form and other accident."[7] But why should this conception of body be any less vain, and why should extension be any less fanciful a property than color or savor? Thomas Spragens points out that, whereas Aristotle had thought that formless matter was unintelligible in itself, Hobbes' claim that "all the universe is Body" was based on the expectation that the resolution of all things into ensembles of matter in motion would render the universe susceptible of intelligibility through quantitative analysis.[8] To reduce body to extension is to resolve substance into quantity and thereby to construe the world as the mirror of mathematical reason. If we focus only on Hobbes' definition of reason as reckoning, we might infer that he held that the geometric method yields truth about nature, whereas ordinary perception yields illusion. Indeed, he often asserts that the aggregate of extended bodies comprises the entire universe, and that Galileo's geometrical method and new model of inertia provide the key to its explanation.[9] But he offers no justification for these claims, beyond pointing to the explanatory sterility of appeal to essences and the relative fertility of the newer method. His main point is that Galileo's approach works better, not that its mathematical language is more truthful. Thus, Hobbes' definition of reasoning as reckoning is

6. Thomas Hobbes, *Concerning Body. English Works.* Vol. I, p. 16.
7. *Ibid.*, p. 118.
8. Thomas A. Spragens, Jr., *The Politics of Motion: The World of Thomas Hobbes* (Lexington: Univ. of Kentucky Press, 1973), p. 90.
9. See, for example, the epistle dedicatory to *Concerning Body:* "Galileus in our time . . . was the first that opened to us the gate of natural philosophy universal, which is the knowledge of the nature of *motion.*" *English Works*, Vol. I, viii.

ultimately subordinated to his definition of reason as an adaptive natural power.

It is only in recent years that a thorough-going pragmatism, combined with a resolutely behavioristic analysis of linguistic usage, has made it possible to retrieve Hobbes' naturalism from its subsequent contamination by residual traces of soul-theory. Contemporary philosophers put forward theories of truth that make no appeal whatsoever to forms, taken either in the ontological manner as modes of presentation or in the language of subjectivity as intermediary representations. To speak, it is claimed, is simply to assign labels to things. There are no natural kinds or fixed essences. Habit and convention are the only constraints, and pragmatic efficacy is the only criterion.[10] The "rightness" of certain descriptions has nothing to do with what is the case. Hobbes' interpretation of reason as an adaptive power has thus finally permitted philosophy to rid itself altogether of traditional notions of truth, and to appreciate, as Richard Rorty puts it, that "modern science does not enable us to cope because it corresponds, it just plain enables us to cope."[11] Of course, the notion of forms has not disappeared entirely. They surface again as the "rules" that govern linguistic performances. The history of philosophy may thus be read as a kind of travelogue of the forms. Indeed, various philosophical eras may be defined in terms of the locus assigned to forms. From Plato's ideal entities, to Aristotle's substances, to the Medieval intentional objects, to Locke's ideas, the forms have been constantly shuffled about, and most recently situated within the "public" domain as the conventional rules guiding the use of contingent signifiers. To a certain extent, this position is a healthy reaction to those theories that ascribe some separate existence to universals, or treat concepts and propositions as exclusively "interior" entities. But many contemporary philosophers tend to blur the ontological difference between linguistic rules and the utterances that they govern, and fail to account for the relationship between the rules and the "looks" of things. There is no need, it is claimed, for a reflective reconstruction of how we intuit the rules in the instance of their implementation, since to know "how to" use a language correctly is a practical skill subject to routinization. In order to formulate a theory of truth, moreover, it is sufficient to determine the precise circumstances under which a sentence

10. Nelson Goodman, *The Structure of Appearance* (Cambridge: Harvard Univ. Press, 1951), pp. 36–42; Nelson Goodman, *Languages of Art: An Approach to a Theory of Symbols* (Indianapolis: Bobbs-Merrill, 1968), pp. 45–74.

11. Richard Rorty, *Consequences of Pragmatism* (Minneapolis: Univ. of Minnesota Press, 1982), xvii.

is typically used by native speakers, and then to ascertain whether or not those circumstances obtain. Linguistic performances are public happenings whose truth-conditions may be specified without appeal to privileged first-person intuitions.[12] This position is obscurantist, for it relies on a sustained ambiguous interpretation of the term 'public'. It is one thing to claim that patterns of sound are publicly available objects of inquiry, and another to say the same of the rules governing their intelligent concatenation. Utterances are public in the sense of "empirically verifiable." Shared meanings are public in the sense of "intersubjectively accessible." Linguistic performances are surely rule-guided and ordinarily public, but this does not mean that there is no role for the individual's consciousness in the production of speech acts. We call speech thoughtful to the extent that it manifests intelligent choices from among linguistic possibilities, rather than routinized responses to stimuli. For the intelligent speaker, "knowing how to" involves an anticipatory sense of what to say next. This is why the right word and the felicitous illustration come to the speaker, and are appreciated by the listener, as fulfillments rather than as associative responses. On the other hand, it is inappropriate to inflate the role of interiority by describing the individual's consciousness as though it were a hidden motor that produces an overt indication of its agency in the linguistic performance. The work of mind cuts across the inside/outside distinction. Consciousness pervades an intelligent performance in the same way that grace pervades a dancer's movements. Both sorts of performance may become routine. But the more thoughtful the speech and the more graceful the dance, the more manifest is the intelligence and freedom of the performance. It follows that the project of deriving the truth-conditions of sentences uniquely from extrinsic observation of the behavior of interlocutors is incoherent. The philosophic investigator necessarily calls upon a prior pre-analytic grasp of the difference between a symbolic expression and a sequence of noises. A complete account of speech acts must discuss the kind of knowing involved in the tacit recognition of linguistic rules, and must specify the relationship between the rules deployed and the "looks" of things.[13]

12. See, for example, Donald Davidson, "Truth and Meaning," *Synthese*, XVII (1967), pp. 304–322.
13. Stanley Rosen makes this point forcefully in *The Limits of Analysis* (New York: Basic Books, 1980), p. 5. For a comprehensive analysis of the way in which propositions "rule" the sentences in which they are achieved and are measured by the facts that are thereby articulated, see Robert Sokolowski, *Presence and Absence: A Philosophical Investigation of Language and Being* (Bloomington: Indiana Univ. Press), pp. 87–115. And for

Proponents of the new behavioral pragmatism have not lost confidence in the explanatory power of the positive sciences. Rorty's attitude is typical: "Some atoms-and-the-void account of micro-processes within individual human beings will permit the prediction of every sound and inscription that will ever be uttered. There are no ghosts."[14] Their emphasis on the limits of procedural reason (science does not provide more perspicacious knowing, but more effective coping) thus seems to leave intact a remarkably dogmatic attitude. While asserting that we cannot know essences, many contemporary philosophers affirm without hesitation that being is reducible to the ensemble of empirical facts. There are no ghosts, no souls, no essences; there is no non-geometrical space of distantiation and freedom; there is no ontological difference. Intentionality is part of the natural world like any other phenomenon. They offer no more justification for these claims than did Hobbes for the thesis that all the universe is Body. These metaphysical claims are really correlates of a methodological preference. Hobbes' nature has no room for any mode of being that cannot be accounted for in terms of the movements and resultant configurations of one-dimensional elements.

We may conclude, therefore, that *Leviathan* was in its way a critique of reason and a philosophy of limit. We now realize that Hobbes was saying that neither intuition nor reckoning yield access to essences. But this discovery of limit was not an occasion for wonder, nor a lesson in the dangers of *hubris*. There is no echo in Hobbes of the prudent admonition of his contemporary, Pascal: "Let us then learn our range."[15] For Hobbes, human nature is *conatus*, impulse, unlimited desire, the incessant drive to acquire power after power. The task of reason, therefore, is management and control; its goal is to maximize the expansion of power and to minimize its side effects. The cunning of reason is, in fact, the cunning of nature's will to power. No doubt, this theme accounts for an odd conjuncture in contemporary philosophy: a stress on limit which takes the form of an insouciant attitude towards relativism, combined with a stress on the unlimited potential of scientific method which takes the form of a militant and confident naturalism. The point is to give up on truth and settle for power.

---

a nuanced interpretation of the "public" status of the work of mind, see Robert Sokolowski, *Moral Action: A Phenomenological Study* (Bloomington: Indiana Univ. Press, 1985), pp. 27–34; 195–199; 219–220.

14. Richard Rorty, *Philosophy and the Mirror of Nature* (Princeton: Princeton Univ. Press, 1979), p. 387.

15. Blaise Pascal, *Pensées*. ed. Louis Lafuma (Paris: Éditions du Seuil, 1962), 199 (72), p. 118. "Connaissons donc notre portée."

Edmund Husserl clearly discerned the link between this exaltation of calculative rationality and the underlying irrationalism of Hobbes' thesis that reason is a scout for the passions. His critique, however, is not the obvious one, that reason discerns goods specific to itself and irreducible to passion's unrestricted drive for power. In the *Crisis*, he shrewdly remarks that one should not be misled by the apparent humiliation of reason suggested by Hobbes' assignment to the soul of the same type of being had by mathematicized nature.[16] He notes that a spirit of rationalism is perfectly compatible with the naturalizing of the psyche. Indeed, Hobbes' revolution seemed to promise that a more developed physics would in the end "explain" what had heretofore been the province of magical or mythical accounts that had postulated odd non-causal relationships and non-physical entities. Hobbes' rationalism, however, is not founded upon the expectation that being is fundamentally intelligible. Reason's hope derives from the sense of power associated with the *esprit de géometrie* rather than from any conviction that the real is rational. As Spragens puts it, "the universe is liberated by Hobbes from the shackles of impenetrable substance only to be delivered into the anarchy of purely inertial motion."[17]

It required a genius such as Hume, says Husserl, to take the critique of essences initiated by Hobbes and further developed by Locke to its logical conclusions. Hume realized that if intuitive reason cannot break out of the circle of impressions and ideas, there is no justification for supposing that calculative rationality can yield any less fanciful results. Thus, the key to Hume's scepticism is his appreciation of the dependence of scientific knowing on pre-scientific experience. All of the categories requisite for a mathematicized version of nature, and for a theory of how matter in motion produces impressions of forms (including the fundamental categories such as identity, resemblance, contiguity, causality) must be derivable from pre-scientific experience which, on Hume's account, remains confined to the zone of immanence. Berkeley had already observed that inferences drawn from immanent data do not justify statements about anything but other such data. Hume concluded that our belief in the identity and existence of extra-mental things corresponding to sensory clusters is unjustifiable: "Hume goes on to the end. All categories of objectiv-

16. Edmund Husserl, *The Crisis of European Sciences and Transcendental Phenomenology*. trans. David Carr (Evanston: Northwestern Univ. Press, 1970), sec. 11, pp. 62–63. *Die Krisis der europäischen Wissenschaften und die transzendentale Phänomenologie*, ed. W. Biemel (The Hague: Nijhoff, 1954), pp. 63–64.

17. Spragens, *The Politics of Motion*, p. 92.

ity—the scientific ones through which an objective extra-psychic world is thought in scientific life, and the pre-scientific ones through which it is thought in everyday life—are fictions."[18] Husserl further observes that Hume says not a word about the status of his own reason (i.e., the reason of the inquiring philosopher) which takes the philosophic positions of solipsism and scepticism, and which gives an account of the mind's workings within the realm of illusion. Husserl thus suggests that, despite his passionate radicalism, even Hume did not comprehend the full collapse of the traditional notion of rationality entailed by Hobbes' model for mind.

Let us consider more in detail the implications of this criticism. The empiricists generally argue that the illusion of perception is induced by processes of association which assemble into configurations those elementary contents that habitually occur together. Thus, Berkeley explains the appearance of unified things as a product of association by contiguity: "a certain colour, taste, smell, figure and consistency having been observed to go together, are accounted one distinct thing signified by the name apple."[19] Moreover, they all appeal to association by resemblance in order to account for re-cognition and the gradual acquisition of a repertory of ideas. Husserl's comment on Hume's failure to call into question the cognitive status of the inquiring philosopher suggests that the deeper incoherence of empiricism lies in the fact that it constantly invokes notions that would be incomprehensible, were it not for our consciousness of transcendent things and objective relationships. How does Hume, qua inquiring philosopher, know in the first place what 'contiguity' and 'resemblance' mean, if we have no consciousness of these relationships? The vague theme of association masks the circularity of his argument. Unperceived objective relationships (contiguity and resemblance) are said to govern associative processes that produce impressions of objective properties and relationships. Now either there occurs a consciousness of properties and relationships somewhere in this circuit, or it is simply nonsense to speak of impressions as though they were anything more than physical traces. Empiricism thus trades on a tacit acknowledgement of conscious acts whose intentional thrust transcends the mind's interiority, while its overt theory reduces those acts to the mere having and processing of intra-mental impressions. Hume understood that any attempt to break out of the circle of ideas is incoherent, because

18. *Crisis*, sec. 23, p. 87. *Krisis*, p. 89.
19. George Berkeley, *A Treatise Concerning the Principles of Human Knowledge* (London, 1910), Part I, p. 1.

there is no standpoint from which we might inspect the relationship between impressions and their alleged extra-mental causes.

Husserl's point is that the empiricist account is even more incoherent than Hume had realized. What seems to lend some credibility to the whole discussion of association is the exemption from the human condition extended to the philosophic inquirer who is presumed to have access to the notions of contiguity and resemblance without ever having to derive them from pre-philosophic intuitions. But this exemption is unwarranted. If pre-philosophic experience does not yield access to these relationships, then we simply do not know about them. We may conclude that empiricism implicitly concedes that the mind somehow registers objective relationships. But to register anything is to transcend containment within the performance of registration. Even to register intra-mental representations would be a transcending act. The passage from the mind's eye to the screen of impressions would necessarily involve some consciousness of a content. If the mind is capable of such transcendence, then why describe it in the first place as a subjective enclosure? Empiricism's explanatory concepts are derived from an intuitive grasp of what is, while its metaphor for mind as a theatre of representations renders such intuition incomprehensible.

Husserl's response to the crisis of reason provoked by its reduction to reckoning and coping was an effort to restore confidence in the rationality of intuition. As early as 1894, he contended that intuitive consciousness reaches out beyond sensory impressions, and grasps the intended object itself: "an intuition is a 'setting before' in an authentic sense, where the object is actually put before us in such a manner that the object is itself the topic of psychical activity."[20] In other words, a perceptual *Vorstellung* is not a representation but a presentation. The centerpiece of *Logical Investigations* (1900) is the theory of categorial intuition, which essentially reaffirms Aristotle's description of intuitive discrimination. When we look at something, we combine two complementary modes of intuition: (1) the intuition that an individual has the "look" (*eidos*) belonging to a family of things; (2) the intuition that the "look" has an indefinite number of instances.[21] What

20. Edmund Husserl, "Psychological Studies in the Elements of Logic," trans. Dallas Willard, *The Personalist*, LVIII (October, 1977), 304. "Psychologische Studien zur elementaren Logik," *Philosophische Monatshefte*, XXX (1894), 159–191.

21. *Metaphysics* Z, 6, 1031b 6–7; 20–21. See Joseph Owens, *The Doctrine of Being in the Aristotelian Metaphysics* (Toronto: Pontifical Institute of Medieval Studies, 1963), pp. 391–393. My formulation of Aristotle's position is taken from Stanley Rosen, *The Limits of Analysis*, p. 60.

presents itself to our intelligence when we look at a particular thing is its species-look. The species-look is thus what we know, when we know this particular thing. We grasp the *what* both as a surplus whose sense exceeds the particularity of this instance, and as the condition for the manifestation of this particular as *x* or *y*. Husserl describes particular and categorial intuition as having a reciprocal founding/founded relationship. There is no insight into essences that is not based on a prior seeing of the *what* and *this* together, and there is no seeing of particulars except as instances or some species-look.[22]

The purpose of Husserl's celebrated *epoché* was not to retract this interpretation of cognitive intuition, but to highlight the incoherence of the naturalistic interpretation of being. Husserl's comments on Kant's theory of the in-itself reveal how inappropriate are those interpretations of the reduction which suggest that Husserl's transcendental turn entailed a reaffirmation of the modern thesis that we know mental substitutes rather than real things. He contends that Kant's historical mission ought to have been to struggle with the enigma that engendered Hume's scepticism. Hume's radicalism led him to shake the foundations of that "dogmatic mathematicizing objectivism, so inspiring to people of the time, which ascribed to the world itself a mathematical-rational in-itself (which we copy, so to speak, better and better in our more or less perfect theories)."[23] Hume saw that the attempt to think of an inaccessible in-itself having any properties whatsoever (e.g., the characteristics ascribed by Hobbes to the realm of nature: materiality, motion, *conatus*) is inconsistent. Moreover, he understood that the postulate of anything whatsoever beyond the circle of impressions and ideas, even a world-horizon within which the circle of ideas might somehow be situated, is equally inconsistent. Seeing that the concepts "world" and "extra-mental reality" had to be derived from information provided by the realm of impressions, Hume fell back into a scepticism. Hume was on the right track, however, to the extent that his radicalism led him to the realization that it makes no sense to posit a realm of being beyond the reach of rationality. His scepticism was the product of unfortunate presuppositions, rather than of the deepest direction of his thought. His mistake was to have decided in advance what is meant by a transcendent thing, and then to have construed the mind itself on that model. In other words, he took it for granted that the processes of mind have the same

22. Edmund Husserl, *Logical Investigations*. trans. J. N. Findlay (London: Routledge & Kegan Paul, 1970), Vol. II, sec. 40–52, pp. 773–802. *Logische Untersuchungen* (Tübingen: Max Niemeyer Verlag, 1968), II/2, pp. 128–164.
23. *Crisis*, sec. 24, p. 90. *Krisis*, p. 93.

sort of reality as the transcendent things that we would reach, if we could somehow break out of the circle of immanence. This is the basic premise of all forms of naturalism. But there can be no solution to the enigma of cognition, if mental processes and their intentional targets are related to one another in the same way as things within the causal network of nature. Intentionality is not a field of force between clusters of matter in motion.

What awakened Kant from his dogmatic slumber, according to Husserl, was the threat posed by Hume's scepticism to the scientific mode of objectivity. He did not take seriously enough Hume's conclusion that even the world of everyday life must be related to the reach of rationality. Had Kant taken the full scope of the problem into consideration, he might have discerned the root error of empiricism, i.e., the illicit transfer of the pseudo-transcendence of things to the acts of the knowing subject.[24] This is strong language indeed, especially as it occurs in the section immediately preceding the introduction of the great theme that dominates the rest of the *Crisis:* modern philosophy as a struggle between transcendentalism and naturalism.

Why does Kant fail to attain the level of insight achieved by Hume? Why is Hume's scepticism, which Husserl surely found abhorrent, a more illuminating protreptic to genuine transcendentalism than Kant's inquiry into the conditions of scientific objectivity? On Husserl's view, Kant's methodological error is this: he set about to justify the mathematicized version of nature, without ever having called into question Hobbes' rejection of the traditional understanding of the relationship between the soul and nature. Having accepted the empiricist premise that sensory affections caused by hidden and unknowable things-in-themselves provide the only link between mind and nature, Kant's strategy was to establish that the same faculties which express themselves in mathematical thinking also function ceaselessly in the rationalizing of sense-data.[25] In this way, he secured the compatibility of the sensibly intuited and mathematically determined realms, but at the price of denying to either prescientific or scientific cognition an access to nature-in-itself. Husserl calls attention in passing to the ambiguity of this philosophy of limit, which thinks the beyond but restricts the range of intuitive rationality.[26]

Throughout the remainder of the *Crisis*, Husserl reproaches Kant for not noticing how the modern mathematical sciences had transformed the meaning of nature. He recognizes, of course, that Kant

24. *Crisis*, sec. 25, pp. 95–97. *Krisis*, pp. 98–100.
25. *Crisis*, sec. 25, pp. 94–95. *Krisis*, pp. 97–98.
26. *Crisis*, sec. 25, p. 95. *Krisis*, p. 98.

repudiates Hobbes' derivation of reason from natural drives. Indeed, he praises Kantian transcendentalism for undertaking to ground scientific objectivity in the syntheses effected by the work of mind. His criticism is that Kant's preoccupation with the transcendental conditions for the appearance of scientific objects led him to neglect the more fundamental problem of relating the everyday surrounding lifeworld to the anonymously functioning performances of subjectivity. He also objects to the inferential character of Kant's transcendentalism, noting that the deductive method yields an excessively elaborate machinery of faculties and functions. Husserl proposes to replace this inferential method with a thoroughly intuitive method, adding that Kant was wrong to have subscribed uncritically to the empiricist account of intuition.[27]

There is a link between these two criticisms and Husserl's earlier claim that Kant's philosophic questioning lacks the radical scope that we find in Hume. Husserl's fundamental insight is this: nothing may be coherently thought of as having a status beyond the range of rationality, not even the horizon of the world or the most anonymous transcendental functions. Any attempt to conceive of a dimension of being beyond the zone of possible consciousness is nonsensical. Consciousness and being belong together. Their ranges are coextensive. Moreover, to make exceptions to this principle is to make concessions to the naturalistic interpretation of being. Neither other persons, nor the domain of culture, nor the conceptual and linguistic matrix of philosophy itself, nor even the contingent status of the reflecting philosopher may be considered as having a being independent of, prior to, or beyond the ken of transcendental consciousness. The transcendental dimension is not a region alongside of other regions; it has no outside.[28]

Husserl's statement that the transcendental sphere has no perimeters, and that it therefore cannot be located within empirical coordinates, introduces an extraordinary image. Commentators have not meditated enough on its significance. Indeed, some have concluded that it testifies to an excessive rationalism. Given the primacy that Husserl ascribes to perception, there can be no question in his work of the typically modern mathematical rationalism, but there is, it is argued, an implicit commitment to an ideal of truth attainable only by

27. *Crisis*, sec. 30, pp. 115–116. *Krisis*, p. 118.
28. Edmund Husserl, *Ideas Pertaining to a Pure Phenomenology and to a Phenomenological Philosophy. Book I*. trans. F. Kersten (The Hague: Nijhoff, 1982), sec. 49, p. 112 sec. 51, p. 116. *Ideen zu einer reinen Phänomenologie und phänomenologischen Philosophie. Buch I.* ed. Karl Schumann (The Hague: Nijhoff, 1976), p. 93; p. 96.

an intellect operating under non-finite conditions. Jacques Derrida finds textual support for this interpretation in those passages of *Ideas* where Husserl comments on the Kantian theme "the object = X." Husserl criticizes the Kantian distinction between the thing-in-itself as known by an infinite mind and the thing as it appears to us, on the grounds that this comparison suggests that human perception delivers images or signs of things, rather than the things themselves. Moreover, he contends that physical things are such that perspectival presentation belongs to their mode of being. Like Bergson who observed that to have the experience of a cup of coffee in its fullness even God must wait for the sugar to melt, Husserl claims that things are necessarily given in successive profiles rather than all at once. He thus defines perceptual givenness as incomplete without measuring its incompleteness against a postulated non-finite mode of knowing. The experience of alternate perspectives requires the positing of the empty "X" as a placeholder for further inquiry, but it does not require that the "X" be taken as a thing-in-itself known by an *intuitus originarius*. However, he does retain the regulative idea of an infinity of profiles. The idea of an endless continuum of perspectives is entailed by the discovery that it is always possible to look at something from a new angle. To refer to the object as "X" is, therefore, to designate it as the inexhaustible subject of alternate perspectives, and also to posit a goal that motivates endless inquiry. Kant had described the idea of the "object = X" as an intention without intuition. According to Husserl, however, all intentions are geared to intuition. Of course, an infinity of profiles is not actually given in the idea of a thing's unlimited determinability, but it does not follow that there can be no intuitive fulfillment of the idea itself. Since the idea of an infinity of profiles is not itself an infinity, the idea can be given adequately: "seeing intellectually that this infinity of necessity cannot be given does not exclude, but rather requires, the intellectually seen givenness of the idea of this infinity."[29] Husserl adds, however, that its mode of intuition is unique. Derrida points out that Husserl does not reflect sufficiently on this uniqueness. The regulative idea of the infinite determinability of the "X" is the correlate of a highly unusual mode of intentionality, for to intend this idea is not to intend some determinate object, but objectivity itself. Phenomenology, Derrida contends, cannot really provide an intuitive founding for the idea of objectivity. An intuition of the non-intuitability of an infinite series is not really a mode of evidence, but an index of an unverifiable premise. Thus, the unique interplay of

29. *Ideas I*, sec. 143, p. 343. *Ideen I*, p. 298.

intending and fulfilling involved in our grasp of the regulative possibility of a thing's appearing reveals an unjustifiable presupposition operative in Husserl's theory of intentionality, the notion that truth is complete adequation or total disclosure.[30]

However subtle, this analysis is a caricature of Husserl's position. Husserl does not claim that truth requires the having of an infinity of perspectives. Indeed, he stresses that inexhaustibility is an essential characteristic of a thing's mode of being, and hence of its truthfulness. Moreover, there are also non-perspectival intuitions. For example, the intuitive grasp of perception's essentially perspectival character is not itself another perspective on the same level as the perspectival presentations of a thing. To grasp the principle governing the endless continuum of profiles is not to enjoy another profile but to identify an invariant structure of appearing. Derrida's analysis seems to be guided by Nietzsche's inflated perspectivalism which obliterates differences in modes of truthfulness, and even undermines the notion of truth itself by reducing presentational modes to a play of illusions generated by the will to power. Husserl would reject this interpretation of truth as will to power for the same reason that he rejects Hobbes' account of rationality. To enjoy the truth is not to be in possession of some more powerful or life-enhancing illusion, but to have discerned the essential from the adventitious in some domain. Truth comes in different forms: there are the clarities attained by mathematical reason, the necessities discovered in moral praxis, the complementary structures uncovered by interpretation and explanation, the perspectives articulated in judgments of perception, and the illuminating distinctions achieved by philosophical reflection. It is just as inappropriate to blur these nuances by asserting that all knowing is perspectival, or that another interpretation is always possible, as it is to look for mathematical certitudes in the ethical and political domains. To say that the regulative idea of an infinity of profiles is essential to the perception of things is not to try to salvage a non-finite standard of objectivity, but simply to acknowledge a condition for the recognition of a perspective as such. There is a difference between saying that truth requires the actual grasp of an infinity of perspectives all at once, and saying that perception entails the regulative idea of an endless series of alternate perspectives. Moreover, the latter statement is more than a "perception" about perception; it articulates an intellectually intuited ne-

30. Jacques Derrida, *Edmund Husserl's Origin of Geometry: An Introduction.* trans. John P. Leavey (Stony Brook: Nicholas Hays, 1978), pp. 139–141. Edmund Husserl, *L'Origine de la géometrie.* trans. and intro. Jacques Derrida (Paris: Presses Universitaires de France, 1962), pp. 152–5.

cessity. Acceptance of finitude does not require the reduction of such necessities to interpretative projections. On Husserl's view, the discovery that there are inexhaustible horizons is enough to teach reason its limits. There is a middle ground between the reduction of reason to coping and the arrogant claim that finite intellects are capable of thematic display of the totality. Phenomenology's goal is to describe the manifold modes of truth available in that properly human intermediary area.

When Husserl claims that rationality and being are coextensive, he is making the same point as Wittgenstein in the *Tractatus:* "Logic pervades the world: the limits of the world are also its limits. So we cannot say in logic, 'The world has this in it and this, but not that.'"[31] In other words, we cannot talk from outside the network of rationality; we cannot consider the limits from the other side too. It is reason itself that always posits or recognizes its limits. Hence, reason has horizons but not an outside. I take it that these spatial metaphors are intended to convey something analogous to what Aristotle meant when he said that the cognitive intellect somehow becomes the forms of things, and what the Medieval thinkers meant by the maxim *anima est quodammodo omnia.* The intellect does not have a structure of its own, but rather enjoys a freedom from structure such that it can become the forms of things in a unique mode of presence combined with detachment.[32] The intellect's formal malleability is the condition of its unique mode of being. If the intellect had a fixed structure, it would be an entity alongside of others; it would have an outside.

To say that rationality has no outside is not to reject finitude, but simply to reject incoherent descriptions of reason's limits. To know in a limited way is to be challenged by an infinite task, rather than to be separated from a radically unknowable reality.

31. Ludwig Wittgenstein, *Tractatus Logico-Philosophicus.* trans. and ed. D. F. Pears and B. F. McGuinness (London: Routledge & Kegan Paul, 1961), 5.61, p. 115.
32. See Stanley Rosen, *The Limits of Analysis,* pp. 35–7.

4

Husserl, Lask, and the Idea of Transcendental Logic

STEVEN GALT CROWELL

The question of a transcendental logic was one of the two great issues to which Husserl devoted himself in the last ten years of his life. Together with the theme of the Lifeworld, transcendental logic seemed to provide a way of articulating what he saw as the universal mission of phenomenology: to re-animate the tradition of Western rationality by establishing philosophy in its historically mandated role as foundational science. Of these two issues, inseparable though they were in Husserl's mind, the problem of the Lifeworld continues to enjoy a currency which that of transcendental logic seems to lack. Yet contemporary debates within epistemology and metaphysics, such as that concerning the nature of realism, come increasingly into the orbit of problems Husserl addressed under the heading of transcendental logic: what it is to be an object, the relation between objectivity and evidence, "categorial frameworks," and the ground of propositional truth. But to appreciate Husserl's contribution to this debate it is first necessary to become clear about the sense in which they are *transcendental* problems, and that means, to become clear about what a transcendental problem is.

In this paper I hope to contribute something to such clarification by contrasting Husserl's conception of transcendental logic with that of Emil Lask, whose major writings on the subject were published just prior to the emergence of Husserl's "transcendental" version of phenomenology.[1] Lask's work involves a criticism of Husserl's pre-transcendental approach to the philosophical problems of logic. At the same time, the shortcomings of Lask's own conception of the tran-

---

1. Emil Lask, *Die Logik der Philosophie und die Kategorienlehre* (1911), and *Die Lehre vom Urteil* (1912), in *Gesammelte Schriften*, ed. Eugen Herrigel (Tübingen: J. C. B. Mohr, 1923), Vol. II, pp. 1–282, 283–463. My references to these works will be incorporated into the text, abbreviated LP and LvU respectively. The translations of all previously untranslated material in Lask and Husserl are my own.

scendental point toward issues which were even then leading Husserl to the phenomenological reduction, his "way" into transcendental thematics. In specifying certain points of convergence and divergence in their views we will be tracing a moment in the archaeology of transcendental philosophy.[2]

1. TRANSCENDENTAL LOGIC AS A THEORY OF MEANING

The origin of the contrast between Husserl and Lask is to be found already in Kant's Transcendental Analytic, or "logic of truth." Whereas general logic abstracts from all content and thematizes the purely syntactical rules knowledge must adhere to lest it contradict *itself*, the "logic of truth" has the task of providing an a priori semantics, or rules without which the formal laws of thought can have no content, i.e., "without which no object can be thought."[3] Transcendental logic thus deals with categories and principles valid of objects a priori, i.e., which truly refer to objects but whose reference cannot be established empirically. How is such a logic possible?

Kant answers with his famous "Copernican Revolution": the categories are valid of objects a priori because they *constitute* objects. Here transcendental logic faces a two-fold task, and subsequent transcendental philosophy inherits a two-fold problem. On the one hand transcendental logic involves the "objective-logical" question of which

2. At the outset a word should be said about what Husserl knew of Lask. Husserl nowhere mentions Lask, a student of Heinrich Rickert, in his published writings. And though Lask sent both of his works on logic to Husserl, the underlinings in the copies preserved at the Husserl-Archive in Leuven indicate that Husserl probably read only the first 18 pages of LP and probably did not read LvU at all. In a letter to Rickert shortly after Lask's death in 1915 at the age of 39, however, Husserl remarks of Lask that "eine der schönsten Hoffnungen der deutschen Philosophie ist mit ihm dahingegangen" (R I/Rickert; 5.11.1915). And on the margin of a manuscript from 1923 dealing with the role of the "persönliche Einstellung" in Kant's doctrine of apperception (F II 7/162b) Husserl notes "auch Lask muss endlich gelesen werden." It is perhaps at this time, when Husserl was finding affinities between his position and Fichte's, that he began to read Lask's *Fichtes Idealismus und die Geschichte* (1902), Husserl's copy of which is heavily underlined, though again only to page 19. There are only three other references to Lask in all of Husserl's unpublished manuscripts, none of them substantial. In a letter from Lask to Husserl (24.12.1911) we learn that Husserl had sent Lask a copy of "Philosophy as Rigorous Science" and had also at some point sent some criticisms of LP as (in Lask's words) being full of "Unexaktheit, Ungründlichkeit, Belastetheit mit Äquivokationen." The present essay will indicate some of the points which might have served as the basis for Husserl's judgment here. I am grateful to Dr. Samuel IJsseling, Director of the Husserl-Archive at Leuven, for permission to examine and quote from this material, and to Dr. Ulrich Melle for his help in deciphering Lask's handwriting in the letter to Husserl.

3. Immanuel Kant, *The Critique of Pure Reason*, tr. Norman Kemp Smith (New York: St. Martin's, 1968), p. 100.

concepts are "forms of an object in general." Which concepts have objective validity a priori? On the other hand it involves the "subjective-logical" question of the "origin"[4] of such non-empirical concepts. Under the Copernican Hypothesis the two questions are related. Certain non-empirical concepts have objective validity because, as originating in the subject, they first of all make possible objects *for* the subject. As subjective forms for the synthesis of a space-time manifold, the "categories" are rules for what it means to be an object at all. But just because the object is seen as a function of subjective synthesis, its transcendental status cannot be that of a metaphysical "in itself," but only that of an objective "representation."

In the wake of the Hegelian criticism of Kant and the emergence of positivism, various Neo-Kantian philosophers sought to renew the project of transcendental logic. But even those who turned "back to Kant" acknowledged significant limitations in Kant's original idea. On the "objective-logical" side, Kant's deduction of the categories from the table of logical judgments was felt to be both artificial and too restrictive. Not only did the emergence of logistics make the table itself obsolete, the categories themselves seemed to provide a foundation only for the knowledge of Nature. If the Kantian project was at all tenable, would there not be categories specific to knowledge in the domain of history and the related cultural sciences as well? On the "subjective-logical" side, the idea that categories were subjective "forms of synthesis" seemed all too reminiscent of the then-current psychologism. What were these syntheses, if not part of a specifically human (and therefore evolving, changing) psychological apparatus? Finally, when taken together, these problems indicated perhaps the most troubling difficulty of all: the failure of Kant's transcendental reflection to account for *itself* as a legitimate mode of "knowledge."

Against the background of such problems Husserl and Lask, each in his own way, seek to re-interpret the idea of transcendental logic. Such a re-interpretation demands a thorough re-casting of both the objective-logical and the subjective-logical dimensions of Kant's project. And it is for our purposes essential to note that both Husserl and Lask do so by appeal to the concept of meaning [*Sinn*]. For both, the concept of meaning comes to supplant the Kantian notion of "representation" as the term for the transcendental status of the object. But though both provide a nonrepresentational theory of meaning, their views on what constitutes the "transcendentality" of meaning present us with a study in contrast, a case of diametrically opposed emphasis.

4. Ibid., p. 96.

For Lask, transcendental logic as a theory of meaning is first of all *ontology*, for Husserl *phenomenology*.

Lask emphasizes the objective-logical side of Kant's project by identifying meaning with the transcendental truth-structure of the object "prior to all contact with subjectivity" (LvU 425). By this he does not mean that the object lies in a "metalogical" region beyond the reach of knowledge. Rather, his point is that knowledge, as the properly subjective activity of making judgments, must be grounded in a transcendental truth-concept that serves as its measure, viz., "meaning" as the objective unity of categorial form and material. Thus Lask's revision of Kant minimalizes the role of the transcendental synthesis, according to which objects are constituted "in" the subject, and moves toward an "a-metaphysical" Aristotelianism, an ontology of the transcendental object as meaning.[5]

Husserl, on the other hand, revises the Kantian project by an ever-deepening concern with its subjective-logical dimension. Husserl's earliest logical works are not works of transcendental philosophy and exhibit a deep distrust of Kantianism. But the subsequent development of his phenomenology comes increasingly under the sign of a Kant mediated by Descartes, the true father of the "transcendental turn."[6] Though Husserl too is concerned with ontological problems, the genuinely transcendental issues of logic are for him contained in the Kantian theory of synthesis, which Husserl makes his own by enriching it with a "Cartesian" theory of evidence in the concept of a phenomenological constitution of meaning.

As important as these differences between Lask and Husserl are, they must not be allowed to obscure the fact that both have in view the same (transcendental) domain of meaning. At bottom their theories of meaning are distinguished by a "nuance," albeit one that spells the "life and death" of genuine transcendental philosophy—the phenomenological reduction. Lask's ontology of meaning already in some sense occupies the field of evidence opened up by the reduction, though it does so "naively" and therefore inconsistently. In contrast to the position of the *Logical Investigations* (the only work of Husserl's with which Lask was familiar), Lask's ontology already sights the prob-

5. For Lask's view of Aristotle see (LvU 403–404) and (LP 223–243). On Lask's attempt to "synthesize" Aristotle and Kant, see Wolf-Dieter Gudopp, *Der Junge Heidegger* (Frankfurt: Verlag Marxistische Blätter, 1983), pp. 30–34.

6. Cf. Edmund Husserl, *Erste Philosophie: Erster Teil*, Husserliana Bd. VII, ed. Rudolf Boehm (The Hague: Martinus Nijhoff, 1956), p. 63. On the interplay between Kantian and Cartesian motives in the development of Husserl's transcendental phenomenology see Iso Kern, *Husserl und Kant* (The Hague: Martinus Nijhoff, 1964), p. 109 pass.

lem of *transcendence,* and does so in a non-metaphysical way. Yet his elision of the transcendental subject, motivated by anti-psychologistic insights he shared with Husserl, involves his account of transcendence in certain "naturalistic" inconsistencies which only an *explicit* application of the reduction can resolve. Just such inconsistencies are what led Husserl to propose the reduction as a *sine qua non* of transcendental logic in the first place, as the newly published *Einleitung in die Logik und Erkenntnistheorie* testifies.[7] In bringing this text to bear on the *aporiae* of Lask's position, therefore, we shall illustrate what Iso Kern has called "the way from ontology"[8] to the phenomenological reduction, and so illuminate one central aspect of a transcendental theory of meaning.

2. JUDGMENT AND THE PARADIGMATIC OBJECT

Both Lask and Husserl conceive transcendental logic as a theory of the conditions for the possibility of knowledge. Thus the conditions for the truth of the judgment make up an important theme for investigation. But again for both, the judgment as such is not the most primordial level of the logical problematic. As Lask puts it, the judgment is merely the *próteron pròs hēmas,* the first with respect to us (LvU 287). It must be clarified by recourse to a level which is first in itself. In specifying what this more primordial level is, however, Husserl and Lask part company. For the former it is the evidence of pre-predicative *experience;* for the latter it is what he calls the "paradigmatic" [*urbildlich*] region of the transcendental *object* itself. Lask's arguments for this position, and the resulting account of judgment-meaning, thus provide a frame of reference for our contrast with Husserl.

Lask takes the significance of Kant's transcendental turn to lie in the insight that the phenomenon of judgment (judgment form) does not exhaust the scope of purely *logical,* non-metaphysical inquiry. Indeed, judgment is a "derivative" or secondary theme presupposing what Lask calls a "doctrine of categories," an objective-logical theory of how "the logical reaches to the level of objects themselves as a constituting moment" (LvU 286). The judgment takes on secondary status within transcendental logic because it is merely a "means for taking possession of the object" on the part of the *subject,* and thus presupposes an investigation into the logical status of this object itself "wholly un-

7. Edmund Husserl, *Einleitung in die Logik und Erkenntnistheorie,* Husserliana Bd. XXIV, ed. Ulrich Melle (Dordrecht: Martinus Nijhoff, 1984). Hereafter abbreviated ELE.
8. Kern, op. cit., pp. 218–239.

touched by subjectivity" (LvU 287). The transcendental object, or what Lask calls the "paradigmatic object" [*gegenständlicher Urbild*], is thus the original theme of transcendental logic.

But if it is not constituted by the subject, in what sense is such a pre-judicative "paradigmatic" object still a *transcendental* concept? Here Lask gives an Aristotelean accent to what he calls Kant's "Copernican Achievement" [*Kopernikanische Tat*]. The Copernican Achievement does not mean that the object is *constituted* by the subject *qua* representation, but that "the concept of being is transformed into a transcendental-logical concept" (LP 28). In other words, Kant's achievement was to have seen that "being" (and *eo ipso* any a priori concept, any "category") is neither a nominalist *flatus vocis* nor a metaphysical element or entity, but "logical content" [*logischen Gehalt*] which constitutes the "objectivity" of an object, the "being" of a being (LP 30). The doctrine of categories is a study of the logical content which belongs to the transcendental structure, the "objectivity" of the object.

Thus Lask's paradigmatic object, as the goal and measure of cognition, is not a "metalogical" transcendent—one whose structure "in itself" would be thoroughly extra-logical—but one in which logical content is already found. Lask argues that this is sufficient to distinguish his transcendental position from the Aristotelian metaphysics with which it shares many features. Both Lask and Aristotle conceive the "paradigmatic" object as an original (not subjectively synthesized) unity of categorial form and material. But whereas Aristotle's "forms" are metaphysical (metalogical) "actualities" existing in things, Lask's categorial form is not a "real" part of the object, but its "objectivity."

To understand the transcendentality of the object here one needs to know how logical and metaphysical "form" are to be distinguished. According to Lask all pre-Kantian theories of logical categoriality were blinded by their commitment to the metaphysical "two world" theory, a fundamental duality within the totality of what is thinkable [*All des Denkbaren*] between the world of "sensible being" and the world of "supersensible being" (LP 5). On such a schema logical form can only remain "homeless," for it is neither a sensible entity nor a supersensible entity. Even Kant's doctrine of categories did not break free entirely from the "two world" picture. According to Lask it was Hermann Lotze who first saw clearly the proper *transcendental* distinction within the totality of the thinkable, between *beings* (physical and metaphysical) on the one hand and *validities* on the other, between "that which *is* and occurs, and that which *holds* [*gilt*] without having to be [*ohne sein zu müssen*]" (LP 6). Logical form is neither a metaphysical element nor a subjective function of synthesis because it "is" not at all;

it is "valid," or "holds" [*gilt*]. To say that the object is "constituted" by logical form is thus simply to have in view the object as a primordial unity of valid form and the material of which it is valid.

To this primordial unity, the *Urverhältnis* of categorial form and material, Lask gives the name "meaning" [*Sinn*], the object in its "truth." Meaning, as Lask notes, is a specifically transcendental-philosophical "predicate," i.e., it denotes what the object shows itself to be from the perspective of transcendental reflection (LP 122–3). Thus "meaning" does not denote a realm of entities *in addition* to the entities of physics and metaphysics (if there are any of these latter). It is just these very entities themselves "in truth," i.e., so far as to be "something" [*Etwas*] at all is to be "material" which "stands in" categorial form: "Particular objects are particular unities of theoretical meaning, particular 'truths'" (LP 41). Further, because Lask defines categorial form in terms of the Lotzean concept of validity and not in terms of a subjective function of synthesis (Kant), the object as meaning cannot be seen as a mere representation. The subject does indeed constitute "representations" [*Nachbilder*] in the act of judging. But transcendental logic is concerned first of all with the truth-structure (meaning-structure) of the object itself, the *ground* of such representing activity.

Meaning is thus a purely transcendental concept whose extension coincides with that of "object in general." The domain of objects, however, is not a uniform field restricted to the "sensibly given manifold," but is differentiated into "regions" on the basis of a purely *functional* conception of the form/material relation. To be a category is to be functionally related to a *certain range* of material as that which provides the "*Klarheitsmoment*" (LP 75), or moment of intelligibility in the object, and to be material is simply to be that which is "clarified" or objectified by categorial form. Thus while it is true that all categorial form is "valid," it is not necessary that all material be "non-valid" or thoroughly alogical (LP 49).

In light of the functional definition of the form/material relation, Lask's doctrine of categories provides what Husserl called "regional ontologies," a theory of the "material logical" forms which ground the object-domains of individual sciences. There is, further, an analogue to Husserl's doctrine of "foundation" in Lask's notion of "tiers" [*Stockwerke*] within the domain of objects in general. At the lowest level lies the thoroughly alogical material which pertains to the category "sensible being" (LP 50). But this "limiting case of alogicity" does not define materiality as such. The unity which is constituted by the relation between "being" and its specific material ("sensibly intuitable" material strictly as such) can itself occupy the "material" place with regard to higher-order categories, for example that of "life." The category "life" presupposes, but is not reducible to, the material of the lower level. Just as the category "being" includes in a logically ordered way the plurality of a priori concepts of physics (thinghood, causality, etc.), so the category "life" indicates a *further* "objective involvement" [*objektive Bewandtnis*] in the material which displays itself in the a priori concepts of biology (organism, development, etc.). And at still higher levels the "material" for psychology, history, and the other human sciences makes its appearance within the more specific categories of "psychic life," "value-individuality," "cultural achievement," "historical event" etc. (LP 60f). At each level the "founded" science takes as *its* material not the material of the previous level, but the categorially formed unity (object) as such, in which the founding material is no longer thematic.

This functional, or "founded," concept of an object accounts for why it is that the object as such is "meaning" only at the level of transcendental logic. For only in transcendental reflection is the category itself (logical form) the specific *material* of investigation. Only in making explicit the logical content itself (as material) by grasping its character as "valid" form does the meaning-character of the "object" at each lower level show itself. At these lower levels, the levels of positive or non-philosophical sciences, knowing consists in "being given over to the object, to categorially formed material, whereby however the validity character of the form and correspondingly the meaning character of the whole object remains unknown. In such knowledge it is never the object, but always the object material which is known" (LP 122). Because the categories are not entities, but simply the clarity of the material itself, a transcendental reflection which thematizes them postulates no new "metaphysical" entities. It merely recognizes explicitly the logical structure which always already made up the objecthood of the objects belonging to the domains of the particular sciences. In these sciences (and ultimately in pre-scientific life as well) there is a certain pre-thematic, pre-predicative familiarity with the categories sustaining the thematic concern with object-material. Positive cognition "experiences" categorial clarity without "knowing" it. Thus, as Lask puts it, we "live in the truth" (LP 86–87).

Upon this pre-predicative domain of truth Lask grounds the structure of the judgment and addresses the question of *propositional* truth. Here again his concern is not with pre-predicative *experiencing* as such, but with the object *experienced* as it becomes available in transcendental reflection, i.e., as an ontological unity of meaning, as "truth" in the paradigmatic sense. The structure of this object must serve to clarify the structure of the judgment and so account for the possibility of a *correspondence* between the judgment and the object. Only because the object itself is "meaning" (i.e., not a metalogical "substance") can meaning in the judgment correspond to it: "The separation between meaning and the object resolves itself into a distance between meaning and meaning" (LP 43).

But if judgment-meaning in some sense corresponds to object-meaning, or "truth" in the paradigmatic sense, it cannot do so by "picturing" it.[9] The "distance" referred to above reflects the fact that the form of the judgment is not the same as the structure of the object, but is a "complication" (LP 291) of the latter which arises through a "decomposition" and a "reconstruction" of the object. This introduces a moment of "compositeness" [*Zusammengesetztheit*] in the structure of the judgment (represented by the copula) which is not found in the object itself. Such a moment renders the grammatical form of judgment unreliable as a "clue" to the structure of objects. Thus if Lask is to preserve the transcendental status of the object as the "measure" (LvU 357) of truth in the judgment, he must show how the grammatical form of the judgment nevertheless conceals within itself a "logical form" which in some sense *does* reflect the structure of the object. Like Husserl in the *Logical Investigations*, Lask seeks to divorce the logical structure of judgment-meaning from the grammatical structure of the "expressions" in which it is articulated. But Lask believes that this can be done in a transcendentally adequate fashion, i.e., in a way which explains the possibility of propositional *truth* (LvU 321), only by deriving the logical "elements" of the judgment from the elements of the paradigmatic object. To this end he offers his "meta-grammatical subject-predicate theory."

In a judgment a predicate is asserted of a subject. Thus, to use Lask's example, in "a is the cause of b," "being the cause of b" is asserted of the subject "a." But this grammatical form conceals the logical achievement of the judgment, the act of knowing itself, which is "to place the material in the categorial determinations in which it stands *an sich*" (LvU 333). The genuine *logical* elements of judgment-meaning are thus the category and the material: the genuine *subject* of which something is asserted is not "a" but the material ⟨a,b⟩, and that which is asserted of this material, the predicate, is the category "causal-

9. Lask rejects the then-current *Abbildtheorie*, but he does not reject an account of propositional truth in terms of "correspondence" [*Übereinstimmung*]. Cf. LvU 353ff.

ity." The logical meaning of the causal judgment, then, is that certain material ⟨a,b⟩ "stands in" the category "causality" (LvU 333).

The logical structure of judgment-meaning thus consists of the same elements as the "ontological" meaning of the object, though it contains them only in the alienated form of individual "pieces" or concepts (LvU 362) between which a relation needs to be *established.* From the point of view of cognitive inquiry the material (which in itself stands in the clarity of logical form and manifests itself as such in pre-theoretical "experience") is not yet recognized *as* standing in some *specific* logical form. It faces us, as Lask says, as "logically naked" [*logisch nackt*]. Revising the Kantian formula to correspond to the *functional* form/material concept Lask writes: "Form without content is empty, content without form is naked" (LP 74). The task of cognition is to "clothe" the material with the category that pertains to it. Thus the problem of knowledge appears as a problem of "choosing" ("discovering") the proper category for given material (LvU 418). Error, on this view, consists in predicating of certain material a category in which it does not stand. At the highest level this would account for even Kant's "error" in conceiving the transcendental object as "representation." For Kant in effect asserts a relation between the given "material" (in Lask's sense) ⟨form, manifold⟩ and the "category" ⟨subjective synthesis⟩, when in fact the proper choice of categorial predicate would have to be "validity."

So far in Lask's theory of the judgment no explicit reference has been made to the role of "subjectivity" or the transcendental subject. This is a consequence of two deep convictions of Lask's objective-logical approach to transcendental logic. The first is that only by tracing propositional truth back to the paradigmatic object, or "truth" in the transcendental sense, can the "positivist" prejudice (LvU 390) of remaining fixed on secondary or "artificial" [*gekünstelt*] judgment-meaning in the account of knowledge be decisively refuted. The second is that any account of the paradigmatic object in terms of a Kantian "synthesis" must lead to psychologism. Lask's claim is that the Kantian synthesis can itself be explained only in terms of the objective *Urbild,* and so can contribute nothing to clarifying the latter (LvU 406–7). Nevertheless, though the subjective-logical aspect of transcendental logic remains undeveloped in Lask's work, it cannot be altogether ignored. In the following section I will approach this issue by contrasting Lask's theory of the judgment with Husserl's position in the *Logical Investigations,* a work in which it is *precisely* the subjective dimension which holds the key to clarifying the problem of knowledge.

3. SUBJECTIVITY AND TRANSCENDENCE

Lask had studied the *Logical Investigations* carefully and makes several references to it in his writings; but from the outset there is a critical tone. On the one hand Lask applauds the anti-psychologistic direction Husserl gives to philosophical logic, and especially the theory of judgment. Husserl's "historical significance" consists in having "pushed through to the separability of meaning—the 'proposition in itself'—from its real substrate" (LvU 425)—i.e., from the psychically occurring, "non-valid" acts which are for Lask merely the "bearers" of logical meaning (LvU 292). Lask goes so far as to say that this "separability" thesis lies at the foundation of his own theory of judgment (LvU 292). And in one sense it does. However, the real foundation of his theory lies in the paradigmatic object, or "measure" of judgment-meaning, while for Husserl the separability of judgment-meaning consists in its being a "species" *of* acts, or "intentional experiences," and can be clarified only by recourse to such acts in their eidetic descriptive character.[10] Like many others who could not see a continuity between the *Prolegomena* and the "phenomenological clarifications" which followed it, Lask had deep suspicions about the relevance of this inquiry into "acts."

This is not because Lask denies the subject any role in the formation of judgment-meaning. But on Lask's view the "separability" of meaning is alone of significance for logic. The subject is "active" not to the point of creating the meaning of the judgment (this is what it is no matter in what language, or under what circumstances, it is found), but only in "breaking up" the undivided unity of the pre-predicatively experienced object into "pieces" or concepts. And although this would seem to be an important problem for transcendental scrutiny, Lask sees it as a psychological issue, dismissing it by saying that he is not concerned with the "origin" [*entstehen*] of the judgment, but only with its "structure" (LvU 309).

As we have seen, this structure gets explained as a "complication" of the more primordial structure of the paradigmatic object. Thus it is not enough for transcendental logic merely to recognize the "separability" of judgment-meaning, as Lask claims Husserl does (LvU 425). This is still only a "quasi-transcendence" which, though it is structurally separable from subjective acts, nevertheless *points back* to

---

10. Husserl soon abandoned this view of judgment-meaning as a species of acts. Already in 1906 he had rejected it. See ELE 45.

an involvement with subjectivity. Only a theory of *genuine* transcendence, completely free from all reference to the subject, can account for the possible *truth* of the judgment. Only ontology can ground apophantics.

It is here that we locate Lask's main quarrel with the Husserl of the *Logical Investigations*. Their differences concerning the structure of the judgment, though significant, are less important than their fundamental disagreement on what the genuine philosophical task is with regard to the question of *truth*. For Husserl, the problem of truth could not be treated ontologically since the paradigmatic object in Lask's sense seemed to lie quite beyond the apodictic evidence available within the sphere of intentional experiences. As Theodore de Boer has argued, the *Logical Investigations* is methodologically structured on the basis of an ontological dualism which has not yet freed itself entirely from naturalism.[11] The realm of intentional experiences was an island of descriptive certainty, so to speak, within a sea of non-intentional nature. Thus the "thing of physics" (as de Boer calls it) does not figure in this work at all. Husserl's sole recourse for treating the problem of truth in the judgment is to carry out a phenomenology of truth-*claims*, of the intentional experiences pertaining to the phenomenon of judgment itself.

Thus Husserl's Sixth *Investigation* yields an interpretation of the correspondence theory of truth by way of a description of the interplay between "assertive acts" and "fullfilling acts," a "synthesis of identification" in which the emptily intended judgment meaning is taken together with the "fulness" present in a fulfilling act of the same intentional sense.[12] On the question of the "object" itself which imparted such fulness, however, Husserl had to remain silent. From the methodological standpoint of a reduction to intentional experiences all discussion of such "transcendent" objects had to be bracketed. At best, the object could be characterized as *wahrmachender*, i.e., "as the ideal fulness for an intention, as that which makes an intention true."[13]

Thus Lask is correct in noting that Husserl's account of truth remains within the sphere of "quasi-transcendence." But this means, for Lask, that Husserl's position is not a *transcendental* one at all. It does

11. Theodore de Boer, *The Development of Husserl's Thought*, tr. Theodore Plantinga (The Hague: Martinus Nijhoff, 1978), p. 223.

12. Edmund Husserl, *Logical Investigations*, tr. J. N. Findlay (New York: Humanities Press, 1970), Vol. II, pp. 764–765.

13. Ibid., p. 766. For more on the relation between Lask and Husserl with regard to the problems we are discussing here, see Konrad Hobe, *Emil Lask: Eine Untersuchung Seines Denkens* (Inaugural Dissertation, Ruprecht-Karl Universität, Heidelberg, 1968), pp. 186–201.

not account for the *possibility* of knowledge, but only analyzes the descriptive psychology of knowledge-*claims*. Of course, Husserl did not consider his phenomenology to be transcendental at this stage. Nevertheless, even as a clarification of knowledge claims "this theory of knowledge is caught in an impasse." As de Boer notes, "It was only later that Husserl saw that a theory of knowledge on a psychological basis is a 'transcendental circle': it seeks to clarify the relation to the world despite the fact that the world is itself presupposed as the surrounding ground of consciousness." [14]

As we shall see, Lask too is guilty of "presupposing the world." Yet with respect to the question of a transcendental theory of judgment he is correct to argue, against Husserl's "phenomenological" conception, that the problem of truth can only be clarified by drawing into the analysis the transcendent object as such, which is not merely a meaning "separable" from the judging subject, but altogether "separate":

> Genuine transcendence is the condition of meaning prior to all contact with subjectivity, while behind the independence of the quasi-transcendent meaning stands the mere redeemability [*Ablösbarkeit*] of meaning *after* its contact with subjectivity. (LvU 425)

Thus even if transcendental logic could thematize the subjective "origin" of the judgment without becoming psychologistic, the transcendental problem of truth would still require a radically different sort of investigation of "transcendent" object-meaning itself.

In the next section we will explore the sense in which Husserl came to agree with this point. [15] But first an obvious question about Lask's own "transcendental" position needs to be addressed. For it is one thing to recognize the need for such a paradigmatic object, and it is quite another to give a philosophical account of its "availability" which is not simply a dogmatic postulate.

Here Lask's position is at its weakest. On the one hand, the paradigmatic object (meaning) is to be considered "prior to all contact with subjectivity." On the other hand, the "transcendence" of this object is not to be construed metaphysically as a Kantian "thing in itself." Lask tries to navigate these treacherous waters by claiming that the subject, in addition to being the source of the "structural complication" into

14. de Boer, op. cit., p. 190.
15. To be sure, not under any impetus from Lask's work. Even if Husserl had studied Lask's position it is unlikely that he would have recognized anything useful in Lask's notion of transcendence. This can be deduced from his response to Lask's mentor *Rickert's* notion of the "object of knowledge," Husserl's fundamental "misunderstanding" of which is discussed in Kern, op. cit., pp. 376–394.

which the object falls in the act of judging, is also a passive "receiver [*Empfängerin*] . . . of the transcendent object," able "to offer a place [*Stätte*] for meaning" (LvU 415). This is what Lask calls the "becoming immanent" of the transcendent object:

> The condition of being there in subjective acts, of hovering before or being contained within experience, may be termed becoming an object or becoming immanent; the condition independent of this situation of becoming experienced may be termed transcendence. Becoming immanent . . . shows itself merely as an external destiny, a chance situation into which the transcendent object or paradigmatic meaning falls. The becoming immanent of what is transcendent in this sense involves therefore no contradiction. It means merely a transition [*Hinübergeraten*] into another situation. (LvU 414)

Given the fact that Lask occasionally mentions Husserl's concept of intentionality with favor, and indeed in a letter to Husserl[16] claims that the "von ihr entworfenen Typ des Subjekt-Objekt Verhältnis als Intentionalität" takes the place of all theories of "Bewusstsein überhaupt," one might expect him to clarify his concept of "becoming immanent" in ways that would bear a resemblance to Husserl's later *transcendental* phenomenology of pre-predicative experience. But again Lask's interests lie in an entirely different direction. In the same passage from which we just quoted Lask is quick to point out that the "standpoint" for his definition of "transcendent" and "immanent" is precisely *not* that of "immanence within experience or consciousness," but that of transcendence itself. Transcendence does not mean "going beyond," but "independence" from the subject (LvU 414). In other words, Lask is not concerned at any point with the *way* that the paradigmatic object "shows itself" *as* transcendence in immanence. An *analysis* of the intentionality of sensibility, perception, and the like is not to be found in Lask. For indeed, in spite of his appeal to Husserl's notion of intentionality, there are indications in his text (though never a direct discussion) that an account of such "becoming immanent" could only be based on a non-transcendental "psycho-physiology" (LP 52).

Thus even though Lask has in view a pre-predicative concept of "experience" as the correlate of paradigmatic meaning, his fear of psy-

---

16. Of 24.12.1911, a copy of which is preserved at the Husserl-Archive in Leuven. As we recall, the occasion for this letter was Lask's receipt of Husserl's "Philosophy as Rigorous Science," a work in which Husserl first indicated a fully universal (transcendental) program for phenomenology. On this point, however, Lask cannot agree with Husserl that phenomenology contains "all of scientific philosophy." It may be a beginning, Lask admits, but it is still only a beginning. Presumably this means that the real problem is to move from the phenomenological standpoint of "transcendence in immanence" to the genuine standpoint of transcendence "untouched by all subjectivity"—i.e., from phenomenology to ontology.

chologism keeps him from recognizing the kind of subjective "achievements" which Husserl investigates in his later transcendental phenomenology of meaning constitution. The genuine problems seem to
him to lie precisely at the level of "transcendence" itself, at the level of
the ontological concept of "validity."

But just for this reason Lask's notion of pre-predicative experience,
of the pre-theoretical subject-object relation as "simple submission to
categorially formed material, . . . to the paradigmatic structural whole
which coincides with the object itself as truth" (LvU 396), remains at
the deepest level ambiguous. Without a functional notion of *intuition*
such as Husserl articulated in his phenomenology of evidence to support the functional concept of the (transcendent) object, the ontological status of this latter remains transcendentally unclarified. It is impossible to say *how* the transcendental object is available, impossible to
specify the *modes* in which it is "given." Thus Lask claims, on the one
hand, that prior to the judgment the subject simply "receives" the
transcendent object. On the other hand he also claims that we "never"
have the object as such, that we "always" operate with pieces (LvU
417). We are "ignorant" of the "simple interpenetration of the transcendental structural elements" of the object, which remains for us a
"lost paradise": "After the original sin of knowledge, it is no longer
ours to possess the transcendent meaning, but only the immanent
meaning [of the judgment]" (LvU 426).

What Lask points to here is of course correct: the transcendent object is never *adequately* given in experience. But if that is so, then it will
not do, as Husserl says in *Formal and Transcendental Logic*,[17] to

stop short with the empty generality of the word consciousness, nor with the
empty word experience, judgment, and so forth, treating the rest as though it
were philosophically irrelevant and leaving it to psychology . . .

The transcendental concept of meaning itself remains homeless if it is
not fleshed out in terms of its own "noetics," in terms of the *evidence*
with which it presents itself. But when this is recognized, the whole
"ontology" of transcendental meaning which Lask saw as the *sole* concern of transcendental logic is transformed into a "transcendental
clue" [*Leitfaden*] for tracing intentional implications, or "modes of
givenness," within a phenomenology of pre-predicative object constitution (FTL 244). The doctrine of categories as an ontology of meaning must become a transcendental *phenomenology*. In the final section

---

17. Edmund Husserl, *Formal and Transcendental Logic*, tr. Dorion Cairns (The Hague:
Martinus Nijhoff, 1969), pp. 244–245. Hereafter abbreviated FTL.

of this paper we will examine how such considerations inform Husserl's own conception of transcendental logic after he, too, had found a way of including the transcendent object in a specifically phenomenological investigation.

4. TRANSCENDENTAL LOGIC AND THE PHENOMENOLOGICAL REDUCTION

For both Lask and the Husserl of the *Logical Investigations,* the question of the truth of the judgment requires an inquiry which goes beyond the level of the judgment as such. For Husserl, however, such an inquiry goes back to the intentional experiences in which signifying and intuiting *acts* come to a synthesis of identification. The question of the transcendent *object* of the intuitive act is, at this stage of Husserl's thinking, explicitly ignored as lying outside the sphere of adequate phenomenological evidence. Lask, on the other hand, sees in just this transcendent object the genuine theme of transcendental logic—it is that meaning-structure whose elements reappear in "atomized" form in the judgment, thus accounting for the possibility of genuine knowledge of what is in truth. With regard to the question of the *object* of knowledge, then, Lask's position is a genuinely transcendental one, while Husserl's is still a "descriptive psychology."

At the same time, *neither* thinker can give an adequate account of transcendental *subjectivity.* This is clear for Husserl, whose eidetic psychology makes no pretension of explaining the *possibility* of knowledge. But it must also be admitted that Lask's conception of the subject is at bottom a psychological one as well—for which reason he excludes it in all but the name from the scope of transcendental logic. As the "real bearer" of judgment meaning the subject is simply discounted as irrelevant; the question of the "origin" of such meaning in the "breaking apart" of the paradigmatic object is a psychological one wholly to be subordinated to the question of the "structure" of judgment-meaning itself. And as the pre-judicative "place" in which paradigmatic meaning is originally "given," the immanence of subjectivity is a mere "chance situation" into which transcendent meaning falls. Lask nowhere gives an *account* of this "transcendence in immanence," the condition of the transcendent object as correlate of the non-active subject. To the extent that any *non-psychological* sense can be given to the subject here, it is simply an abstract "subject-pole" of paradigmatic meaning. For the rest, the givenness of the object seems to be a question for "psycho-physiology."

In writings subsequent to the *Logical Investigations* Husserl came to recognize the need for including this transcendent object in the purview of phenomenology, and precisely as a structure of *meaning*. Thus in the first major work he published after the *Logical Investigations*, the first volume of *Ideas* (1913), we read: "In a certain sense and with the proper care in the use of words we may even say that all real unities are 'unities of meaning'."[18] But as the passage continues we find that while Husserl now stands within the horizon of the Laskian transcendent object, it is not Lask's "perspective of transcendence" which he has adopted, but rather that of a "transcendence in immanence" made possible by the phenomenological reduction: "Unities of meaning presuppose . . . a sense-giving consciousness which, on its side, is absolute and not dependent in its turn on sense bestowed on it from another source."[19] The transcendental field of meaning "presupposes" consciousness; but then, in what sense is meaning "transcendent"? *How* is the transcendent object to be included in a phenomenology of "absolute" consciousness without falling back into psychological representationalism?

Husserl's answer to this question is bound up with the theory of the phenomenological reduction. The concept of the reduction emerges in Husserl's lectures during the Göttingen period. A series of these lectures, given during the summer semester of 1907, was published as *The Idea of Phenomenology*. In this text, as Kern has shown, the reduction is "motivated" primarily through "Cartesian" considerations in the search for apodictic evidence.[20] However, in the lectures of the previous winter semester (1906/7), published now as *Einleitung in die Logik und Erkenntnistheorie*, we find the reduction being discussed in the context of ontological considerations deriving from the idea of transcendental logic.

In this text Husserl explicitly proposes a "doctrine of categories," a logic of the object or "ontology" in the transcendental sense, but in such a way as precisely to bring out the "one-sided" character of any theory of knowledge, like Lask's, which remains at the objective-logical level of categorial "validity." Ultimate transcendental clarification of transcendent meaning is seen to require a radical "change of attitude"; the transcendent domain of meaning is not adequately disclosed simply by recognizing the "validity character" of catego-

---

18. Edmund Husserl, *Ideas: A General Introduction to Pure Phenomenology*, tr. W. R. Boyce Gibson (London: Collier-Macmillan Ltd., 1969), p. 152.
19. Ibid., p. 153.
20. Kern, op. cit., p. 221.

rial form, but requires a reflective modification of the objective ("positivistic," "naturalistic") attitude of thought itself. In what follows, then, I want to chart briefly the emergence of this demand for an *Einstellungsänderung* as the condition for the possibility of transcendental logic.[21]

Husserl begins by considering the role of logic within the context of a theory of science. Here logic makes its appearance first of all as "apophantics," the theory of the formal structure of propositions. Now, it belongs to the essence of any proposition that it "raises a claim to validity" (ELE 70), or truth. Thus, a complete theory of science will not be able to remain within apophantics itself, which studies the forms of the proposition in abstraction from this implicit truth-claim, but will have to investigate "that which in the essence of the proposition grounds it as a unity of validity [*Geltungseinheit*]. In a certain sense," Husserl continues, "the concern here is a logic of truth" (ELE 74).

The logic of truth, which Husserl calls "ontology," is not restricted to a consideration of "objects of a higher order," a purely formal ontology which still abstracts from the "underlying objects" which are bound up in (possible) states of affairs, or "categorially formed objects" in the sense of the *Logical Investigations*. Rather, logic includes "the idea of an apriori ontology, and further not a formal-logical one, but a metaphysical one."[22] This latter has the task of investigating "the fundamental categories in which the Real as such is to be conceived according to its essence" (ELE 101).

Such an a priori ontology of the real as such provides the foundation for "empirically founded metaphysics," or ontologies of the "regions" of the individual sciences. It can do so without becoming "metalogical" in Lask's sense because "logical form points apriori toward material [*Stoff*] which is to be . . . rationalized," toward "something extra-logical, a world of *hyle*" (ELE 104). Thus we find here a *widening* of the concept of "logical form" which appeared in the *Logical Investigations*[23] such that now

21. An important source for understanding how Husserl's view of transcendental philosophy differs from other versions of it, and from other philosophical approaches to the problem of knowledge, is J. N. Mohanty's *The Possibility of Transcendental Philosophy* (Dordrecht: Martinus Nijhoff, 1985). On Husserl's "evidenz-theoretisch" conception (a term Mohanty borrows from B. Grünwald), see especially the essay "The Destiny of Transcendental Philosophy," pp. 213–222.

22. ELE 101. In ELE Husserl uses the term "metaphysics" to refer to a study of the logical structure of the transcendent object, i.e., "ontology" in Lask's sense. He does not mean by it an investigation *other* than a logical one, i.e., a "metalogical" inquiry in Lask's sense. By the time of the *Ideas* Husserl has dropped this use of the term "metaphysics."

23. Cf. Kern, op. cit., p. 385.

one can count within logic all that which belongs apriori to the possibility of knowledge of the real. . . . On this view logic includes a two-fold apriori, one of pure form and one of the formally determined material. (ELE 111)

With the transition from formal apophantics to formal and material *ontology* Husserl for the first time speaks specifically of a "transcendental logic" (ELE 112). Logical categoriality includes not only formal determinations, but also the "essential categories of reality," e.g., "thing, quality, real connection, real whole, real part, cause and effect, real genus and species, etc." (ELE 111).

At this stage, then, Husserl has in view a doctrine of categories along the lines suggested by Lask—a theory of the "objectivity of objects" as an ontology of what is as such. The same view, even more explicitly articulated, is found in *Formal and Transcendental Logic* (1929). There Husserl begins by marking the specific difference between a logic of judgment and a logic of the object: "Categorially formed objectivity is not an apophantical concept; rather it is an ontological concept" (FTL 145). He then reiterates the theory of truth as a "synthesis of identification" found in the *Logical Investigations,* except that now the objects of the fulfilling acts are not simply "true-making," but the things themselves:

> If the fulfillments are ideally perfect then the substrate-objectivities with all their categorial formings are themselves given in the strict sense; the evidence actualizes and seizes upon them themselves as they are in truth. (FTL 145)

This, finally, indicates that there can be no metaphysical problem of "application" in logic; the objects *themselves* are not, as Lask would say, "metalogical":

> Truly existing nature, truly existing sociality or culture, and the like—these have absolutely no sense other than that of being certain categorial objectivities. . . . (FTL 146)

Thus a genuinely transcendental ontology is now part of Husserl's conception of logic. It is necessary (as Lask saw) because the question of possible truth in a judgment implies reference to a concept of the "truly existing" categorially constituted object, *being* in the sense of truth, as the measure of "mere judicial meaning" (FTL 146). But if Husserl has now come to see the need for a transcendental ontology it is by no means the case that this is *sufficient* for a transcendental theory of knowledge as Lask believed. For the possibility of such a "way out" of the problem of truth remains, for Husserl, a mere dogmatic assertion without a corresponding account of the "evidence" in which this paradigmatic object is *given*. If a doctrine of categories is to provide the a priori structure of "logically formed material," then the accessibility of logically formed material must allow for a reflective clarification which is itself "transcendental." There remains the problem of subjective-logic, or what Husserl (in ELE) calls "noetics."

This, as we saw, was precisely the point at which Lask's transcendental logic pulled up short. The question of the evidence in which the object is (pre-predicatively) "given" was left unclarified: how can an investigation into the modes of givenness of the object be anything other than a psychological one? The phenomenology of the *Logical Investigations* tendered no definitive answer to this question. Now, however, Husserl believes that phenomenology can provide the foundations for an ontology—i.e., by way of a differentiated theory of evidence based on a conception of intentionality purified of all psychological elements, a sphere of transcendental "immanence" in terms of which alone the *meaning* of transcendence can be concretely articulated.

The issue of a "noetics" or subjective-logic, as Husserl sees it, is the issue of the *legitimacy* of the "claims to justification" which any mode of knowledge raises. Any genuine theory of knowledge must concern itself with such a problem, including the legitimacy of the claim that the transcendent object is given, as with Lask, in pre-judicative experience (ELE 120). But this means that transcendental logic *must* investigate the subjective dimension:

> All knowledge comes to pass as subjective act, and the subjective act must harbor in itself that which represents and grounds its claim to justification [*Rechtsanspruch*]. (ELE 130)

Only by considering *how* an act of knowledge, of object-consciousness in general, "harbors in itself" its source of validity can "the problems of transcendental philosophy, these most difficult of all scientific problems generally" (ELE 139) be addressed.

Thus on Husserl's view Lask simply presupposes the deepest issues of transcendental logic. What Lask from his "standpoint of transcendence" takes as a simple given, viz., that we have a pre-judicative "familiarity" with the transcendent object, a pre-cognitive experience of ontological meaning, is for Husserl a "mystery" that must be cleared up if philosophical logic is to have a "good noetic conscience":

> The trivially obvious fact that things in themselves are and we merely come to them, apprehend them, consider them, make assertions about them, etc., has become a mystery. (ELE 153)

The question to be raised, then, is "*how* objective being can become conscious and known in subjectivity"; it is a question of *evidence*, for "evidence too belongs to the subjective dimension" (ELE 156).

Husserl's view of evidence overlaps with Lask's concept of experience in one important respect. Evidence, as "givenness" (ELE 155), is *never* the thematic concern of non-philosophical sciences:

> One *lives* in evidence, but does not reflect on evidence. One simply encounters objects, objects are given, one does not however reflect upon, or investigate in reflection what givenness means or how it is possible. (ELE 164)

But how is this level of evidence in which we "live" to be thematized in a non-psychological way? It is here, motivated by ontological considerations, that Husserl introduces the notion of the phenomenological reduction which "seems at first to be an overrefined subtlety." But "here lies the genuine Archimedean point of philosophy" (ELE 211).

The reduction opens up the sphere of transcendental subjectivity, i.e., the descriptive domain of the intentional correlation between noesis and noema. But in ELE such a move to subjectivity is motivated not by the demand for absolute certainty, nor by the demand for a grounding of psychology, but precisely by the recognition that ontology, as an aspect of the transcendental theory of knowledge, rests upon a "field" of evidence which is presupposed, but not investigated, by the sciences themselves. Thus the "method" which will make such a field of evidence available must be specific to an inquiry which "lies prior to all natural knowledge and science and has an entirely different direction from natural science" (ELE 176).

The reduction, as it appears here, is simply the expression of the radical difference between philosophical reflection and all other modes of thought. It is meant to overcome the naiveté of the "naturalistic" attitude, which presupposes the "world" as a pre-given source of validities. The reduction inaugurates an "unnatural direction of thought" (ELE 165) which does not lose itself in "positive" investigation on the basis of worldly evidence, but rather *reflects* on this evidence-structure itself. Thus, the reduction involves the "detachment [*Ablösung*] of all naturalistic theories" (ELE 165), not in the sense of *denying* their validity, but in the sense of refusing to *use* them as premises, or modes of explanation, in philosophical reflection. Such "detachment" is merely to remind us, as it were, that no naturalistic or worldly theory (including psychology) can justify, or even contribute to an explanation of, the correlation between knowledge and the world which constitutes the "unnatural" theme of philosophical reflection, since all such theories presuppose that correlation itself.

Thus this "unnatural" direction of thought, the "critical" direction which investigates *Rechtsansprüche*, does not *exclude* the domain of transcendence from consideration, but *includes* it under a change of signature. Reflection investigates "particular [*beliebige*] sciences, particular theories, particular cognitions not as validities, but as validity-claims, validity phenomena" (ELE 199). A reduction to the sphere of immanence, to transcendental subjectivity in Husserl's sense, thus in no way "brackets" the transcendent object itself. Instead it is what Husserl calls here the "empirical apperception" (ELE 211) of it, the doxic positing of the object in the straightforward attitude of simple experience, that is "reduced" or not allowed to dominate reflection in its presumed "self-evidence."

Such a reduction of transcendence to the status of transcendence-phenomenon alters nothing of its "objectivity," but only clears a space for a non-psychological investigation into the noetic acts in which alone the question of "how such a relation to objectivity is possible" (ELE 212) can be explored concretely:

> From the very beginning it is therefore to be noted that not merely perceptions or other kinds of objectifying acts belong in the sphere of immanence, but also in a certain sense every object, in spite of its transcendence. (ELE 231)

Immanence therefore is itself, in the context of the reduction, a purely transcendental concept, and as such is absolutely necessary for grounding the transcendental concept of the object as meaning. Immanence means neither the real containment of the object within psychological consciousness (as "representation"), nor the "reel" parts of intentional experiences themselves (noesis, hyle), but simply the "givenness" of the object itself, the presence of the transcendent to the (reduced, "transcendental") subject *as* it presents itself, *as* a "unity of meaning."[24]

In conclusion, it is possible to see the ambiguities in Lask's account of the transcendent object as results of his failure to recognize *explicitly* the function of a "reduction," of a change of attitude, for transcendental philosophy. On the objective-logical side Lask does recognize that transcendental philosophy concerns itself with the object as a unity of meaning—i.e., that philosophy deals with the *same* objects as do the sciences and daily life, but in such a way as to recognize the "logical structure" of the object which is merely presupposed in non-philosophical modes of thought. But though this constitutes a "naive" approach to the "difference" between philosophy and natural inquiry,

24. On the various senses of "immanence" in Husserl, see Kern, op. cit., pp. 212–213.

Lask's concept of meaning remains homeless to the extent that the "empirical apperception" of the object is not explicitly "reduced" in his appeal to our "experience" of the object in pre-predicative life. The concept of meaning is not, as Lask assumes, a "worldly" concept which emerges as one ascends *in a direct line* from everyday life to positive science to the theory of knowledge. Its true nature can only be appreciated by bracketing the naturalistic assumptions of such a continuity between positive and philosophical modes of inquiry.

Thus, on the subjective-logical side, Lask's implicit "naturalism," his presupposition of the *world* as the ultimate ground of validities, shows itself clearly in his demotion of all questions of the subject, and thus all questions of evidence, to the status of philosophically irrelevant "psychological" ones. Lask's concept of the subject as a passive "receiver" of the transcendent object forces him to the admission that the transcendent object is indeed a "lost paradise" so far as an investigation into its modes of givenness is concerned. But a reduction of the naturalistic assumption that transcendence constitutes its *own* autonomous sphere of validity would have allowed Lask to recognize that the very "inadequacy" with which the transcendent object is given in immanence is just what serves as a clue to how the meaning of transcendence is constituted *within* immanence. Such "constitution" is in danger of falling back into a psychologistic "creation" of representations only so long as one still thinks of both transcendence and immanence in essentially naturalistic ways. But in that case, the very explication of the transcendentality of the object as a unity of *logical* form and material can only appear as a strange perversion of natural thought, for which the idea of the object "in truth" as meaning must seem no more than a *deus ex machina*.

What it means to practice the reduction in Husserl's sense will always be difficult to grasp—for it is the way to a cultivation of that "non-natural," non-worldly mode of reflection in which philosophy first discovers its own genuine problems. But without it, as our discussion of Lask has begun to indicate, the ultimate concern of even natural thinking to become clear about its own achievements and possibility remains condemned to equivocation.

5   Realism *Versus* Anti-Realism: A Husserlian Contribution

JOHN J. DRUMMOND

1. THE ISSUES: REALISMS AND ANTI-REALISMS

Debates have long centered around the question of whether Husserl was or was not a realist.[1] These debates are complicated not only by the difficulties of Husserl's texts but by the fact that participants frequently appeal to different senses of "realism" and thereby fail to clarify precisely the issues at sake in the debate. There are historical reasons for this:[2] an examination of the history of the controversies surrounding realism reveals that the meaning of "realism" within any

1. I do not intend to survey the various positions in these debates. For a sample of the entire range of positions, see M. M. van de Pitte, "Husserl: the Idealist *malgré lui*," *Philosophy and Phenomenological Research* 37 (1976): 70–78; Karl Ameriks, "Husserl's Realism," *Philosophical Review* 86 (1977): 498–519; Gary Gutting, "Husserl and Scientific Realism," *Philosophy and Phenomenological Research* 39 (1978): 42–56; Roman Ingarden, *Der Streit um die Existenz der Welt* (2 vols., Tübingen: Max Niemeyer, 1965), vol. 2; and "Die vier Begriffe der Transcendenz und das Problem des Idealismus in Husserl," *Analecta Husserliana* (Dordrecht: D. Reidel, 1971), vol. I, pp. 37–74; Guido Küng, "Husserl on Pictures and Intentional Objects," *Review of Metaphysics* 26 (1973): 670–80; and Küng, "The World as Noema and as Referent," *Journal of the British Society for Phenomenology* 3 (1972): 15–26; J. N. Findlay, "Phenomenology and the Meaning of Realism," *Phenomenology and Philosophical Understanding*, ed. E. Pivcevic (Cambridge: Cambridge University Press, 1975), pp. 144–58; W. Morriston, "Intentionality and the Phenomenological Method: A Critique of Husserl's Transcendental Idealism," *Journal of the British Society for Phenomenology* 7 (1976): 36–43; David Woodruff Smith and Ronald McIntyre, "Intentionality via Intensions," *Journal of Philosophy* 68 (1971): 559–61; Richard Holmes, "Is Transcendental Phenomenology Committed to Idealism?," *The Monist* 59 (1975): 98–114; and Harrison Hall, "Was Husserl a Realist or an Idealist?," *Husserl, Intentionality, and Cognitive Science* (hereafter *HICS*), ed. H. L. Dreyfus (Cambridge and London: MIT Press, 1984).

2. See C. F. Delaney, "Presidential Address: Beyond Realism and Anti-Realism," *Realism, Proceeding of the American Catholic Philosophical Association* 59 (1984), ed. Daniel O. Dahlstrom, pp. 2–3, 11. Delaney offers a brief historical sketch of the various debates regarding realism and fills in some details necessarily omitted here. Cf. also Michael Dummett, "Realism," *Truth and Other Enigmas* (Cambridge, MA: Harvard University Press, 1978), pp. 145–65. Dummett catalogs the anti-realistic alternatives for different philosophical issues.

particular debate has generally been defined in terms of some specific non-realistic alternative.[3] Thus, in the Middle Ages, a Platonic or strong realism regarding the separate existence of universals was opposed by nominalism, the view that only individuals, including general terms, exist. Intermediate positions were certainly available. We must, for example, consider Aristotle an ontological realist, although his realism regarding universals is a moderate form asserting that universals have a real existence only as principles or abstract moments of individuals. Similarly, we must consider Abelard's conceptualism a nominalism, although general terms refer not directly to collections of individuals but to an individual idea, a concept or abstract idea, whose extension ranges over similar individuals.

In the modern period, idealism challenged the realist's claim that conscious experience directly or indirectly grasps things whose existence and nature are at least partially independent of the minds which know them. This claim has two inseparable components: (a) an ontological claim that there exists a mind-independent reality and (b) an epistemological claim that we can to some extent achieve reliable knowledge about this mind-independent order.[4] Truth, then, involves an adequation or correspondence between the beliefs we hold regarding existent realities and those realities themselves. The idealist claimed, on the other hand, that what we genuinely know are our own ideas or objects whose categories belong properly to the mind. On this view, experienced "objects" must be reducible to those ideas and the processes—psychological or transcendental—by which we organize them, and truth becomes a function of the formal and material coherence of our ideas. The epistemological realist is committed by (a) to at least a weak form of ontological realism, viz. that individuals exist independently of mind, although to neither strong nor moderate realism regarding universals. But the converse is not true; the ontological realist (in any sense) is not committed to epistemological realism, for the ontological realist can posit an unknowable world-in-itself and proffer an idealistic account of knowledge; this, however, renders impossible a traditional ontology of the mind-independent reality.

The contemporary or logical realist takes the position that linguistic expressions refer to a reality whose nature is not wholly determined

---

3. Dummett, 145–46.

4. I base this formulation of the epistemological realist's claim on a discussion of realism by Nicholas Rescher. It is a cruel irony, however, given the distinctions between ontological, epistemological, and logical realism that I am trying to elucidate herein, that Rescher's paper, delivered at the 36th annual meeting of the Metaphysical Society of America at Vanderbilt University, March 15, 1985, is entitled "Metaphysical Realism."

by the language itself. Thus, a statement reports a true fact if and only if this reality is as described. The anti-realist, on the other hand, denies that language refers to a world whose features are known or knowable independently of the manner in which we characterize them linguistically. And, since language determines our grasp of the known world, a statement can be counted as true if and only if we can justify it in terms of the linguistic and conceptual system in which it takes its place. The truth of any statement, therefore, is always relative to a system of statements, and there is no possibility of a statement's being true by virtue of some reality unknown, and perhaps unknowable, by us. That a statement is not true by virtue of an independent reality implies that the law of the excluded middle does not hold of statements as such, but only of statements relative to a system.

The anti-realist, much like the epistemological idealist, can hold a form of ontological realism, although it would again be impossible to develop a traditional ontology. The relations between anti-realism and epistemological realism or idealism are more complicated. The epistemological realist is committed to the view that the intelligibility of the world is mind-*related*, although not necessarily to the view that this intelligibility is mind-*dependent*. The anti-realist, on the other hand, must take the stronger position that the intelligibility of the world is language-*dependent*, i.e., our world as understood embodies a set of conceptual structures belonging to the language we use to speak about it. Thus, the anti-realist, already committed to the denial of any significant form of ontological realism, appears committed to a view more like epistemological idealism. But this is too strong, for in the case of the anti-realist, (i) the organization at stake is clearly logical rather than psychological or transcendental, (ii) it is statements or propositions which are organized rather than ideas, (iii) language is inherently intersubjective, and (iv) the justification of any statement in terms of other statements within a system necessarily produces a justification which is available and compelling for all who share the system.

It can be claimed that the contemporary debate largely moots other debates about realism and its alternatives,[5] and some would argue that thinkers such as Husserl and Heidegger have participated in the development of this new alternative.[6] In this paper, I shall locate Husserl

5. Dummett, 146–47; see also Nicholas Wolterstorff, "Realism vs Anti-Realism: How to Feel at Home in the World," *Realism*, pp. 190–91.
6. The position of Husserl, however, is decidedly ambiguous, and the ambiguity is illustrated not only by the controversies running through the papers mentioned in note 1. Richard Rorty, *Philosophy and the Mirror of Nature* (Princeton: Princeton University Press, 1979), pp. 3–4, 166–68, for example, places Husserl squarely in the mainstream

with respect to the various debates concerning realism. In order to do so, however, we shall examine two Husserlian doctrines which undoubtedly bear on how Husserl stands relative to the issue of realism: the phenomenological reduction and the noema.

2. THE PHENOMENOLOGICAL REDUCTION AND ONTOLOGICAL REALISM

Ontological realism—and for the moment I consider only the weak version—is not a *theory* about the existence of an extra-mental world to which we argue as a philosophical conclusion, but is instead an *attitude* toward both the world and truth. This realistic attitude forms an implicit part of our experience of the world; our ordinary and scientific experiences of the world simply and naturally posit the existence of a real, intelligible world.[7] Just as the realistic attitude is not the *conclusion* of an argument, it is not logically prior to our ordinary and scientific experiences as their *presupposition*, and it requires, therefore, not justification but clarification. We philosophers reflect upon the *fact* of this attitude in order to clarify its meaning, to disclose those conditions which must obtain if we are to have such contact with a real world as our natural experience involves, and to explore the possibilities and limits of our knowledge of the real. Precisely this project of

---

of philosophers committed to traditional realistic principles such as foundationalism and a notion of absolute, adequational truth. To this tradition Rorty opposes thinkers such as Nietzsche, James, Dewey, the later Heidegger, and the later Wittgenstein. Hilary Putnam, on the other hand, in the first of his Carus Lectures delivered at the 1985 meeting of the Eastern Division of the American Philosophical Association and citing Husserl's Crisis {*Die Krisis der europäischen Wissenschaften und die transzendentale Phänomenologie: Eine Einleitung in die phänomenologische Philosophie* (hereafter *Krisis*), ed. W. Biemel, Husserliana VI (2nd ed., The Hague: Martinus Nijhoff, 1962), [*The Crisis of European Sciences and Transcendental Phenomenology: An Introduction to Phenomenological Philosophy*, tr. D. Carr (Evanston: Northwestern University Press, 1970)]}, enlists Husserl (along with James and the later Wittgenstein!) as an ally in the struggle against scientific realism and the attempt to preserve common-sense realism. Hence, with regard to scientific objectivities, Husserl would be an anti-realist, but with regard to macroscopic, material things, he would be a realist. However, common-sense realism is for Putnam an "internal" realism, pragmatic in character, wherein truth is judged by how indispensable a particular proposition or system of propositions is to living agents.

7. Nicholas Rescher has pointed out this fact in the aforementioned "Metaphysical Realism," although he argues that the realistic postulation must be justified by a non-theoretical, pragmatic argument. As I indicate below, I take this attitude to be a fact of our experience upon which the philosopher reflects. Hall and I, although we disagree on many points, agree (see pp. 170, 184) on this view of ontological realism. I take it also that this notion of a realistic attitude is part of what Putnam has in mind when he speaks of "common-sense realism" as opposed to "scientific realism." I shall discuss below how this attitude operates in science and what the legitimate sense of a scientific realism is.

clarification is involved in Husserl's distinction between the natural and philosophical attitudes and in his theory of intentionality.

The distinction between the two attitudes is revealed in Husserl's discussions of the methodological technique of the phenomenological reduction by means of which we depart the natural attitude and enter the philosophical attitude.[8] Philosophical science, insofar as it is a radical critique of the possibility of cognition, cannot exist on the same plane as the natural and psychological sciences, for these latter sciences—indeed all our ordinary experience and cognitions—merely accept the existence of the world and its objects and the possibility and general validity of our knowledge of them. This general acceptance characterizes what Husserl calls the "natural attitude" (*Ideen* I, §30). The new philosophical science demands, on the other hand, a sceptical attitude toward all cognition which no longer takes its possibility for granted. Just as the natural attitude is characterized by a general acceptance, so universal doubt is accomplished all at once in what Husserl refers to as the "disconnection" (*Ausschaltung*) or "bracketing" (*Einklammerung*) of all transcendent objects (*Ideen* I, 69 [66]).

The distinguishing characteristic of this disconnection is that it annuls the positing of an object's existence or the validity of a judgment (*Ideen* I, 63 [58]). But this annulment is not a negation; it does not transform the positing into its opposite, into the denial of the existence of the object or the validity of the judgment (*Ideen* I, 63 [58]). To doubt universally, therefore, is to *suspend* the affirmation involved in the general positing of the natural attitude. Our participation in the realistic positings characteristic of that attitude is "disconnected," and along with this, the transcendent world and its objects are "bracketed"; it and they are *presumed* existents. The ontological realism at work in our natural attitude is not denied. The world and its objects are all left in place; they are still available for reflection just insofar as

8. Husserl first detailed the methodological technique of the phenomenological reduction in *Die Idee der Phänomenologie: Fünf Vorlesungen*, ed. W. Biemel, Husserliana II (2nd ed., The Hague: Martinus Nijhoff, 1973) [*The Idea of Phenomenology*, tr. W. P. Alston and G. Nakhnikian (The Hague: Martinus Nijhoff, 1970)]. Other important discussions of the reduction can be found in his *Ideen zu einer reinen Phänomenologie und phänomenologischen Philosophie. Erstes Buch: Allgemeine Einführung in die reine Phänomenologie* (hereafter *Ideen* I), ed. K. Schuhmann, Husserliana III/1 (The Hague: Martinus Nijhoff, 1976) [*Ideas Pertaining to a Pure Phenomenology and to a Phenomenological Philosophy. First Book: General Introduction to a Pure Phenomenology*, tr. F. Kersten (The Hague, Boston and Lancaster: Martinus Nijhoff, 1983)], part two; *Erste Philosophie. Zweiter Teil: Theorie der phänomenologischen Reduktion*, ed. R. Boehm, Husserliana VIII (The Hague: Martinus Nijhoff, 1959); *Cartesianische Meditationen* (hereafer *CM*), ed. S. Strasser, Husserliana I (2nd ed., The Hague: Martinus Nijhoff, 1963) [*Cartesian Meditations: An Introduction to Phenomenology*, tr. D. Cairns (The Hague: Martinus Nijhoff, 1970)], §§1–16; and *Krisis*, §§16–20 and part three.

they are posited. Their status as objects has been modified so that they are now viewed exclusively in their being as objects of that conscious experience in which they are posited (*Ideen* I, §§31–32; *CM*, §8).[9]

Philosophical reflection, however, must be distinguished from natural doubt, from natural or psychological reflection, from the critical reflection which focuses on individual experiences, from the logical reflection which focuses on logical content or meaning, and from any reflection which does not turn, in a universal manner, to the experience itself.[10] All these share what Husserl calls the "neutrality-modification,"[11] which is common to and presupposed by a series of attitudinal changes or changes of focus, each of which maintains its hold on the objectivity simply given in the natural attitude, although the index with which this objectivity is given is changed.[12] The

9. This focus on the object as the correlate of experience and conscious activities emerges in *Ideen* I and becomes more prominent in later works such as *Formale und transzendentale Logik: Versuch einer Kritik der logischen Vernunft* (hereafter *FTL*), ed. P. Janssen, Husserliana XVII (The Hague: Martinus Nijhoff, 1974) [*Formal and Transcendental Logic*, tr. D. Cairns (The Hague: Martinus Nijhoff, 1969)] and *Krisis*, especially in the treatments of logical objectivities and the grounding of the natural and mathematical sciences in a prior experience of the life-world.

10. David Woodruff Smith and Ronald McIntyre [*Husserl and Intentionality: A Study of Mind, Meaning, and Language* (Dordrecht, Boston, Lancaster: D. Reidel, 1984)] do not adequately distinguish logical from phenomenological reflection; see pp. 151–52, note 14. While it is true that both logical and phenomenological reflection are directed to sense or meaning, logical reflection is not directed to the noema, i.e. the sense precisely as the objective correlate of an experience, whereas phenomenological reflection is. And Lenore Langsdorf ["The Noema as Intentional Entity: A Critique of Føllesdal," *Review of Metaphysics* 37 (1984: 757–84)] is not specific enough in characterizing the nature of phenomenological reflection. She claims, rightly enough, that the reduction institutes an analytic attitude concerned with the meaning or sense that is involved in our experience of an objectivity. However, she claims that this interest in meaning is an *additional* interest we have in things. But this cannot be understood to mean an additional interest which takes its place alongside our natural interests. I think critical and logical reflection—at least that logical reflection which is ultimately concerned with the soundness of our arguments—is an additional interest of this sort which, while not on exactly the same level as our natural interests, ultimately works along with our natural inclinations. But the phenomenological interest is of a different sort; it exists not alongside but on a different level; it is fully reflective insofar as it is turned not only to the sense but also to the act in which this objective sense is present. And this is to turn our attention away from the world, the things in it, and the correctness of our experiences to the life of transcendental subjectivity, the world as a correlate of the experiences making up that life, and what it is to have this truly or correctly presented to consciousness. It is, in other words and as Langsdorf claims, to reflect on sense, but only in a manner radically distinct from the way logical reflection reflects upon sense.

11. Husserl's discussion of neutralization and its difference from simple belief and the modalities thereof can be found in *Ideen* I, §§109–12; see also Robert Sokolowski, *Husserlian Meditations* (Evanston: Northwestern University Press, 1974), p. 173.

12. A good discussion of the range of different attitudes available to reflection and the foci proper to each can be found in Robert Sokolowski, *Presence and Absence: A Philosophical Investigation of Language and Being* (Bloomington and London: Indiana University Press, 1978); this discussion is nicely summarized in chap. 13.

neutrality-modification, however, does not necessarily involve a departure from our natural concerns; if our concern is simply to confirm or disconfirm the doubted, we essentially remain within the natural attitude. If our concern, on the other hand, is to examine the logical relations of a judgment with other judgments, then we have transformed our attitude—at least for the moment—to the logical attitude in which our focus is turned from the objective state of affairs to the content or propositional sense of neutralized judgments so that we can determine the relations of consistency, inconsistency, implication, and so forth which exist among them. The psychologist, too, in the natural reflection upon the experiences of actual subjects, does not participate in the positings proper to those subjects; he or she neutralizes them, although the psychologist does not neutralize his or her own natural belief in the existence of the world, of the human subjects studied, and of their real, psychological experiences. Even when self-reflecting, the psychologist neutralizes the positings of the experiences studied while maintaining the context of the natural beliefs characteristic of psychological reflection; the experiences studied *are* the experiences of the psychologist, an *actual*, human existent *in the world*.

Neutralization, therefore, is not itself the adoption of the philosophical attitude. The phenomenological reduction involves a change of attitude such that we focus on experience itself and objects just insofar as they are objects, just insofar as they are intended in experience. To say that the reduction focuses attention on experience itself is to say that it focuses attention on experiences *with* their "bracketed" objectivities. We no longer live in our experiences. We neutralize their positings; we step back from our participation therein, and we reflect upon experiences in their full concreteness, as directed to posited or intended objectivities with their doxic characteristics (*Ideen* I, §50). In all this, the ontological realism of the natural attitude is not denied, but is revealed as an aspect of the experience upon which we philosophers reflect.

3. THE NOEMA AND EPISTEMOLOGICAL REALISM

We have seen that epistemological realism involves two claims: (a) an ontological claim which is suspended but not negated by the phenomenological reduction; and (b) an epistemological claim that we can to some extent achieve reliable knowledge about this reality. The phenomenological reduction, however, also addresses (b), for it discloses the correlation between the intentional experience or noesis and the intentional object or noema, the latter of which is irreducible to an inherent component of the subjective experience itself. The object posited in a natural experience with its attitude of ontological realism is the object which is intended or known in the experience, and in clarifying and analyzing the experience itself, we give an account which supports and clarifies epistemological realism, for we explain how it is possible for a transcendent, intended objectivity to be grasped in an immanent experience, i.e. we explain how and to what extent the object as experienced is intelligible in an experience of that type.

The nature of the epistemological realism developed, however, depends upon the understanding of the doctrine of the noema, and there are two interpretations available. One, the Fregean interpretation,[13] which I shall oppose, is committed to two interpretational theses: (1) "the noema is a content [intentional], rather than an object, of intention and . . . is an abstract entity";[14] and (2) "Husserl conceives noematic senses—and, by extension, noemata—as *meanings;* specifically, he identifies noematic senses with the meanings that are expressed in language, which he characterizes basically as Frege did."[15] Noemata, in this view, are intensional as well as intentional entities. Smith and McIntyre argue, in brief, that Husserl, faced with the failure of the object-theories of intentionality found in thinkers such as Brentano, redefined intentionality without appealing to an ontologically distinctive class of intentional objects. Hence, whereas earlier theorists had distinguished the worldly and intentional objects and identified the intended and intentional objects, Husserl—in a manner similar to Frege—identifies the worldly and intended objects (referents) and gives to the distinct intentional (intensional) object a mediating role in the relationship between conscious acts and those intended, worldly objects (referents). Thus Husserl is said to have turned from an object-theory of intentionality to a mediator-theory. Since the theory of sense involved in this formulation entails a theory of reference

13. This line of interpretation was first suggested by Dagfinn Føllesdal, [*Husserl und Frege* (Oslo: I. Kommisjon Hos H. Aschehoug, 1958) and "Husserl's Notion of Noema," *The Journal of Philosophy* 66 (1969): 680–87, reprinted in *HICS*, pp. 73–80], whose study of both Frege and Husserl led him to the conclusion that Frege had decisively influenced Husserl's departure from psychologism and that Husserl's noemata were functionally equivalent to Fregean senses in mediating reference to worldly actualities. This interpretation has been ably developed and extended to issues in semantics in Smith and McIntyre's *Husserl and Intentionality.* For criticisms of the historical aspect of this thesis, see J. N. Mohanty, *Husserl and Frege* (Bloomington: Indiana University Press, 1982) and John J. Drummond, "Frege and Husserl: Another look at the issue of influence," *Husserl Studies* 2 (1985): 245–65.
    14. Smith and McIntyre, *Husserl and Intentionality,* p. 88.
    15. Smith and McIntyre, *Husserl and Intentionality,* p. 154.

to extra-mental and extra-linguistic realities, both epistemological and logical realism are preserved.

The central interpretational tenet of the Fregean approach, viz. that noemata are abstract, intentional entities which mediate the relation of conscious experiences to their intended objects in very much the same way that Frege's abstract senses mediate the relation of linguistic expressions to their referents, is opposed by that view which asserts that the noema or intentional object is the intended object itself, more specifically the posited, worldly object precisely as intended in the act.[16] We must, in other words, understand the reduction not as disclosing a new domain of abstract *existents* called noemata, but as changing the *manner* or *attitude* in which we consider the (presumptively real) object such that we focus on its intelligible presentation to a subject. In the case of perception, this means considering the object in its appearing relation to a perceiver. It also means recognizing that our perceptions of an object are informed by various motives or practical interests and that these determine the degree to which and the manner in which we pursue our investigation of the object. The relationship of certain properties to our interest in objects calls forth those properties for attention and allows us to understand the explicative possibilities inherent in perception. On the basis of such expli-

16. This line of interpretation was explicitly stated first by Aron Gurwitsch, "Phenomenology of Thematics and of the Pure Ego: Studies of the Relation between Gestalt Theory and Phenomenology," *Studies in Phenomenology and Psychology* (hereafter *Studies*) (Evanston: Northwestern University Press, 1966), and is stated most fully in Gurwitsch, *The Field of Consciousness*, Psychological Series 2 (Pittsburgh: Duquesne University Press, 1964). Other important statements occur in Gurwitsch, "Some Aspects and Developments of Gestalt Psychology," "On the Intentionality of Consciousness," and "Contribution to the Phenomenological Theory of Perception," all of which appear in *Studies*, and "Husserl's Theory of the Intentionality of Consciousness in Historical Perspective," *Phenomenology and Existentialism*, ed. E. N. Lee and M. Mandelbaum (Baltimore: Johns Hopkins University Press, 1967), reprinted in Gurwitsch, *Phenomenology and the Theory of Science*, ed. L. Embree (Evanston: Northwestern University Press, 1974). There are certainly difficulties in Gurwitsch's position, especially in his account of the relations between noematic phases and the concrete noema and between the noema and the thing itself. These difficulties, according to Fregean interpreters, undercut his interpretation; see Hubert L. Dreyfus, "The Perceptual Noema: Gurwitsch's Crucial Contribution," *Life-World and Consciousness: Essays for Aron Gurwitsch*, ed. L. Embree (Evanston: Northwestern University Press, 1972), pp. 135–70, reprinted with slight changes as "Husserl's Perceptual Noema," *HICS*, pp. 97–123, and Smith and McIntyre, *Husserl and Intentionality*, pp. 157–65. I do not believe, although I cannot argue here, that all these criticisms are pertinent, and I do not believe, to the extent that the criticism of Gurwitsch's view of the object as a complex whole of noematic parts is pertinent, that it defeats the fundamental thesis of Gurwitsch's interpretation; see John J. Drummond, "On the Nature of Perceptual Appearances or Is Husserl an Aristotelian?," *The New Scholasticism* 52 (1978): 1–22, and Drummond, "A Critique of Gurwitsch's 'Phenomenological Phenomenalism'," *The Southern Journal of Philosophy* 18 (1980): 9–21.

cative perceptions, we can recognize attributes as belonging to the object and frame judgments about objects, judgments which are still related to our practical concerns, even where these "practical" concerns have reached their limit case in a concern with theoretical explanation. But no matter how great the differences ensuing in our perceptions, and even in non-veridical perceptions, we are always in contact with the object itself in one of its appearings.

Since our concerns in this paper include both epistemological and logical realism, we might best investigate Husserl's conception of the judgmental noema, for insofar as this is a propositional sense, it bears directly on the issue of logical realism. Judgments—we might also call them propositions—are for the mature Husserl suppositions or proposals about objects and the states of affairs into which they enter (cf. *FTL*, §§44–48). Judging acts, insofar as they are directed to an object and its determinations, are directed to a predicatively formed complex and thus also to the various *categorialia* which are present to the judger precisely insofar as he or she judges. These categorial determinations are not, in other words, simply available to perception but become available in continued inspections of the object and the predicative activity based thereon. In the straightforward judging of the natural attitude, our attention is turned to the objective state of affairs and we are not aware of any logical reality that we might call the judgment itself or the proposition. However, we can reflectively direct our attention to the judged as such, to the judged state of affairs precisely as supposed; we might do so, for example, in those cases where someone reports his or her judgment to us and we doubt its correctness. In that case, the state of affairs as supposed is not something we posit for ourselves; we simply hold it for confirmation or disconfirmation as the state of affairs supposed and affirmed by someone else. At this point, the judgment takes on for us a double character, that of the categorially formed, judged state of affairs and that of the judgment merely as such, the supposition as supposed (*FTL*, §49).

The problem for logic in this view is its apparent identification of the judged state of affairs and the proposition, and this identification in turn seems to destroy the specifically logical sense of the proposition and to generate problems regarding false beliefs and propositional attitudes. The key for us, therefore, is to determine what Husserl has in mind when he discusses the reflection which turns to the proposition as a logical objectivity. Husserl characterizes this as a "withdrawing" from the judgment its suppositional content, as a focusing on the "meant categorial objectivity as such," i.e. merely as meant. We can recover the logical sense of the proposition, in other words, by recognizing that the state of affairs itself and the proposition are distinguished by means of a distinction in the way we *focus* the meant objectivity. In the straightforward focus on objects, we apprehend the categorial objectivity or state of affairs; in the reflective, abstractive focus on the state of affairs as supposed, i.e. on the supposition itself, we apprehend the proposition.[17]

That this is Husserl's view of the relation between the judged objectivity and the proposition is confirmed by his generalization of the possibility inherent in all experience of turning our attention away from the objectivity straightforwardly experienced to the experienced objectivity precisely as experienced, a possibility which underlies our ability to distinguish appearances from reality, falsity from truth, and, in general, to criticize and evaluate our views (*FTL*, §50).

4. THREE FORMAL SCIENCES, TWO LOGICS, AND LOGICAL REALISM

Both interpretations of the noema apparently yield an epistemological realism, although the Fregean interpretation asserts that our awareness of the object is mediated by noematic entities whereas Gurwitsch's interpretation asserts that we are directly aware of objectivities in the world. Both interpretations also involve some sort of equation between noemata and senses. Thus, the issues of epistemological realism and logical realism are intricately interwoven in Husserl's doctrine of the noema. I shall argue, however, that the Fregean view of the noema entails an erroneous understanding of Husserl's theory of evidence, and this in turn entails a logical anti-realism ultimately incompatible with epistemological (and, for any significant purposes, ontological) realism. The Fregean interpretation, consequently, cannot adequately explain the realism embedded in our natural experience.

Before we can appreciate fully the implications of these interpretations of the noema for a Husserlian position on the issue of logical realism, Husserl's distinction between formal ontology, formal logic, and formal mathematics[18] and that between consequence-logic (i.e. the logic of noncontradiction) and truth-logic[19] must be introduced. The first distinguishes attitudes. Formal mathematics, formal logic,

17. For a similar but lengthier account of the judgmental noema, see Robert Sokolowski, "Intentional Analysis and the Noema," *Dialectica* 38 (1984): 113–29.
18. For an extended discussion of this distinction, see *FTL*, §§23–27, 34, 37–46, and 54.
19. *FTL*, §51.

and formal ontology are each achieved in formalizing abstractions, which focus on those properties and categories that belong to all objects just insofar as they are objects. At the level of formalized systems, therefore, there can be no distinction in content between formal ontology, formal logic, and formal mathematics; the abstractions belonging to these formal disciplines, to put it another way, must be the same abstractions differently considered. When our concern is with articulating the possible forms of relational combination among objects simply as objects, we are engaged in formal ontology, which Husserl defines as "a science of possible objects purely as possible" (*FTL*, §54 b). When our concern is turned toward the theory-form in which such relations are asserted, our concern is logico-mathematical. The mathematician, however, is concerned purely with the consistency of the formal system, whereas the logician is additionally and ultimately concerned with truth.

Hence, we acquire two correlated senses of formal logic. In general, we have an apophantic logic which focuses exclusively on meanings, which abstractively considers objectivities' presented significance for us. When this direction is taken to its limit with an *exclusive* focus on the logical objectivities themselves and the possible forms belonging to non-contradictory senses, we have a pure, formal mathematics. Alternately, we have the possibility of focusing on meanings in order to see in them the forms of possible categorial objectivities, which forms underlie objects and our judgments about them. The fact that the formal activity of the logician is turned to meanings distinguishes formal logic from formal ontology, but this logical focus serves the purpose of a more generalized concern with the objectivities themselves in those sciences for which logic serves as a theory-form (*FTL*, §54 b–c).[20] Hence, this logical attitude stands, as it were, between formal mathematics and formal ontology.

This difference between the formal mathematician and the formal logician is exemplified in the logician's distinction between validity and soundness. The logician, in his or her formal work, is concerned with the validity or consistency of arguments, but the definition of validity already indicates that validity is the formally necessary but not fully sufficient condition for the truth of a conclusion. The logician has a further concern with the soundness of arguments and, con-

---

20. Robert Sokolowski provides a clear discussion of the Husserlian texts dealing with the distinctions between formal mathematics, formal ontology, and formal logic in "Logic and Mathematics in *Formal and Transcendental Logic*," an appendix to his *Husserlian Meditations*, pp. 271–89.

sequently, with a truth beyond mere consistency and validity. The logician's practice, therefore, in its formal aspect coincides with the mathematician's, but his or her concerns point toward the ontological concern with reality, although he or she actually operates in the logical domain of propositions rather than the ontological domain of the states of affairs themselves. This double focus of the logician introduces our second distinction between the logic of non-contradiction or the logic of mere consistency, which is the common concern of the logician and mathematician, and the truth-logic which is the ultimate concern of the logician.

Logic's character as a theory of science indicates its essential connectedness with the idea of truth, i.e. its essential connectedness with the ideal of adequation between propositions as suppositions and the posited states of affairs themselves. Adequation is possible precisely because the formal features of propositions and the formal, categorial features of objects simply are the same features, although in different dimensions, i.e. differently considered. This explains both the correlation between logical forms of propositions and the categorial forms of objectivity as well as the applicability of and scientific benefit to be derived from some mathematical systems for the science of nature.

When the issue of the truth of a judgment arises, we turn our attention to the state of affairs as supposed, therein recognizing it as a supposition which may or may not be in accord with the facts themselves. The determination of truth or falsity is made on the basis of a categorial intuition in which the articulated state of affairs is given bodily, i.e. as actually present to the subject.[21] Upon judging, for example, that S is p when we are distant from S, we can bring ourselves into the presence of S, not merely perceiving S and attending to p, but building upon such simple and explicating perceptions the categorial intuition that S is in fact (as it bodily presents itself to me) p. We "see" *that* p belongs to S. This does not preclude the possibility of error; it does, however, provide a verification over and above the coherence of the judgment 'S is p' with other judgments about the same object or the world. We see herein the distinction between the coherence of a judgment with other judgments, which is judged by consequence-logic, and truth in the sense of verifying presence, toward which truth-logic is teleologically directed.

Nor is it sufficient to say that the merely posited state of affairs 'S is

21. For a detailed account of categorial intuition, see Robert Sokolowski, "Husserl's Concept of Categorial Intuition," *Phenomenology and the Human Sciences: Supplement to Philosophical Topics* (Denver: Philosophical Topics, Inc., 1982), pp. 127–141.

p' *coheres* with the state of affairs actually or "bodily" given in experience, for the phenomenological difference in the two experiences
must not be overlooked. This difference between the absence and
presence of the state of affairs about which we make our proposal indicates that the "coherence" of intended judgment and evidently true
judgment is not mere formal and material coherence. Evident judging includes a *recognized identity* between the merely posited and fulfilled judgments. This teleological concern with the identity of posited
and fulfilled judgments over and above the concern with logical consistency distinguishes, as I have indicated above, the logician from the
mathematician, and we can here understand the role truth-logic serves
in theoretical and ontological pursuits.

The Fregean interpretation of the noema cannot adequately clarify
the distinctions between formal ontology, formal logic, and formal
mathematics, and between consequence-logic and truth-logic. Let us
consider, for example, the views of Robert Tragesser,[22] whose thesis is
that Husserl's phenomenological investigation of the foundations of
logic and mathematics undercuts the basis on which the opposition of
realism and anti-realism is traditionally conceived, but still allows for
the possibility of a modified realism. Husserl achieves this new realism, Tragesser contends, by attempting "to purge logical thinking of
[the] assumption [of the law of the excluded middle] while at the same
time avoiding the pitfalls of psychologism."[23] Interestingly, the rejection of the law of the excluded middle is reminiscent of Dummett's
description of the *anti-realist* position.[24]

Husserl avoids psychologism, according to Tragesser, by means of
his notion of intentionality, specifically his disclosure of the noema as
the intentional correlate of an act of consciousness. Tragesser, however, understands the noema on Fregean lines; according to Tragesser's interpretation of Husserl, our judging acts are directed to
the propositional noema, a "meaning-like entity,"[25] which is a non-
hypothetical, non-theoretical entity instrumental in directing our
judging act to this objectivity rather than some other.[26] Moreover, according to Tragesser, the criterion of a realistic view is that propositions concerning, say, mathematical objects be true or false antecedently to our knowing them. Since the basic thesis of Husserl's
phenomenology, again according to Tragesser, is "no entity (for us)

22. Robert S. Tragesser, *Husserl and Realism in Logic and Mathematics* (New York: Cambridge University Press, 1984).

23. Tragesser, p. 2.   24. Dummett, p. 155.
25. Tragesser, p. 37.   26. Tragesser, pp. 59–60.

antecedently to a way of thinking and thinking in that way,"[27] the truth of our mathematical propositions depends upon their being thought in accordance with non-psychologistic, antecedent principles for the thinking of mathematical objects. Thus, an assertion about a mathematical object is validated not only when it is logically consistent with other justified assertions about that object but when we recognize that it is thought in accordance with the antecedent principles governing the thinking of mathematical objects, principles which are disclosed in the axioms and definitions of the mathematical system in which the object is considered and principles inherent in mathematics as an ideal or formal science. But a consideration of the manner in which mathematical objects are constituted reveals that mathematical choice is free; the mathematician can and may choose to vary an axiom within a system in order to generate an alternative system. And the law of the excluded middle in its traditional interpretation—which presupposes that every proposition or system of propositions is in itself true or false as a consequence of its adequacy to an extra-mental objective order—does not operate in choosing between systems, each of which manifests logical coherence, in each of which there is an asymptotic approach toward completeness, and each of which is thought in accordance with the appropriate transcendental principles. Each system, therefore, can warrant claims about the existence and properties of the mathematical objects named in the propositions belonging to that system.

Tragesser accepts the view, then, that knowledge is cut off from existent things, grasping only judgmental noemata or propositions, but this is not thought to imply an anti-realism, for truth is neither produced solely by our thinking activity nor guaranteed by the coherence of propositions produced within the system. Nor does Tragesser's view involve a traditional realism, for truth is not at all independent of transcendental principles determining our judging activities and does not involve an adequation, correspondence, or identity between propositions and states of affairs themselves. In advancing a modified version of realism, Husserl, according to Tragesser, asserts a relation between propositions and the ideal of a complete and coherent system of propositions about the object or type of object in question. Truth, in other words, is dependent upon the distant (and perhaps infinite or ideal) outcome of future experiences in which the object is presented in noematic aspects which continue to cohere with

27. This thesis controls Tragesser's discussion throughout and is explicitly stated on pp. 14, 75, and 113, although he gives no clear textual references in support of it.

already accumulated experience and whose generation is rule- and telos-governed. If the system is complete or ideally completable, the truth or falsity of every proposition thinkable according to the system's principles and expressible in its language, apart from its being actually thought, would be decidable in principle.[28]

Thus, according to Tragesser, "we have only meanings and validations [fulfilled senses]; whatever objects there are for us are constituted or made manifest on the basis of the latter."[29] But Tragesser's notion of validations does not conform to Husserl's doctrine of fulfillment, in which the objectivity is given in its bodily presence. Instead, for Tragesser—and this must be true for all Fregean interpreters—all we ever achieve are noematic senses distinct from the intended things themselves. Therefore, the confirmation of our assertions about the existence or properties of a mathematical object cannot be achieved in an immediate encounter with that object. We can, in other words, never ascertain an identity or coincidence between the propositions we assert and the mathematical objects and states of affairs themselves. Validation, then, is a function of formal and material coherence of noematic senses and the transcendental principles defining the system. Tragesser concludes: "we are so to speak free to entertain as many objective domains or worlds as our 'logical imagination' is powerful, or as our ability to achieve or construct principles of validation leading to the satisfaction of the criterion for the justifiability of assertions of existence will allow."[30] To each of these worlds, we are justified in attributing an objective existence; consequently, we have the possibility of alternative logical, mathematical, and, by extension, natural sciences.[31]

Hence, Tragesser's view preserves neither epistemological nor logical realism, for there is no relation of either knowledge or propositions to a world which is intelligible and whose existence is independent of mind. What Tragesser preserves instead—and this is the ultimate implication of the Fregean approach—is a notion of rule-governed objectivity, which allows no room for fulfillment by virtue of the actual presence of the objectivity about which we judge and which allows no formal ontology which is not reducible to formal logic and mathematics; what he presents, in other words, is a neo-Kantianized Husserl. What makes Tragesser's Husserl different from Kant is that we can—within the conventions of mathematical and logical choice—

28. Tragesser, p. 116.   29. Tragesser, p. 113.
30. Tragesser, p. 119.   31. Cf. Tragesser, pp. 121–22.

choose validating principles rather than be compelled to work with those intimated in an Aristotelian logic.[32] But, for Husserl, Kantian "transcendental idealism" is "transcendental psychologism," and Husserl was just as opposed to transcendental psychologism as he was to the empirical psychologism of Mill.[33]

5. HUSSERL'S REALISM

I agree with Tragesser that Husserl has undercut the basis on which the issues of realism and its various alternatives are traditionally formulated. But I disagree about the manner in which Husserl has achieved this. I also think Tragesser correct in his implication concerning anti-realistic possibilities in Husserl's view of formal mathematics, although I would not allow the extension of these possibilities to formal logic, formal ontology, or the natural sciences.

Since contemporary physical science is essentially mathematical, our consideration of theoretical unities should begin with mathematics and then move to its physical applications. We should distinguish first two kinds of pure mathematics: (1) that which idealizes the features of a particular region of being, e.g. traditional Euclidean geometry,[34] and (2) that which involves formalizing abstractions and is not restricted to a limited region of being. For Husserl, both the idealizations and formalizations of the pure mathematician, while grounded in the real, can be and are considered apart from their connection with the real. Hence, the mathematician can be concerned only with the logic of noncontradiction, for the disconnection from the real also disconnects the second aspect of logic, the logic of truth. Thus can I agree with Tragesser that the realism/anti-realism issue is mooted in mathematics precisely because only deductive validity or consistency can be at issue when the ideal or the formal is considered apart from its connection with the real. It is possible, therefore, that alternative mathematical systems, each of which is internally consistent but which are mutually incompatible, can both be "true," i.e. "objectively valid," according to the logic of noncontradiction.

This is most obvious in the case of formalized mathematics. Hus-

---

32. Cf., e.g., Tragesser, p. 102.

33. This opposition is clearest in the very work in which Tragesser says Husserl most clearly adopts the position he attributes to Husserl; see *FTL*, §§99–100.

34. For a Husserlian account of the idealizations of traditional Euclidean geometry, see John J. Drummond, "The Perceptual Roots of Geometric Idealizations," *The Review of Metaphysics* 37 (1984): 785–810.

serl's development of the theory of manifolds allows us to distinguish more clearly between geometry as an idealization of intuited structures and geometry as an instance of manifold theory. In the case of Euclidean geometry, the abstraction of the theory-form from the formalization of the idealized Euclidean geometry defines a Euclidean manifold of three dimensions. Other n-dimensional Euclidean and non-Euclidean manifolds can subsequently be constructed by mathematical "choice" with its conventions.[35] We can then view the Euclidean idealizations as a regional ontology of space and the Euclidean manifold as a formal ontology which, while normally applied to space, is theoretically applicable to any region. Since the three-dimensional Euclidean manifold is the formalization of the idealized geometry it can safely be applied in a physical geometry. However, once free mathematical constructions are introduced into the manifolds and once these manifolds are interpreted as "geometries" and applied to the spatial objects of experience, "false" regional ontologies might result. In the case of space, this means that a mathematically derived manifold is applicable as a physical geometry only if, when interpreted, it is consistent with the Euclidean idealizations of the local space in which we live.

It is necessary to recall, however, that even mathematical systems not applicable to the world of direct experience have their roots in the real, for the variations productive of the different formal systems all presuppose the establishment of an original formal system, and this in turn presupposes roots in a more immediate encounter of objects. This is evident in Husserl's arguments concerning the logical priority of the Euclidean manifold and, therefore, of the Euclidean space for which it is the pure categorial form.[36] Since the theory of non-Euclidean manifolds is a logical consequence of the theory of Euclidean manifolds, the non-Euclidean manifolds cannot simply be alternatives to the Euclidean but are modifications of it which do not affect its logical priority. Given the fact, however, that non-Euclidean geometries can have local applications consistent with the idealizations of Euclidean geometry, they can have possible applications to the experienced world. So, for example, the reason for the successful application of Einstein's theory of relativity is that the four coordinates of

35. Edmund Husserl, *Studien zur Arithmetik und Geometrie: Texte aus dem Nachlass (1886–1901)* (hereafter *Studien*), ed. I. Strohmeyer, Husserliana XXI (The Hague, Boston, Lancaster: Martinus Nijhoff, 1983), p. 399.

36. *FTL*, p. 97 n., and for the arguments concerning the priority of the Euclidean manifold, see *Studien*, pp. 337–47.

space-time cannot be arbitrarily interchanged; every point in the four-dimensional continuum involves a splitting apart of three spatial dimensions and a temporal dimension.[37] Thus, even though relativity theory involves the application of a four-dimensional manifold, in its local applications it can satisfy—and does satisfy—this condition of consistency with Euclidean idealizations.

While the issue of realism/anti-realism is mooted in pure mathematics, in formal logic—in the sense of truth-logic—the possibility of alternate and incompatible logics is ruled out because of the teleological concern with verifying presences and because the derivations of propositional forms and deductive unities must conform with possibilities inherent in intuited objects. Furthermore, since formal ontology and interpreted mathematical systems understood as mathematical sciences reestablish the connection between the formal or ideal order and the real order, they must find their truth actually confirmed in verifying presences. These presences occur in categorial—perhaps I should say "theoretical"—intuitions which fulfill the articulated unities posited by the theory. Hence, the choice between competing ontologies and physical theories does not depend so much on the verification of individual judgments within a theory as on the presentation of a unified world which fulfills the posited, theoretical unit. More specifically, the decision between two theories both of which include individual judgments apparently fulfilled in categorial intuitions depends upon the degree of adequacy in the respective theories considered as unified wholes. The more comprehensive theory or the one with the fewest anomalies requires our acceptance. However, theoretical intuiting necessarily involves, as is the case with the categorial intuitions confirming individual judgments, the actual presence of an articulated world to consciousness in a manner which allows us to recognize the identity between the theoretically posited world and this actually present, articulated, real world.

Thus is Husserl's notion of epistemological and logical realism achieved, but it is not the realism of the correspondence theory of truth which asserts a relation of adequation between ideas or propositions which are ontologically distinctive mental or abstract entities and objects or states of affairs themselves. Nor is it an anti-realism which asserts that truth is a coherent system of justified assertions and that

---

37. Oskar Becker, "Beiträge zur phänomenologischen Begründung der Geometrie und ihrer physikalischen Anwendungen," *Jahrbuch für Philosophie und phänomenologische Forschung* 6 (1923): 558. Husserl apparently approved of Becker's account in a letter to Weyl; see Strohmeyer's introduction to *Studien*, pp. lxvii–lxviii.

systems are determined by reference to some ideal of completeness in accordance with axiomatic or transcendental principles (*à la* Tragesser) or chosen on pragmatic grounds (*à la,* for example, Rorty).

Logical, mathematical, and scientific objectivities are not fully formed and waiting to confront us; we must exercise the mind in order to bring them to presence, but our mental activity is grounded in more immediate experiences of the real world and guided by the features of the world and the objects therein. The need for mental activity does not imply that the existence of these higher-order entities depends upon consciousness. The activity does not create the object; it does not produce the state of affairs, the essence, or the mathematical object. The activity is, however, required to bring the objectivity to conscious presence, to bring it to presence *as an object,* as an intelligible, higher-order reality. This activity is, in fact, controlled by the object itself, for it follows at first the clues offered by possibilities of articulation at work within the lower-order objectivity in its presence to consciousness. The constructions achieved in this activity are in turn confirmed in other intuitions, and our scientific knowledge always remains in contact with the real world even as it employs idealizations to render more exact our knowledge and even as it posits theoretical entities to explain more fully and consistently the mechanisms of a physical world. But to conceive truth only as justified assertability relative to an enclosed system is insufficient because it does not adequately take into account the phenomenological differences between the relevant cohering experiences, between the empty and anticipative positings involved in perceiving, judging, and theorizing and the fulfilling intuitions corresponding to the nature of the positings.

So, not a traditional realism, but a realism nevertheless—one (a) in which the ontological realism of the natural attitude, both the weak form with respect to individuals and the moderate form with respect to higher-order objectivities, is preserved; and one (b) which in its theory of intentionality avoids the epistemological problems of the moderns, giving an explanatory account of epistemological realism and taking full account of the activity of a subject in bringing objective unities of all kinds to articulation and presence; and one (c) which allows for an anti-realism only in mathematics. But even in mathematics, this anti-realism can and must be understood only as a modification of and contrasted with the epistemological and logical realism involved in our knowledge of and speaking about the world itself.

6   Husserl on Evidence and Justification*

DAGFINN FØLLESDAL

The problem of evidence and justification is central in Husserl's phenomenology. In nearly all his writings, from the earliest to the latest, it is a recurrent theme.

At first sight Husserl might seem to be a *foundationalist* in matters of justification: one gets the impression that he held that one can reach absolute certainty, at least concerning some matters, and also that he regarded it as a main task of philosophy to attain such certainty. Philosophy should be developed as a "rigorous science" which could provide firm foundations for the sciences and for mathematics. Again and again Husserl emphasizes certainty, a priori knowledge, freedom from presuppositions, and intuition, or essential insight.

In this paper, we will take a closer look at these matters. After a brief introductory exposition of Husserl's notions of intentionality and filling we will review Husserl's notion of evidence and his changing views on the two kinds of perfection of evidence, adequate and apodictic. We will also examine Husserl's seemingly foundationalist statements, and we will conclude that in spite of appearances, Husserl never was a foundationalist. On the contrary, during the last twenty years of his life he developed more and more in the direction of a quite extreme holism, not only in the sciences, but also in mathematics and in ethics, the two disciplines which traditionally have been the strongholds of foundationalism. In fact, I will argue that Husserl's mature view in these matters was very similar to the views that Nelson Goodman, John Rawls and many others were to develop later. My main thesis will be that Husserl embraced what Rawls has called the method of "reflective equilibrium."

*This article springs from a project on Husserl's phenomenology which is presently supported by the Institute for Advanced Study, Princeton. I gratefully acknowledge this support.

1. HUSSERL'S NOTIONS OF INTENTIONALITY
AND FILLING

Intentionality

The central idea in Husserl's phenomenology, which is a key to the understanding of the rest of his philosophy, is that of intentionality. Following his teacher Franz Brentano, Husserl claimed that consciousness is characterized by a certain kind of directedness, that it always appears to be directed towards something, to be consciousness *of* something. When I think, I am thinking of something, when I perceive, I perceive something, and so on. An example from perception may illustrate what Husserl had in mind. Let us consider Jastrow's duck/rabbit picture, which Wittgenstein made famous (Figure 1):

When we look at this picture, we may see a duck or a rabbit. What reaches our eye is the same in both cases, so the difference must be something coming from us. We structure what we see, and we can do so in different ways. The impulses that reach us from the outside are insufficient to uniquely determine which object we experience; something more gets added. This something more that gets added, Husserl called the *noema*. The noema is a structure. Our consciousness structures what we experience. How it structures it depends on our previous experiences, the whole setting of our present experience and a number of other factors. If we had grown up surrounded by ducks, but had never even heard of rabbits, we would have been more likely to see a duck than a rabbit in the above picture; the idea of a rabbit would probably not even have occurred to us. According to

Husserl, all our experience could in principle be structured in different ways; what reaches our senses is never sufficient to uniquely determine what we experience. Only in a few rare cases, such as in the
duck/rabbit example, can we go back and forth at will between different ways of structuring our experience. Usually we are not even aware
of any structuring going on; objects are simply experienced by us as
having a structure.

Filling

The noema of an act of perception can also be characterized as a set
of anticipations: we anticipate different further experiences when we
see a duck and when we see a rabbit. In the first case we anticipate, for
example, that we will feel feathers when we touch the object. In the
latter case we expect to find fur. When we get the experiences we anticipate, the corresponding component of the noema is said to be
filled. In all perception, there will be some filling: the components of
the noema that correspond to what presently "meets the eye" are
filled, and similarly for the other senses.

Such anticipation and filling is what distinguishes perception from
other modes of consciousness, for example imagination or remembering. If we merely imagine things, then our noema can be of anything whatsoever, an elephant or a locomotive standing here beside
me. In perception, however, my sensory experiences are involved; the
noema has to fit in with my sensory experiences. This eliminates a
number of noemata which I could have had if I were just imagining.
In my present situation I cannot have a noema corresponding to the
perception of an elephant. This does not reduce the number of perceptual noemata I can have just now to one, for example, of you sitting
there in front of me. It is a central point in Husserl's phenomenology
that I can have a variety of different perceptual noemata that are compatible with the present impingements upon my sensory surfaces. In
the duck/rabbit case this was obvious; we could go back and forth at
will between having the noema of a duck and having the noema of a
rabbit. In most cases, however, we are not aware of this possibility.
Only when something untoward happens, when I encounter "recalcitrant" experience that does not fit in with the anticipations in my
noema, do I start seeing a different object from the one I thought
I saw earlier. My noema "explodes," to use Husserl's phrase, and I
come to have a noema quite different from the previous one, with new
anticipations. This is always possible, says Husserl. Perception always
involves anticipations that go beyond what presently "meets the eye,"

and there is always a risk that we may go wrong, regardless of how confident and certain we might feel. Misperception is always possible.

2. EVIDENCE

We are now ready to turn to the first of the two major topics of this paper, Husserl's notion of evidence.

In a nutshell, for Husserl evidence consists in one or more components of the noema being filled. His view on evidence can be condensed into four theses:

(i) Evidence is the self-giving of an object in our experience, that is, the object is experienced as being "itself-there," and not merely as imagined, conjectured, etc.

This thesis is uncontroversial, and a number of passages can be quoted to support it, for example the following:

To speak of evidence, of evident givenness, then, here signifies nothing other than *self-givenness*, the way in which an object can be characterized relative to consciousness as "itself there," "there in the flesh"—in contrast to its mere presentification ⟨Vergegenwärtigung⟩, the empty, merely indicative idea of it. For example, an object of external perception is given with evidence, as "it itself," precisely in the *actual* perception, in contrast to the simple presentification of it in memory, imagination, etc.[1]

See also the continuation of this passage, which is quoted in support of our next thesis.

Whenever the noema of an act is partially or totally filled, we have evidence for the existence of the object of the act and for the object's having the kind of properties that are attributed to it according to the noema.

---

1. *Erfahrung u. Urteil*, § 4, pp. 11–12 = Churchill & Ameriks, pp. 19–20. In the following, references to *Erfahrung und Urteil* will be to the edition at Claassen Verlag, Hamburg, 1964. References to works that have been published in the Husserliana edition of Husserl's works will be to page and line in this edition. In the case of the *Cartesian Meditations*, I also give page references to Elisabeth Ströker's edition of this work (Philosophische Bibliothek, Band 291, Felix Meiner, Hamburg, 1977). Where her edition differs from the Husserliana edition, I use her version of the text. In the case of the *Ideas*, I also give references to the first German edition (1913). For works that have been translated into English, I include the translator's name and the page number of the translation. The following translations will be used: *Ideas*, First Book, tr. F. Kersten (Nijhoff, The Hague, 1982); *Formal and Transcendental Logic*, tr. Dorion Cairns (Nijhoff, The Hague, 1969); *Cartesian Meditations*, tr. Dorion Cairns (Nijhoff, The Hague, 1960); *The Crisis of European Sciences and Transcendental Phenomenology*, tr. David Carr (Northwestern University Press, Evanston, 1970); *Experience and Judgment*, tr. James S. Churchill and Karl Amerik (Northwestern University Press, Evanston, 1973).

Husserl emphasizes that

(ii) Evidence does not require complete filling, or *adequacy;* the filling of the noema may be partial.

Husserl warns against the overtones in the direction of perfect evidence that the word 'evident' has in German, as in English:

As *'evident'*, then, we designate *consciousness of any kind which is characterized relative to its object as giving this object itself,* without asking whether this self-giving is adequate or not. By this, we deviate from the customary use of the term 'evidence', which as a rule is employed in cases which, rigorously described, are those of adequate givenness, on the one hand, and of apodictic insight, on the other.
(*Erfahrung u. Urteil,* § 4, p. 12 = Churchill & Ameriks, p. 20. I have translated the German word 'evident' with 'evident' rather than with 'self-evident', as Churchill and Ameriks do. See also *Ideas,* §§ 137–138.)

It is important for Husserl that although evidence is presupposed by judgment, it does not presuppose judgment. It is found already on the prepredicative level, to use Husserl's terminology. That is, we have a lot of evidence concerning matters that we have never thought about, far less explicitly judged about. Such evidence corresponds to the many anticipations in the noema that we have likewise never thought about or made thematic, for example the evidence we have that there is a floor in this room, evidence which we received as soon as we opened the door and stepped in. Hence:

(iii) Evidence is not confined to acts of judgments; an object can be evidently given without having to be judged about in a predicative judgment.

To quote Husserl:

An object, as the possible substrate of a judgment, can be given with evidence without having to be judged about in a predicative judgment. On the other hand, an evident predicative judgment concerning this object is not possible unless the object itself is given with evidence.
(*Erfahrung u. Urteil,* § 4, p. 12 = Churchill & Ameriks, p. 20. See also pp. 21, 23 and 68 of *Erfahrung und Urteil,* corresponding to pp. 27, 29 and 65 of the English translation.)

One important feature of Husserl's notion of evidence that I have not seen noticed in the literature on Husserl is expressed in the following thesis:

(iv) Evidence is not just yielded just by sensory filling, but also by practical activity and by feeling.

By feeling, Husserl here has in mind what the British moral sense philosophers call 'feeling', or 'sentiment', and which for them plays an important role as evidence in moral philosophy. In his early writings Husserl does not devote much attention to practical activity and feeling, but is concentrating on perception and other cognitive activities. However, from 1917 on, he starts to discuss practical activities and feeling and their interconnections with cognitive activities. The following passage from *Experience and Judgment* is typical:

> However, in its orientation on scientific determination and its tendency toward science and scientific theory, this traditional logic has never brought into question the *entwinement of cognitive behavior with the practical and the evaluative* and has never investigated how a judgment is produced which does not serve purely cognitive interest in this way but rather serves the practical in the most general sense of the word; nor has it investigated how predicative self-evidence is built on *this* domain of the prepredicative, on practical evidence and the evidence of feeling. It is indisputable that these are original sources of the giving of existents themselves, of the disclosure of determinations which, by their nature, can take place only in practical activity itself and not in mere contemplation. But it is precisely about these modes of giving a thing itself that we do not ask; we do not ask how it is possible to construct a judicative act of objectification *on them;* rather, we create the fiction that the ego, in a purely contemplative activity without any purpose or interest other than that of contemplation, turns immediately toward what exists as it is passively and affectively given to us. In other words, we create the fiction of a subject that behaves in a purely contemplative way and which is not aroused to any practical activity by the existent by which it is affected environmentally.
>
> (*Erfahrung u. Urteil*, § 14, pp. 68–69 = Churchill & Ameriks, pp. 65–66. My italics.)

3. ADEQUATE AND APODICTIC EVIDENCE

In the passage from *Experience and Judgment* that I quoted in support of thesis 2 above, Husserl mentions two kinds of perfections of evidence: adequacy and apodicticity. These two notions he defines as follows:

Adequate evidence is the kind of perfect evidence we have when there are no unfulfilled components, no expectant and attendant meanings, but where all these attendant meanings have become fulfilled in actual experience.[2]

Apodictic evidence is the absolute indubitability of the affair-complexes that are

2. See *Cartesian Meditations*, § 6, p. 15 of Cairn's translation, p. 55 of the Husserliana edition, p. 16 of Ströker's edition in *Philosophische Bibliothek*, Felix Meiner, Hamburg, 1977. See also *Erste Philosophie*, 31. Vorl., Hua. VIII, p. 33, and *Ideas*, § 137.

given, in the sense of the absolute unimaginableness of their non-being, and thus excluding in advance every imaginable doubt as objectless.[3]

Husserl warns against regarding this notion of "unimaginableness" as a psychological notion. Instead he clarifies it by help of Bolzano's notions of consistency and self-contradictoriness, notions that were later rediscovered by Quine and Ajdukiewicz in their work on logical truth.

Husserl also points out that having perfect evidence is not a matter of psychology and feelings:

We may not rely upon the *feeling* of knowledge-satisfaction in the manifestation of evidence. The evidence that we have, must also *justify* itself to us as evidence.

That [the evidence is adequate] we therefore recognize only in a second, *reflective evidence*, which in its turn must be adequate. That it can be carried out adequately, that in this way adequate reflections are possible *ad infinitum* and also, it seems, justifications are required *ad infinitum*, shall not worry us here, although at the proper time we will have to consider the problem that lies here. We shall also have to consider the problem that ensues from the possibility of adequate givenness. For it might turn out that such adequate givenness is a mere "idea," in a sense analogous to the way in which we call pure red an "idea": seen red is, we think, always only red in more or less imperfect purity, belonging to incremental scales through which we may come closer to pure red, although we finally nevertheless remain (more or less) far from it. (*Erste Philosophie*, 31. Vorl., Hua. VIII, 33.8–34.1)

Husserl hence tends towards the view that adequate evidence is not attainable, it is only a goal, a Kantian "idea," which guides our search for knowledge. Already in the *Ideas*, § 143, he characterizes the adequate givenness of a *physical thing* as a Kantian idea, but in his lectures on First Philosophy in 1923–24 he seems to hold that this applies to adequate evidence generally, regardless of what kind of object one is experiencing.

In the *Ideas* Husserl further states that errors are possible in any sphere of validity (*Ideen I*, § 87, Hua. III/1, 201.34–35 = First ed., 180 = Kersten, 212).

In *Erste Philosophie* (1923–24) from which the above quotation was taken, Husserl maintained that adequate and apodictic evidence go hand in hand: every adequate evidence is apodictic and every apodictic evidence is adequate (*Erste Philosophie*, 31. Vorl., Hua. VIII, 35.22–

3. *Cartesian Meditations*, § 6, pp. 15–16 of Cairn's translation, p. 56 of the Husserliana edition, p. 16 of Ströker's edition. See also *Erste Philosophie*, 31. Vorl., Hua. VIII, p. 35, and *Ideas*, § 137.

25). This is a view that he appears to have held all the time from when he introduced these notions in the *Ideas* (1913) until he gave these lectures in the mid twenties. However, in the *Cartesian Meditations* (1929) Husserl has changed his view on this point. He there holds that apodictic evidence can occur even in evidences that are inadequate.[4]

In the *Cartesian Meditations* Husserl says about his new view that *adequacy and apodicticity* of evidence *need not go hand in hand:*

Perhaps this remark was made precisely with the case of transcendental self-experience in mind. In such experience the ego is accessible to himself originaliter. But at any particular time this experience offers only a core that is experienced "with strict adequacy," namely the ego's living present (which the grammatical sense of the sentence, *ego cogito,* expresses); while, beyond that, only an indeterminately general presumptive horizon extends, comprising what is strictly non-experienced but necessarily also-meant. To it belongs not only the ego's past, most of which is completely obscure, but also his transcendental abilities and his habitual peculiarities at the time.
(*Cart. Med.,* § 9, Hua. I, 62.9–20 = Ströker, 24 = Cairns, 22–23)

This remained Husserl's final position with respect to perfection of evidence: adequate evidence is an unobtainable ideal, apodictic evidence may be possible in one special case: our knowledge of our own existence. However, even in the latter case our knowledge of ourselves is so obscure as to be very far from being adequate.

4. FOUNDATIONALIST STATEMENTS IN HUSSERL

In view of this meager sphere of perfect evidence in Husserl, one should not expect him to be a foundationalist in epistemology, as Husserl interpreters invariably claim.

I could quote any of a number of Husserl scholars who hold that Husserl was a foundationalist. However, I shall instead quote two representative passages from a prominent philosopher who is not a Husserl scholar, but has a strong interest in Husserl. Hao Wang says in his latest book, *Beyond Analytic Philosophy:*[5]

[H]e [Husserl] spent most of his energy in the struggle for securing a 'true beginning.' The indiscriminately applied pejorative term 'foundationalism' is a quite appropriate label for his work." (p. 32)

[H]e looks for the absolutely certain or synthetic a priori foundation once and

4. *Cart. Med.,* § 6, Hua. I, 55.31–32 = Ströker, 17 = Cairns, 15; see also Hua. I, 56.36–37 = Ströker, 18 = Cairns, 16.
5. Hao Wang, *Beyond Analytic Philosophy,* Bradford Books, M.I.T. Press, Cambridge, Mass., 1986.

for all, while I feel such a quest for an unattainable goal is doomed to failure, however useful and interesting its by-products might be. (pp. 37–38)

Wang makes no pretension to being an expert on Husserl; his book is, as the title indicates, primarily a discussion of central issues in analytic philosophy. However, his characterizations of Husserl reflect the universally accepted view that Husserl was a foundationalist. This view is, as far as I can ascertain, shared by all who write on Husserl, Husserl scholars and other philosophers alike.

There are excuses for this interpretation in Husserl's own writings. Husserl often writes as if he held that we can attain some infallible, absolutely certain insight from which the rest of our knowledge can be built up in a Cartesian fashion. Thus, in *Formal and Transcendental Logic* he praises Plato and others because they would

accept no knowledge that cannot be accounted for by originarily first principles, which are at the same time matters of perfect insight—principles such that profounder inquiry makes no sense.
  (*Form. u. transz. Logik,* Einl., Hua. XVII, 8.6–9 = Cairns, 4)

The concluding words in this passage, that one should strive for principles such that profounder inquiry makes no sense, seem foundationalist. However, as I shall argue in the last section of this paper, this is not the way it should be interpreted.

Also, Husserl characterizes in all his writings phenomenology as a study of the *a priori.* This makes it natural to assimilate him to Kant and Kant's foundationalism. However, Husserl means something different with '*a priori*' than does Kant. For Husserl, the *a priori* is that which we anticipate, that which we expect to find, given the noema we have. Phenomenology studies and attempts to chart these anticipations, but as we know, our anticipations often go wrong, our experiences turn out differently from what we expected, and again and again we have to revise our views and our expectations.

The way I interpret Husserl, his seemingly foundationalist statements are mere surface appearances. I shall now argue that far from being a foundationalist he is on the contrary a "holist" and has a view on justification very similar to the view that has been set forth by Nelson Goodman, John Rawls and others, and which I will call the "reflective equilibrium" view. I shall first state the view and then argue that Husserl had it.

5. REFLECTIVE EQUILIBRIUM

I am borrowing the label 'reflective equilibrium' from John Rawls, who introduced the label in *A Theory of Justice*[6] for a method that he had started to develop already in his article "Outline of a decision procedure for ethics" (1951).[7] Using this label for a method of justification may be misleading, since when Rawls uses this label in *A Theory of Justice* and his later writings he does not have in mind a theory of justification, but a method for obtaining agreement. There is some vacillation in Rawls on this point; in "Outline of a decision procedure for ethics" Rawls regards the method as providing justification (p. 186); he talks about the method helping us to attain moral knowledge (p. 177) and about moral rules being validated through the use of this method (p. 177), and he states that he is not concerned "with the problem of how to make it psychologically effective in the settling of disputes" (p. 177). However, in his later writings Rawls is more cautious, and he distinguishes more clearly between achieving agreement and providing justification. He no longer contends that the method provides justification, but settles for the more modest claim that it is a practical way of achieving agreement.

However, we will use 'reflective equilibrium' for any method that has certain general characteristics that we will now list, whether it be conceived of as a method of justification or as a method of settling disputes. There is no other label that approximates more closely what we find in Husserl. 'The hypothetico-deductive method' is less appropriate, since that method contains only some of the ingredients of Husserl's view, ingredients that we find in a very large number of philosophers and which therefore do not help to characterize Husserl's view in any detail.

The basic characteristics of the method of reflective equilibrium, as I will use the term, are the following six features:

(i) It is usually a method of *justification*. As we noted, Rawls in his later writings regards the method as merely a practical way of *reaching agreement*, and there are some who regard the method as yielding only *explanation* or *prediction* but not justification. However, all versions of the method have the remaining five features in common:

6. John Rawls, *A Theory of Justice*, Harvard University Press, Cambridge, Mass., 1971.
7. John Rawls, "Outline of a decision procedure for ethics," *Philosophical Review* 60 (1951), 177–191.

(ii) The method emphasizes the *coherence* of one's views. The coherence is of the kind that we typically strive for in scientific theories; deductive logical inference plays an important role, and so do simplicity and other considerations: some might, for example, want to make use of what is often called 'inference to the best explanation'. Typically, particular statements are justified by being deduced from more general statements, but on the other hand, the general statements in their turn are justified by the fact that the desired particular statements follow from them.

So far, the method is nothing over and beyond the hypothetico-deductive method. However, now we come to its distinctive features, which set the method of reflective equilibrium apart as being one specific variant of the more general hypothetico-deductive method:

(iii) *Total corrigibility.* No statement in one's "theory" is immune to revision (I use the word 'theory' in a broad sense, which does not require a theory to be fully worked out into a deductive system, but only requires the statements to be sufficiently related to permit transfer of evidence between them). Any statement may be given up when we find that giving it up brings about simplifications and greater coherence in our overall theory. The views of some of the logical empiricists on "protocol statements" as non-revisable and unaffected by theory are incompatible with this, and their methods are therefore not examples of reflective equilibrium, although they are examples of the hypothetico-deductive method. The method of reflective equilibrium is also incompatible with a theory of "sense data," where statements about sense data are supposed to be incorrigible. Adherents of reflective equilibrium are fallibilists not only with respect to some or most statements, but with respect to all.

(iv) The method of reflective equilibrium can be applied in a number of different *fields*, four prominent ones being empirical science, mathematics, logic and ethics. Philosophers can regard the method as appropriate for one, two, three, or all four of these fields. They can also be distinguished according to whether they regard these four fields as separate fields, where evidence from one field does not transfer to the other fields, or whether they are what we could call "unbounded" holists, and regard all four fields as part of one whole, where coherence considerations involve all four of them and where evidence accordingly is transferred from one area to the other. Evidence from the empirical sciences will thus be relevant for questions of values and norms, and more remarkable, evidence from ethics may have a bearing on questions in mathematics, logic or empirical science.

The foremost representative of such unbounded holism is Morton White, in *Toward Reunion in Philosophy* (1956), pp. 254–58 and 263, and in *What Is and What Ought To Be Done* (1981).[8] White here argues that all the four areas mentioned are interrelated in such a way that statements from all four areas can be put to test together, and that sometimes "we may reject or revise a *descriptive* statement in response to a recalcitrant moral feeling." (*What Is and What Ought To Be Done*, p. 122). By including statements from all four areas in the body of statements to be tested White includes more than Quine, who does not discuss ethics, and much more than Duhem in *The Aim and Structure of Physical Theory*,[9] who does not include mathematics and logic and does not discuss ethics.

In *Science and Sentiment in America*,[10] White shows that William James vacillated between a "trialistic" view and a holistic view. The former predominates in the *Psychology* (which Husserl got acquainted with in 1891 and studied carefully in the mid-nineties) and in *The Will to Believe*, where natural science, logic/mathematics, and ethics are three separate fields, each subject to a method like that of a reflective equilibrium, but with no transfer of evidence between the fields. The latter, holistic view White finds advanced in some parts of *Pragmatism* and in *A Pluralistic Universe*, where all three fields are regarded as part of one unified whole, one stock of beliefs, in a broad sense, with evidence being transferred between the fields: strains in one field may be increased or reduced by what is happening in the other fields. According to White, "an unsatisfied desire may challenge the stock as much as the discovery of a logical contradiction or a recalcitrant fact, and it is James' belief in the parity of unsatisfied desire with the two other creators of strain that distinguishes his later position." (White, *op. cit*, p. 205)

8. Morton White, *Toward Reunion in Philosophy*, Harvard University Press, Cambridge, Mass., 1956; and *What Is and What Ought to Be Done*, Oxford University Press, New York, 1981.

9. Pierre Duhem, *La Théorie Physique: Son Objet, Sa Structure*, Rivière, Paris, 1906, English translation, as *The Aim and Structure of Physical Theory*, Princeton University Press, Princeton, N.J., 1954.

10. Morton White, *Science and Sentiment in America: Philosophical Thought from Jonathan Edwards to John Dewey*, Oxford University Press, New York, 1972.

Husserl, as we shall see, used the method of reflective equilibrium within each of the four fields separately, but he did not try to combine them.

Quine's oft-quoted characterization of his holism at the end of "Two dogmas of empiricism" is a nutshell description of the method of reflective equilibrium as applied to a broad field, comprising empirical science, mathematics and logic, but with nothing being said about ethics:

> [T]otal science is like a field of force whose boundary conditions are experience. A conflict with experience at the periphery occasions readjustments in the interior of the field. . . . Having reëvaluated one statement we must reëvaluate some others, which may be statements logically connected with the first or may be statements of logical connections themselves. . . . No particular experiences are linked with any particular statements in the interior of the field, except indirectly through considerations of equilibrium affecting the field as a whole.[11]

Before proceeding to the last two features of the method it may be instructive to consider an example of an application of the method of reflective equilibrium to the problem of justification in logic. Let me quote Nelson Goodman's classical description of the method, in his *Fact, Fiction and Forecast* (1955):

> How do we justify a *deduction?* Plainly by showing that it conforms to the general rules of deductive inference. . . .

> But how is the validity of rules to be determined? Here again we encounter philosophers who insist that these rules follow from some self-evident axiom, and others who try to show that the rules are grounded in the very nature of the human mind. I think the answer lies much nearer the surface. Principles of deductive inference are justified by their conformity with accepted deductive practice. Their validity depends upon accordance with the particular deductive inferences we actually make and sanction. If a rule yields inacceptable inferences, we drop it as invalid. Justification of general rules thus derives from judgments rejecting or accepting particular deductive inferences.

> This looks flagrantly circular. I have said that deductive inferences are justified by their conformity to valid general rules, and that the general rules are justified by their conformity to valid inferences. But the circle is a virtuous one. The point is that rules and particular inferences alike are justified by being brought into agreement with each other. *A rule is amended if it yields an*

---

11. W. V. Quine, "Two dogmas of empiricism," *Philosophical Review* 60 (1951), 20–43. Reprinted in Quine, *From a Logical Point of View*, Harvard University Press, Cambridge, Mass., 1953, 2d. ed. 1961. The passage quoted occurs on pp. 42–43 of *From a Logical Point of View*.

inference we are unwilling to accept; an inference is rejected if it violates a rule we are unwilling to amend. The process of justification is the delicate one of making mutual adjustments between rules and accepted inferences; and in the agreement achieved lies the only justification needed for either.[12]

Note here the three features of the method of reflective equilibrium that we have discussed so far: justification, coherence and total corrigibility. The passage from Goodman brings into focus a further, highly important feature, to which we shall now turn: pre-reflective, intuitive acceptance as the basic source of evidence:

(v) The method of reflective equilibrium makes crucial use of our *pre-reflective, intuitive acceptance* of various statements. Through reflection, systematization and observation it seeks to gradually modify our acceptances, strengthen some of them and weaken others, but it does not attempt a whole-sale rejection of all of them in order to replace them with something radically new. There is no source of evidence upon which such a new edifice could be built; all the evidence there is is imparted through these intuitive acceptances.

(vi) *Sources of evidence.* Only a careful study of how various observations, experiences, and changes in our system affect our acceptance can tell us whether, in addition to coherence considerations, which are crucial to the method of reflective equilibrium, there is any source of evidence that is of particularly great importance. Perception would, at least by empiricists, be looked upon as one such privileged source, which, although not infallible, provides whatever evidence there is, in addition to the coherence considerations. Rawls, in "Outline of a decision procedure for ethics," seems to hold that the *particular* moral judgments have such a privileged status: the general ethical principles have whatever acceptability they have in virtue of how well they systematize our particular moral judgments. Our acceptance of some of the particular judgments may be modified through this systematization, but the particular judgments remain the ultimate source of evidence for the ethical principles, much as in science the particular observation statements are the ultimate source of evidence for the general hypotheses of the theory.

12. Nelson Goodman, *Fact, Fiction and Forecast,* Harvard University Press, Cambridge, Mass., 1955 and later editions. Here quoted from the second edition, Bobbs-Merrill Company, New York, 1965, pp. 62–64.

While most philosophers would attribute to perception and observation such a privileged role in the sciences, the situation is not so clear in ethics. There have been philosophers who have treated moral feelings, or sentiments, as an ethical counterpart to perception. As we shall see, Husserl had this view. However, Rawls, in his later writings, no longer gives particular moral judgments a privileged status when compared with the general judgments, but gives judgments of both kinds the same status. This change of view accompanies his change from regarding the method of reflective equilibrium as a method of justification to regarding it merely as a way of settling disagreements.

6. REFLECTIVE EQUILIBRIUM IN HUSSERL

What evidence is there that Husserl accepted the method of reflective equilibrium, and in which fields did he accept it? We will now take a look at the diverse features of the method, and I will show by quotations from Husserl's writings that Husserl accepted all these features, that he did so separately within all the four areas that we have described, and that he gave a special twist to the method, reflecting his views on perception and on the Lebenswelt.

(i) *Justification.* In his whole discussion concerning coherence, corrigibility, etc., from which discussion excerpts follow, Husserl is always concerned with justification and validity; he is never, like the later Rawls, merely interested in reaching practical agreement within a community. 'Justification', 'evidence', 'validity', 'truth' are terms that recur in his discussion.

(ii) *Coherence.* Husserl again and again emphasizes the importance of coherence for validity and for truth. The following passage from his *Lectures on First Philosophy* (1923–24) is typical:

> A judgment-unity penetrates all the individual judgments. . . . they have a unity which builds itself up in the progression of judgment, tying together judgment-sense with judgment-sense. This unity confers on all of them an intrinsic, interrelated validity. In this way the multiple statements in a treatise have a comprehensive judgment-unity, and so has in its way every theory and every entire science.
> (*Erste Philosophie*, 3. Vorl., Hua. VII, 19.24–36)

Already in the *Logical Investigations* Husserl emphasizes coherence as a source of validity. He refers to Ernst Mach's idea that a scientific theory *sums up* the multiplicity of sensations, perceptions and intuitions into *one* unitary conception. Mach called this the principle of economy of thought. Husserl accepted economy of thought; however, he did not, like Mach, regard it biologically, but as a principle of the greatest possible rationality of our experience.[13]

Notice how Husserl in the preceding passage does not merely point out that the different judgments in a treatise, a theory, a science and in our whole web of belief have a unity, but that this unity confers validity upon all these judgments, justifies them. Husserl uses the phrase 'interrelated validity', making explicit the central idea in the Goodman-Rawls theory of a reflective equilibrium, that through the coherent unity the individual judgments confer validity on one another.

(iii) *Total corrigibility.* This may seem a difficult point to defend in an interpretation of Husserl, with all his foundationalist talk. However, Husserl is a foundationalist only on the surface. If we study him carefully, we discover that he adheres to the method of reflective equilibrium. We shall now look at some of the crucial passages, and we shall deal with empirical science, logic and mathematics, and ethics in that order.

First, lest one be misled by Husserl's foundationalist way of talking, note the following question from the *Crisis:*

Can I begin with a truth—a definitive truth? . . . If I already had such 'immediately self-evident' truths, then I could perhaps mediately derive new ones from them. But where do I have them?
(*Krisis,* § 73, Hua. VI, 269.24–29 = Carr, 335)

The only case where we might possibly have a definitive truth may, as we noted at the end of Section 3, be the case of our own existence. However, even here, Husserl added a "perhaps," and he immediately pointed out that even our self-experience is in any case inadequate, partial and obscure.

(iv) *Justification within different fields.* In the case of *empirical science,* Husserl again and again emphasizes that we always risk to be in error. I can be certain of something, but there is always a risk that I may be wrong:

It is certain; but this certainty can modalize itself, it can become doubtful, it can dissolve in the course of experience into illusion: no im-

13. See in this connection the following studies of Mach and Husserl: Hermann Lübbe, "Positivismus und Phänomenologie (Mach und Husserl)," in *Beiträge zu Philosophie und Wissenschaft, W. Szilasi zum 70. Geburtstag,* Francke, München 1960, pp. 161–184; Klaus Düsing, "Das Problem der Denkökonomie bei Husserl und Mach," in U. Claesges and K. Held (eds.), *Perspektiven transzendentalphänomenologischer Forschung, für Ludwig Landgrebe zum 70. Geburtstag von seinen Kölner Schülern* (Phenomenologica 49), Nijhoff, The Hague, 1972, pp. 225–254; and especially Manfred Sommer, *Husserl und der frühe Positivismus* (Philosophische Abhandlungen, Band 53), Klostermann, Frankfurt am Main, 1985.

mediate experiential assertion gives me an entity as what it is in itself but only something meant with certainty that must verify itself in the course of my experiencing life. But the verification which lies merely in the harmonious character of actual experience does not prevent the possibility of illusion.
(*Krisis*, § 73, Hua. VI, 270.2–9 = Carr, 335)

Everybody nowadays would agree with Husserl about this. However, Husserl gives, through his theory of perception, a more detailed account of the many ways in which we may go wrong. Husserl does not merely, like Popper and so many other philosophers of science, tell us that our hypotheses may be wrong, he also gives an illuminating account of how our observational statements may be wrong. Quine points out how "even a statement very close to the periphery can be held true in the face of recalcitrant experience by pleading hallucination or by amending certain statements called logical laws" (Quine, "Two dogmas of empiricism," *From a Logical Point of View*, p. 43). However, Husserl's theory of noema and filling, which I sketched earlier, gives us a much simpler way out. Only rarely do we need to invoke hallucinations or revise our logic. Usually what happens is that we get a new noema, as when we go over from perceiving a duck to perceiving a rabbit, or a mannequin instead of a man. The impingements on our sensory surfaces remain the same, what we see becomes different. Philosophers of science have been talking much about the theory-ladenness of observation. However, they have been skimpy on examples, and they have rarely provided a theory to account for the phenomenon. Husserl does so.

So much for empirical science. Let us now turn to *mathematics and logic*. According to Husserl, the possibility of mistake is found here, too. The following passage is representative of the many places where he discusses the status of these two areas:

[T]hus all descriptive assertions are necessarily relative, and all conceivable inferences, deductive or inductive, are relative.
(*Krisis*, § 73, Hua. VI, 270.28–29 = Carr, 336)

Hence, even deductive inference, that is *logic*, can require correction! Husserl again and again comes back to this unavoidable possibility of mistake. Thus in *Formal and Transcendental Logic* he says:

Even an ostensibly apodictic evidence can become disclosed as deception and, in that event, presupposes a similar evidence by which it is "shattered."
(*Form. u. transz. Logik*, § 58, Hua. XVII, 164.32–34 = Cairns, 156)

Note the last part of this quotation, where Husserl points out that the "shattering" is not due to some special, privileged sort of insight, but always is a result of ~~more evidence of the same kind~~. We shall come back to this under our next point, but let us first turn briefly to *ethics* and see how the situation is there:

Husserl wrote relatively little on ethics compared to what he wrote on epistemology and the philosophy of logic. However, from what little he wrote one may gather that he also in ethics had views on justification similar to those that he had in logic.

By way of introduction, Husserl sets forth the question of what kind of evidence one has in ethics:

And thus also in ethics we have to ask: where is the source of the primitive ethical concepts, where are the experiences [*Erlebnisse*], on the basis of which I can grant these concepts the evidence of conceptual validity?
(Husserl-manuscript F I 20, p. 106. Quoted by Alwin Diemer in *Edmund Husserl. Versuch einer systematischen Darstellung seiner Phänomenologie* (Monographien zur philosophischen Forschung, Band XV), Anton Hain, Meisenheim am Glan, 2d. ed., 1965, 316)

For Husserl, acts of sentiment (*Gemüt*) are the source of evidence for values. (Husserl-manuscript F I 23, p. 77 (Diemer, 316, n. 3). For

How can the unconditional validity of 'ought' be recognized, if not by some relations or peculiarities of sentiments, and indeed acts of sentiment, lying at the bottom, which the one who is judging is looking to?
(Husserl-manuscript F I 20, p. 227; Diemer, p. 317, n. 6, and p. 48, n. 48)

Further, Husserl says:

The English moral sense philosophy [*Gefühlsmoral*] has after all established beyond doubt: If we imagine a being, who is *sentiment-blind* in the same way as we know beings who are *color-blind,* then everything moral loses its content, the moral concepts become words without sense.
(Husserl-manuscript F I 20, p. 227; Diemer, p. 317, and p. 48, n. 106)

Thus it is

obvious that there can be no talk of 'good' and 'bad' when one abstracts from sentiments.
(Husserl-manuscript F I 20, p. 107; Diemer, p. 317, n. 6)

Not as if we can accept the content of his ⟨Hume's⟩ argumentation *in its entirety,* but one thing it makes certain, one thing is thereby completely evident: sentiment is *essentially* involved in the coming about of ethical distinctions.
(Husserl-manuscript F I 20, p. 99; Diemer, p. 317, n. 7)

Finally, let us look at the method to be used in ethics. Here Husserl is more scanty, but he surmises that the method in ethics is parallel to the method in logic:

If there really is a philosophical axiology which has a status as first philosophy similar to that of logic, then it refers back to empirical values and relations between such values in a way similar to that in which philosophical logic refers back to empirical objects and relations between them.
(Husserl-manuscript F I 14, p. 110; Diemer, p. 46, n. 102)

Is there an analogue to logic as ethics? An analogue to formal logic as formal ethics? On the other hand, the ethical norms have meaning exclusively in the empirical realm? How do the empirical and the apriori relate to one another in ethics? . . . How can one clarify the relation between sentiment ⟨Gemüt⟩ and intellect with regard to the objects of understanding and the objects of sentiment? How far extends the analogy between acts of object-appearance and acts of value-appearance?
(Husserl-manuscript F I 20, p. 7; Diemer, p. 46, n. 102)

In another place Husserl says:

We are now reflecting upon the relation between *reason in the realm of intellect* and *reason in the realm of sentiment.*
(Husserl-manuscript F I 23, p. 58; Diemer, 317, n. 4)

The method is not axiomatic and fundamentalistic, but clarifying and reflecting. Like Rawls, Husserl finds his method anticipated by Socrates:

Socrates . . . recognized the fundamental sense of this method, expressed in a modern way, as intuitive and *a priori* critique of reason. Or, more accurately, he recognized its fundamental sense as a method of clarifying stocktaking of oneself. . . .
(*Erste Philosophie*, 2. Vorl., Hua. VII, 11.10–14)

Immediately before this he says:

Truth and falsehood, genuine and non-genuine, are separated through making reflectively evident what it is that one really is aiming toward, and what one thereby unclearly has presupposed concerning putative beauty and ugliness, usefulness and harmfulness. They are separated because the essential content of the things themselves come to intuitive realization just in the perfect clarity, and united with this essential content value and disvalue themselves.
(*Erste Philosophie*, 1. Vorl., Hua. VII, 10.12–20)

Since thus our concrete particular intuitions are the last source of validity in ethics, Husserl avoids, like Rawls, a danger that often comes up in connection with fanaticism and totalitarianism: one acts against common sense morality in the name of some higher moral principle.

(v) *Pre-reflective, intuitive acceptance.* As we just noted, Husserl held that evidence can only be corrected through other evidence, and that there is no deeper source of justification. The set of all these intuitive acceptances makes up what Husserl called the "life-world," and in the *Crisis* Husserl emphasizes the crucial role of the *life-world* in the process of justification:

> There has never been a scientific inquiry into the way in which *the life-world constantly functions as a subsoil*, into how *its manifold prelogical validities act as ground for the logical ones*, for theoretical truths. And perhaps the scientific discipline which this life-world as such, in its universality, requires is a peculiar one, one which is precisely not objective and logical but which, as *the ultimate grounding one*, is not inferior but superior in value.
>
> (*Krisis*, § 34, Hua. VI, 127.13–20 = Carr, 124. The italics are mine.)

Note how Husserl here expresses a view very similar to that of Goodman: the prelogical validities act as ground for the logical ones, the life-world functions as a subsoil. Remember how, according to Goodman, "principles of deductive inference are justified by their conformity with accepted deductive practice. Their validity depends upon accordance with the particular deductive inferences we actually make and sanction." (Goodman, *op. cit*, p. 63) Rawls, too, appeals ultimately to "what seem to be intuitively acceptable and reasonable moral decisions" ("Outline of a decision procedure for ethics," p. 194.) Similarly, Husserl says:

> Just as other projects, practical interests, and their realizations belong to the life-world, presuppose it as ground, and enrich it with their activity, so it is with science, too, as a human project and praxis. And this includes, as we have said, everything objectively a priori, with its necessary reference back to a corresponding a priori of the life-world. *This reference-back is one of a founding of validity* ⟨*Geltungsfundierung*⟩. A certain idealizing accomplishment is what brings about the higher-level meaning-formation and ontic validity of the mathematical and every other objective a priori on the basis of the life-world apriori.
>
> (*Krisis*, § 36, Hua. VI, 143.9–19 = Carr, 140, my italics)

And also:

> every objective logic, every a priori science in the usual sense . . . is to be grounded . . . no longer "logically" but by being traced back to the universal prelogical apriori [i.e. the life-world] through which everything logical, the total edifice of objective theory in all its methodological forms, demonstrates its legitimate sense and from which, then, all logic itself must receive its norms.
>
> (*Krisis*, § 36, Hua. VI, 144.27–34 = Carr, 141)

There are a number of similar passages in the *Crisis*, the most important of which are the following ones:

> [T]he *subjective-relative* is on the other hand still functioning for him, not as something irrelevant that must be passed through but *as that which ultimately*

grounds the theoretical-logical ontic validity for all objective verification, i.e., as the source of self-evidence, the source of verification.
    (*Krisis*, § 34b, Hua. VI, 129.11–15 = Carr, 126, my italics)

It is of course itself a highly important task for the scientific opening-up of the life-world to bring to recognition the *primal validity of these self-evidences* and indeed their *higher dignity* in the grounding of knowledge compared to that of the objective-logical self-evidences. One must fully clarify, i.e., bring to ultimate self-evidence, how all the self-evidence of objective-logical accomplishments, through which objective theory (thus mathematical and natural-scientific theory) is *grounded* in respect of form and content, has its *hidden sources of grounding* in the ultimately accomplishing life, the life in which the self-evident givenness of the life-world forever has, has attained, and attains anew its prescientific ontic meaning. From objective-logical self-evidence (mathematical "insight," natural-scientific, positive-scientific "insight," as it is being accomplished by the inquiring and grounding mathematician, etc.), the path leads back, here, to the primal self-evidence in which the life-world is ever pregiven.
    (*Krisis*, § 34d, Hua. VI, 131.2–18 = Carr, 128, my italics)

The knowledge of the objective-scientific world is "grounded" in the self-evidence of the life-world.
    (*Krisis*, § 34e, Hua. VI, 133.19–20 = Carr, 130)

There is also a brief Goodmanesque remark on induction in the *Crisis:*

Inductions can be confirmed by other inductions, working together.
    (*Krisis*, § 34d, Hua. VI, 130, note = Carr, 127, note. I have deviated from Carr's translation by translating Husserl's "*bewähren*" by "confirmed" rather than by "verified.")

Also in *Experience and Judgment* there are several similar passages:

[T]he retrogression to prepredicative experience and the insight into what is the deepest and ultimately original level of prepredicative experiences signifies a *justification of doxa*, which is the realm of ultimately original self-evidence, not yet exact and physicomathematically idealized. Thereby, it is also shown that this realm of doxa is not a domain of self-evidence of lesser rank than that of *episteme*, of judicative knowledge and its sedimentations [*Niederschläge*], but precisely the domain of ultimate originality to which exact cognition resorts for its sense, such cognition (it must be recognized) having the characteristic of being a mere method and not a way leading to knowledge by itself.
    (*Erfahrung und Urteil*, § 10, p. 44 = Churchill & Ameriks, 46)

I would like to end the discussion of this point by quoting a long passage from the *Crisis*, where Husserl expresses ideas very similar to those of Goodman:

What is actually first is the "merely subjective-relative" intuition of prescientific world-life. For us, to be sure, this "merely" has, as an old inheritance, the disdainful coloring of the *doxa*. In prescientific life itself, of course, it has nothing of this; there it is a realm of good verification and, based upon this, of well-verified predicative cognitions and of truths which are just as secure as is necessary for the practical projects of life that determine their sense. The disdain with which everything "merely subjective and relative" is treated by those scientists who pursue the modern ideal of objectivity changes nothing of its own manner of being, just as it does not change the fact that the scientist himself must be satisfied with this realm whenever he has recourse, as he unavoidably must have recourse, to it.

(*Krisis*, §34a, Hua. VI, 127.31–128.10 = Carr, 125)

(vi) *Sources of evidence.* It may seem that we now have already said what there is to say about the sources of evidence: the sole kind of evidence is our prescientific acceptances in the life-world. However, Husserl presses on further. These prescientific acceptances are not just a matter of internal coherence, they depend ultimately on what is going on at our sensory surfaces, that is on perception. So, for Husserl, perception plays a very special role in the justification of scientific theories, just as sentiment plays a special role in justification in ethics. Yet, there is not a one-way dependence. As we noted in section 1, perception is not uniquely determined by the impingements on our sensory surfaces, but depends also on our various other pre-reflective acceptances. Similarly for sentiments. I shall not go further into Husserl's theory of perception here, but shall end this paper by noting two important features of our prescientific acceptances: they are affected by our scientific theories and they form an ultimate court of appeal behind which it makes no sense to ask for a further justification.

7. TWO IMPORTANT FEATURES OF THE LIFE-WORLD

For Husserl, our prescientific acceptances, that is, the life-world, is not a realm separate from that of the sciences. As we have seen, the sciences have the life-world as their evidential basis, and on the other hand, the sciences gradually change the life-world. As Husserl puts it in *Experience and Judgment:*

[E]verything which contemporary natural science has furnished as determinations of what exists also belongs to us, to the world, as this world is pregiven to the adults of our time. And even if we are not personally interested in natural science, and even if we know nothing of its results, still, what exists is pregiven to us in advance as determined in such a way that we at least grasp it as being in principle scientifically determinable.

(*Erfahrung u. Urteil*, § 10, p. 39 = Churchill & Ameriks, p. 42)

In *The Crisis of the European Sciences* he says similarly:

[A]ll these theoretical results have the character of validities for the life-world, adding themselves as such to its own composition and belonging to it even before that as a horizon of possible accomplishments for developing science. The concrete life-world, then, is the grounding soil [*der gründende Boden*] of the "scientifically true" world and at the same time encompasses it in its own universal concreteness.
(*Krisis*, § 34 e, Hua. VI, 134.13–19 = Carr, 131)

The reason why science belongs to the life-world is, according to Husserl, that it is conceived of as being valid, as making a claim to truth:

Though the peculiar accomplishment of our modern objective science may still not be understood, nothing changes the fact that it is a validity for the life-world, arising out of particular activities, and that it belongs itself to the concreteness of the life-world.
(*Krisis*, § 34 f, Hua. VI, 136.18–22 = Carr, 133)

Finally, I come to the important point that the life-world for Husserl is an ultimate court of appeal, behind which there is no point in asking for further justification. The main reason Husserl gives for this is that most of the life-world consists of acceptances that we have never made thematic to ourselves and which have therefore never been the subject of any explicit judicative decision:

[W]here such completely self-giving intuition of the judicative substrates takes place, there is absolutely no possible doubt with regard to the "so" or "otherwise" and hence no occasion for an explicit judicative decision. (*Erfahrung u. Urteil*, § 67, p. 330 = Churchill & Ameriks, p. 275)

Every claim to validity and truth rests upon this "iceberg" of largely unthematized prejudgmental acceptances. Every request for justification ultimately has to lead back to this same sort of acceptances. There is nothing more ultimate to turn to, and there is nothing more that can be asked for:

[T]here is nothing to "postulate" or to "interpret suitably," but only something to bring to light. Thus alone can that ultimate understanding of the world be attained, behind which, since it is ultimate, there is nothing more that can be sensefully inquired for, nothing more to understand.
(*Form. u. transz. Logik*, § 96 b, Hua. XVII, 249.17–20 = Cairns, 242)

7   Truth and Freedom

KARSTEN HARRIES

1. INTRODUCTION

Many philosophers today like to hear talk of the end of philosophy, as if this end could not only liberate them from a burden they have been carrying all too long and free them for a thinking more edifying and poetic than traditional philosophy, but also help lift the oppressive shadow cast by the possibility of technology's final victory over the earth and over humanity. Especially Heidegger's reflections on this end have been received with an at times almost evangelical fervor. In work after work Heidegger invites us to take a step beyond philosophy understood as metaphysics and, at the same time, beyond the scientific-technological world in which, if he is right, metaphysics triumphs, even if this triumph appears to have left metaphysics far behind as something no longer relevant to the world we live in. Inseparable from this attempt is Heidegger's effort to show that the traditional understanding of truth as correspondence is derivative and to appropriate the supposedly more original Greek experience of truth as *alētheia* or unconcealment.

This effort, however, is put into question by some remarks in what is Heidegger's last major essay, "The End of Philosophy and the Task of Thinking." This prospective and retrospective meditation once again restates Heidegger's understanding of *alētheia*, but with a difference. *Alētheia*, he now insists, while it does indeed "first grant the possibility of truth," should not therefore be equated with truth (*EP, BW* 389).[1] "To raise the question of *alētheia*, of unconcealment as such, is

---

1. References to Heidegger's writings use the following abbreviations: *EP, BW:* "The End of Philosophy and the Task of Thinking," tr. Joan Stambaugh, in *Basic Writings*, ed. D. F. Krell (New York: Harper and Row, 1977), pp. 369–392. *ET, BW:* "On the Essence of Truth," tr. John Sallis, in *Basic Writings*, pp. 113–141. *H, BW:* "Letter on Humanism," tr. Frank A. Capuzzi with J. Glenn Gray, in *Basic Writings*, pp. 189–242. *OWA, BW:* "The Origin of the Work of Art," tr. Albert Hofstadter, in *Basic Writings*, pp. 143–187. *SZ: Sein und Zeit*, 7th ed. (Tübingen: Niemeyer, 1953). Tr. John Macquarrie and

not the same as raising the question of truth. For this reason, it was inadequate and misleading to call *alētheia* in the sense of opening, truth" (*EP, BW* 389). This may not seem a very significant admission: of course we should distinguish between what is usually called "truth" and the unconcealment that makes such truth possible; this having been pointed out we can return to Heidegger's interpretation of *alētheia*.[2] But more is at stake. In this late essay Heidegger grants that the traditional understanding of truth does not derive from some more original understanding, but is itself the original and natural one. "The natural concept of truth does not mean unconcealment, not in the philosophy of the Greeks either. It is often and justifiably pointed out that the word *alēthes* is already used by Homer only in the *verba dicendi*, in statement and thus in the sense of correctness and reliability, not in the sense of unconcealment" (*EP, BW* 389–390).[3] As Heidegger recognizes, with this admission his "assertion about the essential transformation of truth, that is, from unconcealment to correctness, is also untenable" (*EP, BW* 390). Heidegger thus explicitly revokes what he had so often claimed, especially in "Plato's Doctrine of Truth."[4] This forces us to reconsider his account of the origin and history of metaphysics, and that means also his determination of the triumph of metaphysics in the form of technology.

The following is an attempt to think through some of the implications of Heidegger's acknowledgement that truth cannot be equated with *alētheia* for the path from phenomenology to a thinking beyond philosophy that he has travelled and bids us follow. In a footnote to the cited passage Heidegger himself speaks of having strayed:

How the attempt to think a matter can at times stray from what a decisive insight has already shown is demonstrated by a passage from *Being and Time*, 1927 (p. 219): "The Translation [of the word *alētheia*] by means of the word 'truth,' and even the very theoretical-conceptual determinations of this expression [truth], cover up the meaning of what the Greeks established as basically 'self-evident' in the prephilosophical understanding of their terminological employment of *alētheia*. (*EP, BW* 389 fn)

E. Robinson, *Being and Time* (New York: Harper and Row, 1962). *GA* 20: *Gesamtausgabe*, vol. 20, *Prolegomena zur Geschichte des Zeitbegriffs* (Frankfurt: Klostermann, 1979). *GA* 24: *Gesamtausgabe*, vol. 24, *Die Grundprobleme der Phänomenologie* (Frankfurt: Klostermann, 1975). *GA* 26: *Gesamtausgabe*, vol. 26, *Metaphysische Anfangsgründe der Logik* (Frankfurt: Klostermann, 1978).

2. See Walter Biemel, *Martin Heidegger, An Illustrated Study*, tr. J. L. Mehta (New York and London: Harcourt Brace Jovanovich, 1976), p. 176.

3. See Paul Friedländer, *Plato*, vol. 1, *An Introduction*, tr. Hans Mayeroff, 2nd ed. (Princeton: Princeton Univ. Press, 1969), pp. 221–229.

4. Martin Heidegger, "Platons Lehre von der Wahrheit," in *Wegmarken, Gesamtausgabe*, vol. 9 (Frankfurt: Klostermann, 1976), pp. 203–238.

How are we to understand this "decisive insight"? How are "truth" and the phenomenon Heidegger, following the Greeks, calls *alētheia* related? I shall argue that if we are to do justice to what Heidegger himself came to call the natural understanding of truth, we have to challenge his starting point, his understanding of Dasein's being-in-the-world. Such thinking with Heidegger against Heidegger has to challenge also his final meditation on the task of thinking.

2. THE TRUTH OF ASSERTIONS

Traditionally truth is thought to reside first of all in judgments or assertions. The essence of truth is thought to lie in the agreement of the judgment with its object. As Thomas' much quoted definition puts it: *Veritas est adaequatio rei et intellectūs*, "Truth is the adequation of the thing and the understanding."[5]

How are we to understand such adequacy? To help us approach this problem Heidegger offers this example: "Let us suppose that someone with his back turned to the wall makes the true assertion that 'the picture on the wall is hanging askew': This assertion demonstrates itself when the man who makes it turns around and perceives the picture is hanging askew on the wall" (*SZ* 217). He recognizes the perceived as just what his assertion meant. To recognize this fit of perception and assertion is to be certain of its truth. The perception, we can say, fulfills the intention. There are of course obvious objections. How reliable are our perceptions? Are they not by their very nature partial? And do expectations and preconceptions not help to determine what we "see"? Thus we often "see" what we want or perhaps fear to see. How are we to distinguish such a wishful or fearful seeing from a seeing that discloses the entity as it really is? And what do we mean by this "as it really is"? Such questions suggest that certainty is rarely absolute. Often it can be shaken by the introduction of other evidence. A true assertion, it would seem, has to fit all possible relevant evidence. This is recognized by Kant's definition of formal truth as the fit of knowledge with itself.[6] The necessity of such a fit may well force us to question the reliability of perception. But bracketing such questions for the time being, we can agree with Heidegger that "To say that an assertion 'is true' signifies that it uncovers the entity as it is in itself" (*SZ* 261). From this Heidegger concludes that "The Being-true (truth) of an assertion must be understood as a Being-uncovering" (*SZ* 218).

5. Thomas Aquinas, *Quaestiones disputatae de veritate*, qu. I, art. 1.
6. Kant, *Logik*, A 72.

As Ernst Tugendhat has pointed out, the second formulation does not quite say the same as the first. While the first insists that the true assertion uncovers the entity "as it is in itself," the second elides this phrase and thereby leaves open the possibility of a false uncovering, a disclosing of the entity as other than it is.[7] Thus it elides just what distinguishes true from false assertions. So understood, being-uncovering can hardly be said to capture the essence of the being true of our assertions.

Tugendhat links this elision to Heidegger's replacement of Husserl's understanding of intentionality with his own much broader notion of *Erschlossenheit* or disclosure. As long as one understands the assertion as intending or meaning, "it is of course impossible to say: an assertion is true when it means an entity; for the manner in which it means it, can also be false: One will have to say: an assertion is true, when it means the entity as it itself is."[8] The matter becomes quite different, however, when an assertion is understood as a disclosing of what is. "Disclosing" already suggests a successful exhibition of the thing as it is. Unfortunately Heidegger often uses the term in a broader sense. Consider for example his claim that first of all and most of the time "That which has been uncovered and disclosed stands in a mode in which it has been disguised and closed off by idle talk, curiosity and ambiguity" (*SZ* 222). Disguise and covering up, too, are understood here as modes of uncovering. But then, if we want to understand the essence of truth, we have to distinguish different modes of uncovering, only some of which would seem to allow what is to be uncovered to show itself as it is in itself. Only such privileged uncovering could be identified with the being-true of assertion. But how are we to understand this privilege? This returns us to the question: how are we to understand "the thing as it really is" or the "the thing as it is in itself"? Must we not, if we are not to fall prey to the concealment that, Heidegger tells us, usually accompanies disclosing, attend not only to *what* shows itself, but to *how* it shows itself, that is to say, also to how this mode of showing conceals? Must we not attend to appearance as appearance and thereby open ourselves to the way all that deserves to be called real transcends the way it gives itself to us?

Think of vision and of the way it involves perspective. What sense does it make to claim that when we see something it discloses itself to

7. Ernst Tugendhat, *Der Wahrheitsbegriff bei Husserl und Heidegger* (Berlin: de Gruyter, 1967), pp. 331–337. See also Tugendhat, "Heideggers Idee von Wahrheit," in *Heidegger, Perspektiven zur Deutung seines Werks* (Cologne and Berlin: Kiepenheuer und Witsch, 1969), pp. 287–297.

8. Tugendhat, *Wahrheitsbegriff*, p. 333.

us as it is? The presence of something I see is necessarily a presence
for me, dependent on my particular point of view, the makeup of my
eyes and particular light conditions, shaped by my preconceptions
and prejudices. Its presence is governed by a particular perspective.
Implicit is the possibility of other possible perspectives, which may
give me or someone else a different, perhaps better access to what I
see. But when I make an assertion such as "the picture is hanging
askew," I not only claim that the picture looks to me that way, but I
claim it as a fact. How does this fact present itself? I see the picture
hanging askew, but this is not to say that I see the fact that it is hanging askew. The evidence that fulfills assertion of the fact demands
more than a simple seeing; it demands a particular appropriation of
what is seen. This appropriation presupposes something like an interpretation of what has presented itself to me as there for everyone to
see. This being there for everyone to see cannot present itself to me as
the picture on the wall can. Can it present itself at all? At this point the
notion of presence begins to blur. Given an understanding of presence based on the paradigm of sight, is it not more plausible to say of
facts that they are not present at all, that they are not so much something seen as constituted or constructed from necessarily inadequate
evidence? Inseparable from such construction is a projection of what
I now see onto a background of other possible ways in which it could
be seen or experienced. Assertion of a fact is thus never fulfilled just
by what now presents itself, but presupposes the power of transcending what appears to me towards what is appearing.

Enough has been said to establish the following: we cannot say that
an assertion is true when it discloses; rather we must say it is true only
when it discloses what is as it is, where the meaning of that phrase remains problematic. This suggests that the phenomenon Heidegger
calls *alētheia* does not capture the essence of truth at all. What should
concern us more than the appropriateness of our word "truth" to
what the Greeks understood *alētheia* to mean is the appropriateness of
alētheia as Heidegger understands it to the meaning of "truth."

In just what sense can *alētheia* be said to grant the possibility of truth?
If the truth of assertions may be understood as a being-uncovering, can
the same not be said of their falsehood? False assertions, too, presuppose that something hidden has emerged into light, if in a way inappropriate to the entity in question. This is to say: *the truth of assertions
must be given its foundation in the uncoveredness of entities as they are in
themselves or in what Heidegger sometimes calls "the truth of things."* But does
it even make sense to speak of this "uncoveredness of entities as they
are in themselves"? How are we to understand the "truth of things"?

3. THE TRUTH OF THINGS

Heidegger founds the truth of assertions in the truth of things in *On the Essence of Truth*. That essay, too, begins with a consideration of what we usually mean by "true," but this time Heidegger starts by calling attention to the way we often call something true to suggest that it is genuine or real rather than counterfeit or illusory. Thus we speak of the true God, of a true love, of true gold. The assertion of truth here serves to dismiss a suspicion that something might be other than it presents itself as being. Presupposed is some preconception of what God, love, or gold really are. To call something true is to assert that it fits our preconception. Truth is here thought as the agreement of the thing with an idea.

To be sure, as Heidegger is quick to remind us, usually we think of the agreement going the other way.[9] As we have seen, we call an assertion true or false when it agrees or fails to agree with the matter in question; here it is not the thing that fits the understanding, but rather the reverse. The traditional definition of truth as *adaequatio rei et intellectūs*, as "the adequation of the thing and the understanding," invites both the reading *veritas est adaequatio intellectūs ad rem*, "truth is the adequation of the understanding to the thing," and the reading *veritas est adaequatio rei ad intellectum*, "truth is the adequation of the thing to the understanding."[10] Indeed, the second would seem to have a certain priority: if we are to measure the truth of an assertion by the thing asserted, this thing must somehow disclose itself as it is. This presupposes that in some sense it can accommodate itself to the understanding. This idea of an adequate disclosure of the thing we can call its truth. In this sense we can agree with Heidegger when he insists that the truth of assertions presupposes the truth of things (*ET, BW* 120).

But once more the question returns: how are we to understand this truth of the thing, the *adaequatio rei ad intellectum*? Should we call things true insofar as they receive their measure from human knowers? We might thus appeal to Kant's insistence that "objects conform to our knowledge."[11] As Heidegger points out and as the Latin formulation hints, talk of the truth of things need not be linked to Kant's Copernican revolution. It has its origin in a quite different understanding: in the "Christian theological belief that, with respect to what

---

9. Gerold Prauss insists that all talk of the truth of things must in principle remain unintelligible. See his *Erkennen und Handeln in Heideggers 'Sein und Zeit'* (Freiburg and Munich: Alber, 1977), p. 96.

10. Thomas Aquinas, *De veritate*, qu. I, art. 1 and 2.

11. Kant, *Kritik der reinen Vernunft*, B xvi. See *ET, BW* 120.

it is and whether it is, a matter, as created (*ens creatum*), *is* only insofar as it corresponds to the idea preconceived in the *intellectus divinus*, i.e., in the mind of God, and thus measures up to the idea (is correct) and in this sense is 'true'" (*ET, BW* 120). Created in the image of God, the human knower does justice to his own essence when he measures what he thinks by the matter to be thought, which in turn possesses its measure in the divine idea. On this view the truth of things, understood as *adaequatio rei (creandae) ad intellectum (divinum)* secures truth understood as *adaequatio intellectūs (humani) ad rem (creatam)* (*ET, BW* 121). Human knowing is given its measure in the divinely created order of the cosmos.

But can we today still accept any of this? What happens to the thought of the truth of things when recourse to a divine creator no longer carries conviction and has become unavailable to philosophy? How are we then to understand the truth of things?

This much seems certain: if the truth of assertions is to be given its measure in the truth of things, these things must disclose themselves in such a way that they can function as such measures. The truth of assertions, it would seem, must be given its foundation in the presencing of the things themselves. Such presencing presupposes that we *let* these things present themselves without imposing on them our preconceptions, that we open ourselves to what they have to tell us so that our speaking can find its measure in that speech.

In spite of Heidegger's fondness for similar expressions,[12] one may well wonder whether "speech" is not here an unwanted metaphor, one that unduly anthropomorphizes the presencing of things. But recall the definition of discourse Heidegger gives in *Being and Time:* Discourse (*Rede, logos*) is defined there as the "articulation of understandability" and is said to be presupposed by all asserting (*SZ* 161). Discourse may thus not be equated with language (*Sprache*); in *Being and Time* at least, the latter names a human product, something human speakers send forth into the world as one thing among others. But if this thing is to disclose others, as language must to be language, it must also be discourse (*Rede*), that is to say, language must give voice to a prior understanding, an understanding that, if it is not to be a misunderstanding, must let things present themselves as they are. What our language discloses is always something already articulated. That is to say, what presents itself does so as something definite, as

---

12. See especially "Die Sprache," in *Unterwegs zur Sprache, Gesamtausgabe*, vol. 12 (Frankfurt: Klostermann, 1985). Also Karsten Harries, "Metaphor and Transcendence," in *On Metaphor*, ed. Sheldon Sacks (Chicago and London: Univ. of Chicago Press, 1979), pp. 71–88.

being this and not that. If we are to be open to the thing, such definition may not be our own work, but has to issue from the thing itself. To be open to the truth of things is to be open to the self-definition of things.

Such talk of openness and letting be, where such letting be does not mean indifference or lack of concern but, on the contrary, disciplined attention, recalls traditional discussions of aesthetic distance, which also is said to involve a letting be of the aesthetic object. Such distance, too, is supposed to open our eyes as it frees us from our usual cares and preconceptions; because of this it is supposed to let us attend to what is present and to its presencing as never before. It is thus not surprising that in "The Origin of the Work of Art" Heidegger should understand art as a setting into work of truth. But it would be a mistake to understand aesthetic experience as a simple opening to what is in its mysterious presence, an interpretation that would invite us to understand art as privileged language, at least if we understand language, with Heidegger, as the sending forth into the world of a prelinguistic logos. Schopenhauer held some such view. We must, however, keep in mind that the same object may elicit very different aesthetic responses. Is the aesthetic observer ever a clear mirror of what he beholds? How he is open to what he appreciates would seem to depend on how he stands in the world. Heidegger thus suggests that the point of the work of art is not so much to picture some particular thing as it really is, as to disclose a way of being in the world.

Think of the way Van Gogh paints a pair of peasant shoes. I emphasize the painter's way of painting or his style because it is just this style that discloses not just a pair of shoes, but more importantly, a particular stance towards things, a particular projection of their being. The painting reverses the way we usually see and understand things. Heidegger thus understands the truth of art in opposition to a fascinated concern with things that so absorbs us that we forget the way we stand in our world. Think of someone preoccupied with discovering the make-up of some substance or the workings of some mechanism. His very effort to understand prevents him from attending to the way this effort presupposes a particular way of standing in the world and that is to say, a particular blindness. As Heidegger says in "On the Essence of Truth": "Precisely because letting be always lets beings be in a particular comportment which relates to them and thus discloses them, it conceals beings as a whole. Letting-be is intrinsically at the same time a concealing" (ET, BW 132). Just by focusing our attention on things, we inevitably limit our access to what they are. Precisely our concern to find out the truth about things lets us be in error. We are in error because we fail to attend to these things' mode of presencing, to their being.

As Heidegger points out in *Being and Time,* first of all and most of the time we have already lost ourselves to our world, subjected ourselves to the way "they" understand (*SZ* 222). Yet, he adds, even if all human seeing and understanding is inevitably dominated by the way things are publicly interpreted, such domination does not completely obscure these things. "They are precisely the sort of thing that has been uncovered, but at the same time, they have been disguised" (*SZ* 264). Because of this, we face the task to "explicitly appropriate what has already been uncovered again and again. The uncovering is never done on the basis of something completely hidden, but takes its departure rather from uncoveredness in the mode of semblance" (*SZ* 265). Access to the things themselves must be wrested from our usual inadequate understanding. *The truth of things demands that we learn to attend not just to the things that present themselves to us but also to their mode of presencing and that is to say, to the way we ourselves stand in the world.* In this sense Heidegger can say of the art work that it lets what it presents stand in the light of its being (*OWA, BW* 164).

But does attention to our way of standing in the world really help us to seize the truth of things? Do most ways of standing in the world not do violence to things as they are? Mere attention to these ways would not seem to get us closer to the truth of things unless such attention allows us to gain a freer access to things. If, as Heidegger insists, the presencing of things is inseparable from some particular way of being in the world and if we take seriously his admonition that we must wrest the truth of things from semblance and disguise, then we face the task of critically examining our being in the world.

4. TRUTH AND WORLD

Heidegger uses "truth" to refer both to the uncovering and to what is uncovered. The former is said to ground the latter and in this sense is said to be more fundamentally true. Yet all uncovering presupposes being in a world, which Heidegger thus calls true in a still more fundamental sense (*SZ* 220). But if our being-in-a-world grants the possibility of truth, it equally grants the possibility of error. The truth of things demands that we distinguish being-in-a-world from a being-in-the-world that gives proper access to what is. At the same time we should try to understand Heidegger's reluctance to pursue this distinction.

When Heidegger thinks the world as the necessary condition of disclosure, "world" cannot mean the totality of facts. Think rather of what we mean when we speak of "the world of the baseball player." "World" here means not just bases and balls, ball parks and hotels, players and umpires, wives and children, but first of all a mode of existing (*GA* 26, 233), a way in which the baseball player relates to things and persons and to himself. His particular actions and thoughts presuppose this world. It circumscribes his possibilities.

World then may be understood as a realm of possibilities that both embraces and surpasses whatever presents itself to an individual, claims, and moves him. In *Being and Time* Heidegger defines "the world" as "that 'wherein' a factical Dasein as such can be said to 'live'" (*SZ* 65).[13] World here means first of all the life-world constituted by care. As Heidegger puts it in "The Origin of the Work of Art," "The world is not the mere collection of the countable or uncountable, familiar and unfamiliar things that are at hand. But neither is it a merely imagined framework added by our representations to the sum of such given things. . . . World is the ever-nonobjective to which we are subject as long as the paths of birth and death, blessing and curse keep us transported into Being" (*OWA, BW* 170). World is that open yet always structured space of intelligibility in which we live and in which all that can present itself to us and all that we can think, decide, and enact must take place.

Heidegger's world invites comparison with language or with what has been termed logical space. These, too, may be understood as realms of possibilities. Logical space thus has room not only for what is, but for all that may be, while language has been thought of similarly as a transcendental condition of all that can present itself to those who "live" in it. But the phenomenon Heidegger terms "the world" is both wider than logical space and deeper than what we usually call language—wider than logical space in that it is thought not just as that realm in which Dasein can be said to think, but as the realm in which Dasein can be said to live, and living includes thinking; deeper than language in that lived experience is richer than what words can capture.

We begin to understand what is at stake when Heidegger calls Dasein's being-in-the-world the primordial phenomenon of truth. That formulation promises an understanding of truth no longer bound up with theoretical understanding. Just as Heidegger's "world" is wider than logical space, so his understanding of truth is wider than the tra-

---

13. Heidegger in that place distinguishes four different senses of "world," corresponding to his distinction between ontic, ontological, existentiell, and existential, only to privilege the third, which alone concerns us here.

ditional understanding of truth as correspondence or correctness. That width challenges the assumption that experience narrowly conceived in terms of a subject encountering objects furnishes a privileged mode of access to what is. Heidegger invites us to think our being in the world in all its breadth, of love, for example, and of the understanding it grants, or of faith, or of aesthetic rapture. To these different modes of disclosure correspond different senses of truth. The hegemony of scientific-technological thinking appears to have been broken. The question, however, is whether this extension, if perhaps justified by Heidegger's broad understanding of truth as disclosure, must not lose sight of what Heidegger himself finally came to call the natural sense of truth.

It is important to keep in mind that the openness granted by what Heidegger calls the world is never a pure clearing, but structured. Thus our baseball player stands differently in his world than some peasant ploughing his field or a scientist trying to understand the structure of the atom. Bound up with this difference are different modes of access to what is, different projections of possibilities, different ways of understanding the being of things. The way we stand in the world inevitably limits that openness to things which it grants. Disclosure and concealment inevitably intertwine.

But how then can the world be said to allow things to present themselves as they are? Does the pursuit of truth as we usually understand it not demand that we open ourselves more radically to what is than our being-in-the-world allows, that we transcend ourselves in our being-in-the-world? The truth of things requires that we learn to see and understand for ourselves. But to do so we must gain possession of ourselves, must free ourselves from the tyranny of the "they" and of "their" world. *The truth of things would thus seem to have its foundation in that genuine freedom that is inseparable from authenticity* and that means for Heidegger from resolute being unto death. "In resoluteness we have now arrived at that truth of Dasein which is most primordial, because it is authentic" (*SZ* 287). Authentic Dasein stands in the truth.

But what does it mean to stand in the truth? Does it even make sense to speak of a completely open access to things that rules out semblance and disguise? Are we not asking the impossible when we demand that Dasein transcend and in a sense free itself from its being-in-the-world? Yet Heidegger, too, claims that "the essence of truth is freedom" (*ET, BW* 125). How are we to understand his claim that freedom grants the possibility of truth?

5. FREEDOM AS THE ESSENCE OF TRUTH

Heidegger knows how strange this claim is likely to sound. Does truth not imply independence from all subjective choice? What does truth have to do with freedom?

There is, however, a way in which truth and freedom are sometimes linked: we may say of a person that he lacks the freedom necessary to see things as they are. What binds him may be a particular upbringing or social status, special needs or interests, fear or love—which, as the proverb has it, makes blind. Freedom gives an open mind. In this sense truth can be said to presuppose freedom.

Plato's Myth of the Cave gives voice to this link between truth and freedom: his cave is a prison; his prisoners, having always lived in their cave, chained so that they cannot see more than shadows cast on the wall before them by hidden images, live in a very limited world, which determines their very inadequate understanding of the being of what is. Truth to them is "literally nothing but the shadows of these images."[14] The progress towards an ever more adequate understanding, of which the myth tells, begins when some prisoner's fetters are loosened; forced to stand up and turn around, he sees the images that cast the shadows he mistook for reality; later he is dragged out of the cave and forced into the presence of the sun, which illuminates the land of truth. Freedom appears as the necessary condition of looking beyond the appearances of things to their true being. The myth also tells of the ill will which those who, having themselves been liberated, would liberate their fellow prisoners, are likely to meet. It is more comfortable to remain with long established and taken for granted ways of seeing and to let such understanding determine what is to be done and understood.

Heidegger tells a similar story. First of all and most of the time we are captive to long established and usually taken for granted ways of seeing and understanding. Our access to what is is determined by the world we have inherited.

From this world [Dasein] takes its possibilities, and it does so first in accordance with the way things have been interpreted by the "they." This interpretation has already restricted the possible options of choice to what lies within the range of the familiar, the attainable, the respectable—that which is fitting and proper. This levelling of Dasein's possibilities to what is proximally at its everyday disposal also results in a dimming down of the possible as such. The average everydayness of concern becomes blind to its possibilities and tranquilizes itself in what is merely "actual." (SZ 194–195)

14. Plato, *Republic*, VII, 515 c.

Caught up in the everyday world we are in a state of unfreedom, which is at the same time a state of untruth. Yet we are haunted by the possibility of escaping from this cave. That we are so haunted presupposes that at least our understanding is not imprisoned in the cave. We can at least dream of stepping into a clearing that would allow us to see things as they really are, illuminated not by a false fire, but by the sun. Such freedom could be said to be the essence of truth in that it founds the truth of things, which, in turn, founds the truth of assertions.

But is this how Heidegger understands freedom? In "On the Essence of Truth" we learn that we fail to do justice to the phenomenon he has in mind when we think of what we usually call freedom, the ability to do or leave undone whatever we please; or when, following Kant, we think of a positive freedom that gives itself its law (*ET, BW* 128). Heidegger thinks freedom more fundamentally as the ground of our being-in-the-world: to understand human being as being-in-the-world is to understand it as transcending whatever entities or persons it encounters towards that open space Heidegger calls the world. Freedom is this transcendence. Never bound by what is, we have always already transcended it towards what may be. Whatever appears does so against a background of possibility. As free beings we exist *sub specie possibilitatis,* haunted by contingency and by the need to defeat it. To assert a truth is to battle against contingency, is to dismiss competing possibilities. Such assertion is necessarily a choice, but this choice would be unable to banish the specter of contingency, were it groundless. As the free being, man is the being who faces alternatives and therefore gives and demands reasons and grounds.

Heidegger understands freedom as transcendence towards the world (*GA* 26, 234). The world here plays a part analogous to that Plato assigns to the realm of forms. Heidegger calls Plato's forms an ontic misrepresentation of the former, a misrepresentation because it takes what is "ever non-objective" to be a collection of things present-at-hand, open to a special kind of intuition (*GA* 26, 236). The analogy is nonetheless instructive: as the forms determine the essence of things, so the world determines the being of whatever can present itself; thus both structure and thereby limit the realm of possibilities. And as attention to the form of some entity not only discloses along with it a class of possible beings to which it belongs, but also provides a measure that allows us to judge how well or ill it succeeds in being the sort of thing it is, so attention to the world does not disclose mere possibilities, but, since our being-in-the-world is marked by care and we are always up to something or other, possibilities disclose themselves as possibilities that invite or discourage or rule out actualization. To understand freedom as transcendence towards the world is to understand it as essentially bound, i.e. as finite. And just as, according to Plato, the turn from particular things to the governing forms lets human beings transcend their bondage in space and time—the *Phaedo* shows how this power of transcendence robs death of its sting—so, according to Heidegger, the turn from particular beings to their being, and that is to say, from entities to the world, frees us from the cave in which we live first of all and most of the time—although Heidegger understands this freedom not as a freedom that transcends the power of death, but as a freedom unto death. I shall have to return to this point, which turns out to be intimately connected with the problem of truth.

Heidegger pushes the analogy still further. If Plato grounds the realm of forms in the form of the Good, which as the form of forms presides over them, as they preside over entities in space and time, Heidegger grounds the world in freedom (*GA* 26, 237–238). Just as the form of the Good transcends the forms and at the same time organizes them as that for the sake of which they not only are, but are just what they are, so freedom transcends the world and at the same time gathers it into a whole. This claim should not seem surprising if we remember how in *Being and Time* Heidegger understands Dasein as the being whose being "is an issue for it" (*SZ* 12). All we do is ultimately for our own sake.[15] To say that Dasein's being is an issue for it is to say that it faces its own being in the world as a possibility. But this is to say that freedom constitutes Dasein. As the ground of all projections of possibilities, this freedom transcends the world; it gathers these possibilities into a whole because all of our possibilities are circumscribed by death as the final possibility that cannot be surpassed. The freedom that gathers the world into a whole must be understood as a freedom unto death.

Heidegger's conception of freedom as the ground of the world or as the "primordial projection of a world" invites misunderstanding. Projection should not be understood as the work of some subject who does the projecting. We would come closer to what Heidegger has in mind, were we to think of this subject as itself the product of a particular projection. But all particular projections presuppose Dasein's projective being, i.e. freedom. We should also keep in mind that, if the way a thing discloses itself presupposes the projection of a world, it is nonetheless the thing that discloses itself. Thus in "On the Es-

---

15. See *SZ*, pp. 84–88. Also *Logik. Die Frage nach der Wahrheit. Gesamtausgabe*, vol. 21 (Frankfurt: Klostermann, 1976), pp. 220–234.

sence of Truth" Heidegger understands freedom as "engagement in the disclosure of beings as such" (*ET, BW* 128). This projection of a world, which inevitably means concealment as well as disclosure, is the price of such engagement.

We may well wonder whether Heidegger's understanding of freedom does not leave behind what we usually mean by that term. Heidegger admits as much when he writes that in considering the essence of freedom it is "inessential, to what extent a being determined as free is in fact free, or to what extent it knows about its freedom" (*GA* 26, 247). If the phenomenon he has exhibited is the ground of what we usually mean by freedom, it is equally the ground of its opposite. But so understood freedom no more founds the truth of things than its opposite. Thus while Heidegger, too, sketches a progress from an inferior to a superior understanding—the development of his thinking may indeed be understood as just this progress—"superior" here means only that understanding has become more thoughtful, more open to the way a particular mode of being determines what can present itself and to the questionable character of all disclosure. Such understanding may be said to be more lucid in that it knows that our world cannot claim to be *the* world. For what could this mean? Are there not indefinitely many ways in which what is can become present, can be? To speak of a thing as it is in itself, apart from the questionable being that belongs to it as belonging to some world would seem to make no sense.

Another way of making what is essentially the same point is to suggest that Heidegger's progress is a progress within the cave. What separates the enlightened prisoner from his fellows is his knowledge of the way their prison-world determines the way things can disclose themselves. There is a sense in which the freedom of his thought pushes against the prison's walls, but he cannot oppose to the world they share a better world, cannot tell them what would be a more adequate way of life or what would constitute more adequate access to what is. All he can do is keep his distance from this world, let it be, console himself with the thought that the ontological truth he has discovered is far deeper than the merely ontic truths that occupy them.

But *if we are to give a meaning to* what following Heidegger I have called *the truth of things, there must be,* as the Platonic myth suggests, *an open space beyond the cave that allows us to understand things as they are.* Only if freedom can be understood as a self-transcendence that transports us into such an open space does it make sense to found the truth of things in freedom.

6. FREEDOM AND CURIOSITY

We find hints of such a freedom in an unexpected place, in Heidegger's discussion of curiosity, which, together with idle talk and ambiguity, is said to characterize the falling of everyday Dasein (*SZ* 170–173, 346–349; *GA* 20, 378–384). Heidegger speaks there of our strange desire to see and know for its own sake, without concern for what good this does us or anyone else. The phenomenon is familiar. Periods of rest and leisure are part of everyday life and leisure awakens curiosity. For a time we cease to worry about what should or should not be done. Instead we attend to what is not our business at all. Thus we concern ourselves with the affairs of individuals we neither know nor care about, read about far away places, experiment with new sensations. Curiosity refuses to be bound by the familiar. It wants to open closed doors. Think of the woman in the fairy tale who just has to enter the room forbidden to her to see what secrets it may hold; or of Dante's Ulysses, who, unable to restrain his longing to learn ever more about the world, journeys beyond the pillars Hercules had set up to warn men that they should not pass beyond; or of the star-gazing Anaxagoras, who thought "viewing the heavens and the order of the universe" sufficient to justify life.[16]

Heidegger understands curiosity as a deficient mode of Dasein's care. Surrendering to curiosity, "Dasein lets itself be carried along solely by the looks of the world; in this kind of Being, it concerns itself with becoming rid of itself as Being-in-the-world and rid of its Being alongside that which, in the closest everyday manner, is ready-to-hand" (*SZ* 172). But we hardly do justice to this desire to be rid of one's engagement in the world when we characterize it merely as a deficient mode of Dasein's care. To be sure, curiosity dislocates, but dislocation also opens our eyes; curiosity thus lets us attend to what is usually overlooked or too remote to be bothered with. Think of Anaxagoras and his stars. Curiosity can be characterized positively as a self-liberation, as the beginning of our escape from Plato's cave. Such liberation promises just the kind of openness needed to seize the truth of things.

Something very much like this is suggested in paragraph 69b of *Being and Time,* where Heidegger sketches the projection of being that governs science. The aim of such projection is said to be "to free entities we encounter within-the-world and free them in such a way that they can become 'Objects'" (*SZ* 363). The similarity of this aim and the

16. Aristotle, *Eudemian Ethics,* I, 5, 1216 a.

concern of curiosity is apparent. Without curiosity there would be no science. Like curiosity, science presupposes a transformation of our usual being-in-the-world. But science goes beyond mere curiosity in that Dasein now "projects itself towards its potentiality-for-Being in the 'truth'" (*SZ* 363; cf. *GA* 24, 455). The resolve to seize the truth transforms curiosity into the theoretical curiosity of the scientist.[17] Such resolve has to objectify whatever presents itself. This objectification is the price that must be paid by him who would be in the truth.

Heidegger's sketch of "the way in which circumspective concern becomes modified into the theoretical discovery of the present-at-hand" does not mention curiosity. Quite the opposite: science is said to have "its source in authentic existence," although how this is to be understood is left undeveloped. I fail to see how it could have been developed. Science remains bound to its origin in "inauthentic" curiosity. We may want to claim that science arises from an authentic appropriation of curiosity, but the subjection of curiosity to a concern for truth cannot be understood as such an appropriation. The commitment to science has to transform the care that binds the authentic person and lets him discover his place in the world into a care concerned to be rid of just this place. To the objectification of what is corresponds the subjectification of Dasein, which is transformed from a being engaged in the world into a being that stands before and in this sense transcends the world. Such transcendence cannot be reconciled with Heidegger's understanding of curiosity.

That curiosity should be the ground of truth understood as the disclosure of things as they really are should not seem strange, if we recall the opening sentence of Aristotle's *Metaphysics:* "All men by nature desire to know. An indication of this is the delight we take in our senses; for even apart from their usefulness they are loved for themselves; and above all others the sense of sight."[18] Theory raises this curiosity to a higher power. No longer content just to see, it wants to know what really is, wants to know "the truth." Theory gives birth to philosophy when it turns to "the first causes and principles of things." As Aristotle understands it, philosophy appears to be just potentiated curiosity. It, too, is loved for itself. Human beings philosophize just "to escape from ignorance," that is to say, "in order to know, and not for any utilitarian end." Philosophy is thus the most useless of all the sciences, but just because of this, it stands highest. For "as the man is free, we say, who exists for himself and not for another, so we pursue

17. See Hans Blumenberg, *Der Prozess der theoretischen Neugierde* (Frankfurt: Suhrkamp, 1973).
18. Aristotle, *Metaphysics*, I, 1, 980 a.

this as the only free science, for it alone exists for itself." [19] Freedom and philosophy go together.

"Freedom" here cannot mean what Heidegger has in mind: the primordial projection of a world. Nor can it mean that freedom unto death only those know who have freed themselves from the tyranny of the "they" and truly gained possession of themselves. The freedom of philosophy is the freedom of curiosity. That freedom cannot but be inauthentic in Heidegger's sense in that it presupposes that care has turned away from the self towards whatever curiosity wants to see or know. Curiosity thus lets us forget our mortality. As the Socrates of the *Republic* asks of the philosopher: "How can he who has the magnificence of mind and is the spectator of all time and all existence, think much of human life?" [20]

We may well wonder whether when elevated into philosophy curiosity does not reach for what lies beyond man's grasp. As Aristotle remarks: "in many ways human nature is in bondage, so that according to Simonides 'God alone can have this privilege,' and it is unfitting that man should not be content to seek the knowledge that is suited to him." [21] But Aristotle raises this objection only to dismiss it: God is not jealous. The highest science is the one which it would be most fit for God to have, a science free of the cares and concerns that are part of our engagement in the world and of the prejudices and the blindness that accompany such engagement.

Heidegger would seem to be more on the side of Simonides, although in his discussion of curiosity he cites a far weightier authority, Augustine, who not only noted the curious priority of seeing in everyday life, but placed it in the context of a discussion of *concupiscentia*, of lust, and that is to say of sin. The lust of the eyes and the intellect lets us betray our mortal selves and lets us forget what alone can save from the power of death, not the philosopher's wisdom, but faith. And even though Heidegger disclaims that his characterization of phenomena as inauthentic is meant to imply a negative judgment, he also insists that his discussion of authenticity "is based on a factual ideal of Dasein" (*SZ* 310). The rhetoric of *Being and Time* communicates very effectively what kind of life Heidegger would have us choose. That he gives Augustine so much room in his characterization of curiosity presupposes a deep affinity between the thinker and the church father. This suggests that if Heidegger does indeed go astray in his discussion of truth, such going astray may be due not so much to a failure to heed what the natural concept of truth demands, as to an ideal of human life that has to consider all single-minded pursuit of such truth inauthentic. *The kind of openness presupposed by the truth is a gift of curiosity, and that is to say of inauthenticity.*

As Heidegger emphasizes, the price of such openness is profound rootlessness. Curiosity is "everywhere and nowhere" (*SZ* 173). Bracketed are the care and concern that normally bind us to persons and things. Curiosity does not want to engage or cultivate what it sees, but bids us push restlessly from one thing to the next until we resemble the unhappy Peter Schlemihl of Chamisso's story, the man who lost his shadow, who has become ghostlike and insubstantial, and spends the rest of his life as a scientist, travelling the earth with his seven league boots, collecting specimens. Heidegger speaks of the *Aufenthaltslosigkeit* of curiosity. *Aufenthalt* is Heidegger's translation of the Greek *ethos*, which he understands as the place that lets us dwell in the world (*H, BW* 233). In this sense we can say that curiosity lets us become unethical.

The tall man in Chamisso's story who robs Peter Schlemihl of his shadow is of course the devil. This association of curiosity with the devil recalls the fateful curiosity that let Adam and Eve lose their place in paradise. The snake's promise that by eating the fruit of the forbidden tree of knowledge their eyes would be opened and they would be like God suggests that, as Aristotle also points out, curiosity has its telos in a divine, and that is to say a superhuman, seeing and understanding. This leaves the question whether the sought-for truth will not prove a will-o'-the-wisp or a castle in the clouds. And it leaves the challenge posed by the association of truth so understood and curiosity: is this pursuit not by its very nature unethical in that its price is the loss of man's proper place, his human ethos?

7. TRUTH AND OBJECTIVITY

Dislocation discloses. Think of the way a tool that breaks while we are using it calls itself to our attention. How is the job to be finished? The breakdown invites us to consider what we are up to. In Heidegger's words, "The context of equipment is lit up, not as something never seen before, but as a totality constantly sighted beforehand in circumspection. With this totality, however, the world announces itself" (*SZ* 75). Not only that: as we wonder about what is to be done and look at the now useless tool it acquires a strangely insistent presence; it falls, so to speak, out of its world—Heidegger speaks of *Entweltlichung*—and just because of this presents itself as something that now is just there, simply present. Heidegger does not want to say that now the tool presents itself as it is "in itself"; just the opposite: the tool presents itself as it is "in itself" when we actually use it. What the tool is "in itself" is thought here relative to a particular context of activities, and that is to say also, relative to a particular world. But as the tool falls out of this world, it calls for a different understanding of this "in itself." What the thing is "in itself" now means what it is regardless of the place it is assigned by those concerned to use it and by their world. So understood the thing's being-in-itself is essentially *worldless*. But since Heidegger refuses to separate the being of things from their being-in-a-world, to say that the thing's being-in-itself is worldless is to say that it transcends Being as Heidegger understands it. *Beings transcend Being.* Such transcendence announces itself whenever our world fails us and things call themselves to our attention in their now mute presence. That may sound like nonsense. But we should note that Heidegger is forced to say something very much like this. Thus he writes, "Being [*Sein*] (not beings [*Seiendes*]) is dependent upon the understanding of Being," that is to say, on Dasein (*SZ* 212; cf. *SZ* 226). This forces us to think the transcendence of beings over Being, where transcendence may not be understood formally, as we do when we speak of the transcendental subject or of Heidegger's freedom, but materially, as we do when we speak of the transcendence of the thing-in-itself or of Heidegger's earth. If this is hardly sufficient to dismiss the charge that to speak of beings transcending Being is to talk nonsense, it should at least suggest that such odd formulations point to a difficulty that Heidegger, too, needs to address.

If what Heidegger calls the *Entweltlichung* of things makes them conspicuous and discloses them in their mere being there, such dislocation need not be the result of the things in some sense failing us, as a broken tool fails us; we can imagine an *Entweltlichung* of which we are the authors. Our concentration may flag; as our mind wanders, we begin to look at the tool in ways that have nothing to do with the job to be done. Think of a shoemaker who, moved by the leather's strangely insistent presence, puts down his awl. Imagine the shoemaker given to philosophical musings: he begins to wonder what the seemingly so familiar materials he is working with are really made of. The transformation of things ready-to-hand into things merely present-at-hand presupposes such dislocation. No longer bound into the world by care and concern, we become its spectators. The being of things is transformed into being for a subject, being-in-the-world into subject-encountering-objects.

Such transformation, however, still does not provide for an openness that would allow us to grasp things as they really are, for "objectivity" is still thought here relative to a particular subject and to its standpoint. If we are to do justice to the truth of things, we have to attempt to free our understanding from such relativity. True objectivity implies freedom from perspectival distortion. The being of objects is not a being for a subject imprisoned in a particular here and now, but for a subject that transcends the accident of location. Objectivity and truth both presuppose that human beings can transcend themselves in reflection. Experience is indeed bound to the body and to its location in space and time; seeing is inescapably perspectival. But as soon as curiosity makes what we see an object of reflection, the difference between appearance and reality has to open up, and with it the desire to know things as they really are, as they are "in themselves." Kant thus distinguishes subjective appearance, thought relative to the embodied self and hence inescapably perspectival, from the object itself, thought relative to the transcendental subject, which as the form of all possible experience is not tied to any particular point of view.[22] *This allows us to think the truth of scientific propositions as their correspondence to the objects themselves, where such objects in principle cannot be given in experience, but must be reconstructed in thought.* This is the task of science and there is no reason to think that its reconstructions can or should be fully adequate to the objects themselves. The idea of such objects functions only as a regulative ideal.

The pursuit of this elusive truth demands a willingness to test our reconstructions by how well they fit not only our other judgments, but also those of others. Kant criticizes the "logical egoist" who thinks it unnecessary to test his judgment by holding it up to the judgment of others and claims not to need this *criterium veritatis externum*.[23] Not only freedom of thought, but freedom to publish is an indispensable condition of the pursuit of truth. To commit oneself fully to this pursuit is to commit oneself also to the freedom of those who might join us in this search. A strategy of emancipation, of helping others find their way out of the cave, is part of this commitment.

Similar considerations apply to Heidegger's being-in-the-world. First of all and most of the time we are indeed caught up in the world and in its language-games. Our understanding is in this sense bound by perspectives. But we are beings of reflection. As soon as a perspective is thought by us as such, its hold on us is loosened. Reflection has to disclose the gap that separates reality from appearance. Such dis-

---

22. Kant, *Kritik der reinen Vernunft*, B 70 fn; see also A 29 fn.
23. Kant, *Anthropologie*, BA 6.

closure has to deny us the "ground" that Heidegger's world-bound "in itself" seemed to promise. Coupled with our restless curiosity, our power of reflection has to deny us every paradise.

But does Heidegger himself not make this power of self-transcendence constitutive of Dasein? And does he not found truth in just this transcendence? Citing Calvin and Zwingli, he even calls our attention to the traditional view that God created man in his image and that man gains his measure only by looking up to Him (*SZ* 49). But his analysis of Dasein's transcendence fails to do justice to the vertical dimension of human existence that is here suggested. Thus philosophy's conception of a godlike pure subject and with it the conception of objective truth are said by Heidegger to rest on a confusion of theology and philosophy. He speaks of a jumbling together of Dasein's phenomenally grounded "ideality" with an "idealized subject" as "residues of Christian theology within philosophical problematics that have not as yet been radically extruded" (*SZ* 229). There is indeed a historical and a systematic connection between the Christian idea of God and the Cartesian determination of the essence of man as *res cogitans* or the idealized subject of transcendental idealism. Kant's transcendental subject plays at least some of the part that the tradition had assigned to God, even if it provides only the form of the totality of what is, not its matter. But to point out this connection is not in any way to discredit the idea of such an ideal subject. With this idea reflective consciousness attempts to give itself a measure. *Heidegger's own temporal account of the ecstatic being of Dasein fails to do justice to that power of reflection which allows human beings to think a worldless knowing, free from the accident of place and time, and by so doing transcend themselves.*

To do justice to everyday experience, we have to recognize the role curiosity and reflection play in it, to the way human beings will again and again struggle to escape whatever caves may hold them. This role becomes conspicuous whenever someone has lost his way or just from curiosity has come to doubt the reliability of the maps he has been given. Much of philosophical reflection has been a groping for forms of representation less bound to particular points of view, less likely to keep us imprisoned in the cave, than those generally accepted and taken for granted. In this sense the mathematical language of modern science stands unambiguously higher than the language used by its Aristotelian predecessor, which remains closer to everyday language and more intimately bound to the senses and thus to appearance. Copernican revolutions are not just paradigm shifts, but steps in this process of the spirit's self-elevation. Richard Rorty's suggestion that we cannot call Cardinal Bellarmine's objections to Copernican theory, on the grounds that it conflicted with Scripture, unscientific, that we do not know how to draw the necessary distinction between theological and scientific discourse, must be rejected.[24] Careful examination of the two kinds of discourse involved will show them not just to be different, but to be on different levels. There is an unambiguous sense in which science has progressed since Aristotle. The measure of this progress is given by the idea of objectivity or, and this is to say the same thing, by the idea of the truth of things. That idea has its foundation in reflection spurred on by curiosity.

8. THE ESSENCE OF TRUTH AND THE TASK OF THINKING

I have argued that the ground of truth must be located not just in the phenomenon Heidegger calls freedom, but in a special mode of that freedom, in the freedom of theoretical curiosity, which is the freedom to know for the sake of knowing. This, however, does not answer the challenge that has shadowed the pursuit of truth from the very beginning: as Nietzsche insists, we have no organ for "the truth."[25] Nor does it answer the challenge that the pursuit of truth for its own sake is, by its very nature, unethical.

The first challenge is given an answer by the history of science and technology. Both continue to demonstrate that Aristotle's confidence that potentially the human mind is all things was not misplaced. To be sure, we have no organ for the truth. Whatever presents itself to eye or ear, to taste or touch, is never more than appearance. But precisely because we are in this sense shut off from what is as it is, we face the task of reconstructing it in thought. Such reconstruction invites suspicion: might there not be a misfit of the mind and what is so radical that all our attempts to arrive at a coherent reconstruction of reality are doomed? There can be no argument that would demonstrate the required fit once and for all, for such an argument would have to consider what is as it is in itself, apart from our reconstructions; yet only in these reconstructions do we approach what would have to be presupposed. That is to admit that the pursuit of truth that continues to give such reconstructions their direction rests on faith. It presupposes the confidence that the human mind is attuned to what is, even though it will never be able to seize the ground of such attunement. Our life, more especially the life of science, justifies such confidence.

More serious is the second challenge. If our science and technology

24. Richard Rorty, *Philosophy and the Mirror of Nature* (Princeton: Princeton Univ. Press, 1979), p. 32.
25. Friedrich Nietzsche, *Die fröhliche Wissenschaft*, V, 354.

demonstrate daily the very real power that the pursuit of truth has granted us, they also have proved to threaten our being in the world, even in the most literal sense. Scientific rationality is finally unable to understand the nature of this threat, let alone to meet it. Needed is a critique of science that recognizes both its legitimacy and its limits. Its legitimacy is bound up not only with the legitimacy of theoretical curiosity, but also of that will to power that technology manifests; its limits are bound up with what I have called the "unethical" character of the pursuit of truth. The world of objects has no place for anything like value.[26]

This is not to deny the possibility of reflection ascending higher than empirical science, of a truth "higher" than ontic truth. Take, for example, the truths of mathematics. Was Plato not right to place mathematical knowledge higher than knowledge of nature? But how are we to understand this "higher" standing? We unduly reify the phenomenon of number when we make numbers into strange things that transcend space and time and exist independently of the mind. Numbers lack reality; they are constituted in thought, objectifications of our ability to count. The truth of "$2 + 2 = 4$" presupposes a certain skill. The evidence that supports this truth is our ability to add. As Wittgenstein suggests, the answer to the question, Do we need intuition for the solution of mathematical problems? is given by our command of the language of mathematics. "The process of *calculation* brings about just this intuition."[27] Mathematics is transcendental. The propositions of mathematics have their ground in the form of experience, not in what is the case.

Besides material truths, we thus have to recognize formal truths, truths that have their measure not in what is experienced, but in the form of experience, or, as Heidegger might say, truths that have their measure not in beings, but in Being. We can thus distinguish ontic from ontological truth (*GA* 24, 455–461). We can also show that one form of description, one projection of the being of things, is more adequate to things as they are than another, where the measure of such adequacy is given once again by the idea of objectivity.

If the positive sciences presuppose ontological reflection, projections of the being of things, further reflection shows that, as Heidegger reminds us, an ontology "remains itself naive and opaque if it fails to discuss the meaning of Being in general" (*SZ* 11). Such a discussion will seek to ground ontology, more especially that projection of Being

26. Ludwig Wittgenstein, *Tractatus*, 6. 41.
27. *Tractatus*, 6.2331; see also 6.13, 6.2, 6.233.

which finds expression in the commitment to objectivity, in a richer concept of experience. Heidegger can thus claim that "*fundamental ontology*, from which all other ontologies can take their rise, must be sought in the *existential analytic of Dasein*" (*SZ* 13). What we cannot do, however, is claim that just because objectivity or, more generally, presence-at-hand, derives from readiness-to-hand, the latter is therefore more adequate to what things are in themselves. That phrase is itself inseparably intertwined with the commitment to objectivity and becomes meaningless when separated from it.

The commitment to objectivity liberates. But it also has to raise the specter of contingency. The stronger this commitment, the more the persons and places we are tied to will present themselves to us as places and persons we just happen to be tied to. As Kierkegaard knew, reflection threatens to rob us of our sense of belonging. The hope that further reflection will restore that place to us is vain. But just because reflection can reveal this vanity it can awaken us to the necessity of putting reflection in its place. That self-elevation of the human spirit,[28] which finds expression in the very idea of things as they are and of truth as adequacy to this idea, has to bring with it a profound self-dislocation. Man, and especially modern man, is both constituted and threatened by his spiritual mobility. Reflection is finally impotent to meet this threat. Only an affect such as love or faith can deliver us from the sense of contingency, from the suspicion of the vanity of our existence, that is inseparable from the life of reflection.

28. See Theodor Litt, *Mensch und Welt. Grundlinien einer Philosophie des Geistes* (München: Federmann, 1948), pp. 214–231.

8   Husserl, Hilbert, and the Critique of Galilean Science

PATRICK A. HEELAN

Edmund Husserl's later philosophy of science is contained in his critique of "Galilean science." [1] 1. What is Galilean science? 2. On what grounds did Husserl claim that the prevalent scientific practice of his own time was Galilean? 3. To what extent did Husserl share the attitude of his Göttingen colleagues, particularly of David Hilbert, towards scientific theory-making? 4. Did he attribute to theory an ontological significance beyond computational power? 5. If the ontological significance of theory, as both Husserl and Hilbert assert, lies in the fact that theoretical values are just the limits of "infinitely perfectible" measuring processes, then what if this is a mistaken fact? 6. How is the "prescientific" life-world the "soil," "origin," and "ground," as Husserl claims, of all theory? 7. How satisfactory can Husserl's account of the "historical origins" of theoretical science in the life-world be, given that science produces ever new basic phenomena seemingly without precedent in the life-world? 8. Should we accept the uncritical assumption made by Husserl, Hilbert, and the physicists of his time that sensible quality X and measured quality X are denotationally the same differing only in their connotation or *Sinn*? 9. Does Husserl's account not suggest the need for development in the direction of a hermeneutic phenomenology, both with respect to the way phenomena come to be understood through theory and with respect to the cre-

---

1. For Husserl's discussion of Galilean Science, see his *The Crisis of European Sciences and Transcendental Philosophy* (1934–1937), the "Vienna Lecture" (1935), and the "Origins of Geometry" (1936). All of these works were written after the publication of Martin Heidegger's *Being and Time* (1927) and may have been influenced by Husserl's reading of this great work. "The Vienna Lecture" and "The Origins of Geometry" are included in the English translation of the *Krisis* by David Carr. These works are referred to in the notes in the following way: C for *Crisis*, VL for "The Vienna Lecture," and OG for "The Origins of Geometry"; the number following is the page number in Carr's English translation. For an important review article on the *Crisis*, see Gurwitsch (1966).

ation of new scientific phenomena through instrumentally assisted perception?

1. *What is Galilean science?* Galilean science is what Husserl took to be the philosophical core of the mainstream tradition of physical science.[2] This mainstream science he took to be the thrust toward the "mathematization of nature." The "new" "unprecedented" characteristic of mathematical natural science, he says, is that "through Galileo's *mathematization of nature, nature itself* is idealized under the guidance of the new mathematics; nature itself becomes . . . a mathematical manifold," that is, there is "the surreptitious substitution of the mathematically substructed world of idealities for the only real world, the one that is actually given through perception, that is ever experienced and experienceable—our everyday life-world."[3] The philosophical core of this position is today called "Scientific Realism."[4]

Such a project included the "direct" geometrization of space-time and the "indirect" mathematization of sensible qualities ("sensible plena") by the mathematization of their measurable indices.[5] The link between perceptual phenomena and theory was measurement. He accepted an assumption virtually unquestioned in his time against which I shall argue forcefully below that measured qualities were (denotationally) the same as perceptual qualities though (connotationally) they acquired by measurement a theoretical *Sinn* (or meaning). "Objective science . . . sets itself the task of transposing knowledge which is imperfect and prescientific in respect of scope and constancy into perfect knowledge—in accord with an idea of a correlative which is, for sure, infinitely distant, i.e., of a world which in itself is fixed and determined and of truths which are *idealiter* scientific ('truths-in-themselves') and which predicatively interpret the world."[6]

The philosophical core of this project of mathematization is uncovered when it is shown that such a project has its roots in the philosophical tradition of Galileo, Descartes, and Kant.[7] Within this per-

2. The thesis of Pt. I of the *Crisis* is that, within the historical context of European civilization, science is a part of the history of philosophy.

3. C 23; 48–49. See also VL 277–278.

4. For a classic defense of Scientific Realism, see "Philosophy and the Scientific Image of Man," pp. 1–40 in Sellars (1963). See also, for example, Hooker (1986).

5. See my paper, "Husserl's Later Philosophy of Science," Heelan (1987).

6. C 111; cf. C 139.

7. See the *Crisis*, Part II, on Galileo, Descartes and Kant. Galilean science is a philosophical ideal type, some would say a reconstruction. It is of the kind used, for example, by Alexandre Koyré, a pupil of Husserl at Göttingen and strongly influenced by Husserl's early work on phenomenology, in his *Galileo Studies* (1939/1978). Historians of science today treat their historical sources more flexibly and do not feel constrained to use them just to determine the "origins" of present sedimented scientific traditions, but also to recover lost traditions.

spective, the mathematization of nature is a philosophical project concerned with the ontology of nature. Galilean science would claim that the ontology of nature is the ontology of scientific theory apart from the life-world and the load of history and culture that constitutes the life-world. He calls this thrust "objectivism." Objectivism implies that the description provided by scientific theory (and its mathematical model) ought for the purposes of philosophy to replace the language of the direct experience of the life-world.[8]

2. *On what grounds did Husserl claim that the prevalent scientific practice of his own time was Galilean?* This question is to be understood as one for genetic phenomenology.[9] Only through the historical method (as Husserl understood it) can one find the essence of a tradition.[10] The scientific tradition then *as it exists* is to be understood through a study of the historical origins that presently direct it and give it meaning and goals. "What is historically primary in itself is the present."[11] Such a study supposes intimate familiarity with the existing practice of science in so far as it embodies a past that gives it present direction toward its future accomplishment.

Husserl's familiarity with the scientific practice of his time was a privileged one.[12] While at Göttingen during the period 1901–1916 he was a close associate of the group of mathematician-physicists who were to transform physics in the 20th century. These included Felix Klein (1848–1925), Hermann Minkowski (1864–1909), Richard Courant (1888–1972), Hermann Weyl (1885–1955), and especially David Hilbert (1862–1943), whose energies after 1911 were almost totally

8. Most phenomenological studies of theoretical science emphasize the Cartesian and objectivist character of Galilean science, for example, Kisiel (1970a) and (1970b), Kockelmans (1970). The phenomenological tradition, as carried on through the works of Martin Heidegger, Maurice Merleau-Ponty, and their students, has seen itself as a movement that directly confronts "science" as its philosophical antagonist—the "science" in question is, of course, Husserl's Galilean science that is the philosophical core of the prevalent scientific tradition; see, for example, Boehm (1964) for such a polemic, and Merleau-Ponty (1962), p. viii–ix.

9. The principal text dealing with genetic phenomenology is Husserl (1929). See, for example, the excellent commentaries in Sokolowski (1964), Landgrebe (1977) and (1981), and Welton (1983).

10. See Carr (1974) and Kisiel (1970a) for studies of Husserl's notion of history, especially in the *Crisis*. See my forthcoming paper "Husserl's Later Philosophy of Science" for Husserl's notion of history as this applies to the history of science.

11. OG 373. See also OG 371.

12. The primary sources for this section are Husserl's *Logische Untersuchungen* I, sects. 69 and 70, and *Hussrliana* XII, *Abhandlungen* VI and VII in Husserl (1970), pp. 445–457 and Hilbert's *Gesammelte Abhandlungen* (1932–35), III. The secondary sources are the biographies of Hilbert, Reid (1970) and of Courant, Reid (1974); also Mahnke (1966, orig. 1923), Van Dalen (1984), Miller (1982), chap. 6, Schmit (1981), Kap. IV, and Mohanty (1982).

devoted to solving the fundamental problems of physics. One finds, not unexpectedly, that Husserl's understanding of the tradition of physics coincided with the one that ruled the Göttingen school in the early part of this century and that came to dominate physics—and serve as model *par excellence* of science for all disciplines—in this century up to our own time. Not that this model of science was the only one to be found in the scientific community of Husserl's time, nor has it the monopoly today, but it is surely the dominant one, and continues to enjoy paramount respect.

Gauss's university at Göttingen was one where the use of mathematics in natural science was always held in high esteem. This interest in physics was carried forward by the geometer Felix Klein whose *Erlanger Programme* for geometry was extended to physics through the work of Eugene Wigner.[13] If according to Klein geometry is about the invariants of the space (or space-time) transformation group, then physics according to Wigner is about the invariants of *representations* of the space (or space-time) group, i.e., of systems that co-vary with the space (or space-time) coordinate system used. It is not hard to see in Husserl's method of variation of profiles the extension of the *Erlanger Programme* to the analysis of perceptual invariances (or essences).

The second aspect of Göttingen mathematics and mathematical physics to which Husserl was deeply attuned was Hilbert's program of *axiomatic thinking*. Already at the turn of the century in 1900, in a famous lecture to the Second International Congress of Mathematicians in Paris, Hilbert listed among the 22 outstanding problems to be resolved by mathematicians in the 20th century the following, "To axiomatize those physical sciences in which mathematics plays a significant role."[14] Eventually Hilbert was to devote more and more of his energies to the task of axiomatizing physics, for "physics," he said in all earnestness, "is too hard for physicists."[15] It was Hilbert and the circle of mathematicians around him at Göttingen that were responsible for giving physics the impetus it experienced in the first half of this century.[16]

13. For Klein's theory of geometry, see Klein (1932–1939), and *Bull NY Math Soc*, 2 (1893), pp. 115–149. For Wigner's theory of physics, see Wigner (1967), Part I.

14. Reid (1970), p. 82. Hilbert's lecture *"Axiomatisches Denken,"* is in *Bull Am Math Soc*, vol. 8 (1902), 437–445, 478–479, and in *David Hilbert: Gesammelte Abhandlungen* (1932–35), vol. 3, pp. 146–156. A translation, "Axiomatic Thinking," is in Fang (1970), pp. 187–198.

15. Cited in Reid (1970).

16. The direct influence of Göttingen thinking is seen in the work of R. v. Mises and A. N. Kolmogorov on the foundations of probability, G. Hamel on the axiomatization

3. *To what extent did Husserl share the attitude of his Göttingen colleagues towards scientific theory-making?* Husserl shared Hilbert's view that the theory of any field of knowledge, mathematical or physical, should be expressible as a deductive system based on a few fundamental propositions—or axioms—that are consistent with one another but mutually independent. The theory of theory is, according to Husserl, the axiomatic theory of (what he called) "manifolds" (*Mannigfaltigkeiten*). These are, roughly, in modern terminology, algebraic models. A manifold (in Husserl's language) is a structured set; but not a set of real or ideal objects given apart from the structure among them but rather a set of possible ideal objects given only in so far as they fulfil the functional relationships specified by the algebraic model. Note that the elements of the set are *ideal* and not real, and they are not ideal essences, such as number integers, of what is simply given in primitive experience. While for Hilbert, the elements of an axiomatic theory were just the "signs" that are manipulated in the model, to the contrary for Husserl, the elements were the possible ideal objects represented by those signs.[17] Husserl and Hilbert, however, were in rough agreement as to how the elements of axiomatic theory related to the objects of physics.

The view they shared was that what made theoretical axiomatization possible for physics was that measurement yielded a unique measure of sensible qualities. This was what the elements of a theory stood for. That the measures were unique was, in Husserl's analysis, due to the fact that measurements were "infinitely perfectible" and could be made as precise as one wished. Measuring is the praxis that links the real to the geometrical and the numerical. As long as measurement is governed merely by practical interests, he says, there is no need for an ideal limit, but "out of the praxis of perfecting, of freely

---

of mechanics, and J. v. Neumann on the axiomatic theory of quantum mechanics. Courant and Hilbert's *Methoden der Mathematischen Physik* (1924) astonished the new generation of quantum physicists by anticipating brilliantly the needs of the new physics and became the text from which directly or indirectly all theoretical physicists have been taught down to our own time. Cf., for example, Einstein (1954), and (1949), "Autobiographical Notes," pp. 20–21, 48–49; also Heisenberg (1952); and v. Neumann (1955).

17. The broad extent of the agreement between Hilbert and Husserl on the theory of theory as well as the subtle differences between them on this topic have been studied by Mahnke (1977), Van Dalen (1984), Miller (1982), chap. 6, Schmit (1981), chap. IV, and Mohanty (1982), pp. 91 and 96. For Husserl's explicit references to Hilbert, see Husserl (1929), p. 96 in Eng. trans., *Abhandlungen* VI and VII in Husserl (1970), pp. 445–457. Implicit references to Hilbert are found on pp. 45 and 55 of the *Crisis*. The philosophical differences between Husserl and Hilbert centered on two issues, (1) *logicism* in the foundations of mathematics that Husserl rejected, and (2) *objectivism* in physics.

pressing toward the horizon of *conceivable* perfecting 'again and again,' *limit-shapes* emerge toward which the particular series of perfectings tend, as toward invariant and never attainable poles."[18] Measured values then are unique and they are the limiting values of perceptual processes.

That such a view was common to the Göttingen physicists is clear from Hilbert's words. In his famous lecture "Axiomatic Thinking" (1918),[19] he states that a *Stetigkeitsaxiom* or Axiom of Continuity "expresses the essence of experimental physics" and "has always been assumed by physicists who, however, have never formulated it." The axiom goes: "If a certain arbitrary degree of exactitude is prescribed for the validity of a physical assertion, a small range shall then be specified, within which the presuppositions prepared for the assertion may freely vary such that the deviation from the assertion does not overstep the prescribed degree of exactitude."[20] This axiom attempts to give practical meaning in terms of experimental criteria to a concept of continuity necessary (as it was thought by Hilbert and his colleagues) for theory formation.

4. *Did Husserl attribute to theory an ontological significance beyond computational power?* We need to make a distinction. On the one hand, his critique of Galilean science is precisely a rejection of the position that the mathematical models of science *independently of the life-world* provide an ontology for nature. Mathematical models according to Husserl provide technical computational power but, of themselves, independently of the life-world, do not illuminate the things that comprise nature or provide the categories for natural objects.[21] On the other hand, taken in conjunction with the life-world processes for which

18. C 26. See also C 111, 139, 343–351; also OG 376 where Husserl comments on the praxis of making even surfaces by polishing.

19. *"Axiomatisches Denken,"* Hilbert (1932–35), vol. 3, pp. 146–156; Fang's translation, "Axiomatic Thinking," in Fang (1970), p. 187–198.

20. Hilbert (1932–35), vol. 3, p. 150; in Fang's translation, Fang (1970), p. 191.

21. Associated with objectivism is *technicism* or the view that to know lies in the *techné* of calculating. Such a view reduces real causality to no more than the manifestation of a functionality between numerical values in an ideal space-time (C 46). Technicism is the view that science contributes no ontological understanding to real perceptual life and that its function in human affairs is no more than to provide effective *technical control* over the environment. Many in the phenomenological tradition, such as Edward Ballard, Rudolf Boehm, Hans-Georg Gadamer, Maurice Merleau-Ponty, seem to be persuaded that all science is essentially and incorrigibly objective and theoretical, and would agree with Jürgen Habermas that the cognitive interest of the empirical-analytic sciences is technical control over objectified processes. Such a view, of course, reflects only one part—the negative part—of Husserl's critique of (the most prevalent tradition of) positive science.

mathematical models serve as "idealizations" and "limits," science does provide an ontology, and the ontology comprises the (experimental) phenomena ordered by theory.[22]

We need to distinguish, however, between idealizations that are limits of convergent processes and idealizations that are not. Only among mathematical entities—all ideal entities—can there (strictly speaking) be convergent processes. Physical processes such as measurements can be perfected but not "infinitely" and therefore do not converge on a limit, much less on a unique limit. If nevertheless one wants to introduce a notion of convergence to physical processes, the physical processes must be measurement processes since these produce numbers that can then be studied for convergence. But it is clear that no purely causal or physical process can produce a number, since numbers are timeless spaceless ideals. Numbers can only come to be attached to measuring processes by an act of interpretation performed by a competent observer. The measurement instrument is a "text" that is to be "read," and the occasion of the "reading" is a scientific phenomenon to be experienced.

Interpretation introduces into the context of reading a measuring instrument the limited purpose of the inquiry. This background purpose is to explore the scientific phenomenon that is revealed in and experienced through measurement. Such a phenomenon, as, for example, an electron packet of definite momentum, does not occur naturally (unless, of course, its occurrence is controlled by instrumental measurement so as to fulfil appropriate criteria) but is produced by canonical processes called the "preparation of state" and is stable only within generally unspecifiable constraints. Such preparations of the scientific phenomenon to be studied, while dependent on theory, are also constrained by unspecifiable non-theoretical factors—both hermeneutical and aesthetic—embodied in the competences of skilled scientists.

Husserl also mentions a different kind of idealization that is not a limit. Such is the idealization that gives the ideal essence of a perceptual object, the kind of thing the object is perceived to be.[23] Husserl describes such an essence as the invariant law among the set of perspectives through which a perceptual object reveals itself to a perceiver

22. For Husserl's notion of the *ideal*, see Husserl (1900–01), volume II of the German edition. For the controversy surrounding its interpretation, see, for example, Mohanty (1969).

23. For the notions of essence and specific essence, see Husserl (1950) and (1952a). For an excellent commentary, see Stevens (1974), pp. 103–128.

who explores it actively with his or her body.[24] The living human body (*Leib*), says Husserl, is "essentially different" from inanimate physical bodies (*Körper*) because it is self-moving, it has bodily kinestheses through which it explores the bodily characteristics of other bodies and in which these bodily characteristics are represented.[25] Such exploration can, of course, use technological equipment.[26] The exploration of a bodily essence is not a limiting process in a mathematical sense, and it is not reached by mathematical convergence, but it is pursued by studying the variations—subjectively induced or objectively discovered—that leave the perceptual object intact as to its kind. Such a process is experimental ("inductive"[27]) but at the same time hermeneutical and phenomenologically intuitive, since what counts as continuity and change is to be judged by a competent observer on the basis of perceived presence (fulfilment) or experienced absence (unfulfilment).

Although there may be confusion as to whether one should follow one Husserl in taking scientific theory to be the limit of a sequence of perfectible perceptual processes (measurements) or to follow the other Husserl by taking theory to be the essence of scientific perceptual phenomena (already in the life-world), it is clear that for Husserl the ontology of science is *in the life-world*—therefore, perceptual— while at the same time being *organized by theory*—therefore, theoretical. That Husserl's argument in favor of this position is confused should not obscure the fact that this is what he concluded.

5. *If the ontological significance of theory, as Husserl and Hilbert assert, lies in the fact that theoretical values are just the limits of "infinitely perfectible" measuring processes, then what if this is a mistaken fact?* I have argued above that there are no infinitely perfectible measuring processes. Consequently, theory cannot borrow ontological significance from such a relationship. Is theory then no more than an arbitrary convention or just a means of environmental control? I argue it is neither! Theory, though not a limit of perfectible perceptual processes, does provide the perceptual essence (in the Husserlian sense) of scientific phenomena in the life-world and so has ontological significance on that account. Not that Husserl made such an argument clearly and

24. See C 106–108, 161–162. See also Heelan (1987), "Husserl's Later Philosophy of Science," for an interpretation of these as related to the representations of active and passive transformation groups.

25. C 107. See also C 161–162.

26. Technological equipment belongs to the prescientific life-world according to Husserl; see below.

27. See C 40. Husserl's induction is more akin to C. S. Peirce's *abduction* than to Mill's *induction;* see below note 33.

explicitly, but such an argument can be made from the standpoint of Husserl's position.

6. *How is the "prescientific" life-world the "soil" and "ground," as Husserl claims, of all theoretical science?*

Husserl places the "origin" and "ground" of theory in (what he calls) the "soil" of the "prescientific" life-world.[28] For Husserl, the life-world is "the intuitive surrounding world of life, pregiven for all in common."[29] It "includes all our goals, all our ends, whether fleeting or lasting, in a flowing constant manner, just as an intentional horizon-consciousness implicitly 'encompasses' everything in advance."[30] It is not an object—if it were, it would fall prey to Kant's critique—it is not a particular of a kind, nor is it any kind of thing, nor above all is it a conceptual framework. Rather is it the universe of what is; its universality, however, is not ideal but concrete. It is the ultimate pregiven horizon of all perceptible objects and practical goals.[31]

The prescientific life-world is not the life-world as it was before modern science existed, but the present life-world as it is (or would be) experienced without the intervention of theory. It is then the pre-theoretical world for those who know no theory. Many of the technologies of science, however, remain and much of its "inductive praxis," such as "[seeing] measuring instruments," "[hearing] time beats," and "[estimating] visible magnitudes."[32] Such is the life-world of a child or of a scientifically unlettered person today. Such persons like all others in our culture find themselves surrounded by the instruments and artefacts that science has deposited in our environment. They can play with them, use them, experience the phenomena they generate, and even gain a certain practical understanding of the effects these produce or measure. How many of us are like children with just a practical understanding of thermometers and temperature while ignorant of thermodynamics? A child may be able to use the vocabulary of science but not as a scientist would use it. Since a child does not understand theory, he or she does not understand the theoretical substructure that makes such artefacts work the way they do. A child is ignorant of the theory of forces and fields, particles and waves that explain what these artefacts do and what the phenomena are that they gener-

28. Cf., for example, Husserl (1954), pp. 28–40. For discussion of Husserl's notion of the life-world, see, for example, Mohanty (1974), Natanson (1964), Landgrebe (1981), Essay 4, pp. 122–148, Ströker (1979), as well as the work of Alfred Schütz on the social world.
29. C 121.
30. C 144.
31. C 142–3.
32. C 121.

ate. This pretheoretical life-world is the "soil," however, in which the child—with the help of a mentor—discovers theory. Theory for the child has its origins in this kind of life-world and grows out of (usually a tutored) experience with such artefacts.

Attending to the origin of scientific understanding in a child, we see the movement from a practical understanding of stable scientific but pretheoretically understood phenomena (e.g., of rulers and compasses, or the use of photographic emulsions, or the action of electron beams in video tubes) to an understanding of the theory (e.g., geometry, or optics, or atomic theory, or electron theory) that explains such phenomena. Ruled straight lines, emulsion changes produced by light, etc., are truly perceptual phenomena as I shall argue below. They are produced by instruments, controlled, varied, made to interact with other phenomena, and all of this can be learned by anyone equipped with standard equipment who knows no theory.

What gives such a perceptual phenomenon as, say, an electron beam an essence is in part theory, for theory provides the name ("electron") for the scientific phenomenon, and theory gives the essential law that, subject to the purpose and art of experimental inquiry, connects the variety of manipulations that yield the sensible appearances characteristic of the scientific phenomenon (in this case, the phenomenon of the electron beam). The pretheoretical scientific phenomenon mediates for the child the past of science and brings forth for him or her a historical understanding of the theory—perhaps, revised and reinterpreted—that accounts for the phenomenon, and prepares for the production of new phenomena that in their turn will mediate theory for a future generation of children. Scientific phenomena are then historical entities.

When the theory of the phenomenon is retrieved, it is not by means of a simple-minded "induction." The connection between the theoretical essence and the phenomenon is more subtle than would be accounted for by a Baconian or a Millian induction. The process is more akin to (what C. S. Peirce called) "abduction," for deeply involved in the discovery and use of theory is interpretation (hermeneutics)—knowing when the purpose of the inquiry is fulfilled—and a sense of the aesthetics—knowing how to produce the phenomenon and how not to exceed the bodily constraints of disinterested experimentation.[33]

7. *How satisfactory can Husserl's account of the "historical origins" of theo-*

33. Cf. Peirce (1931–1958), 1.338, 2.228–2.308. For abduction as an interpretative act leading to a transformation of the perceptual field, see 5.182–5.184. Cf. also Heelan (1988), where I trace the interpretative and esthetic components of the kind of induction based on the prescientific life-world.

retical science in the life-world be, given that science produces ever new basic phenomena seemingly without precedent in the life-world?

Having followed the progress of a child from the scientifically enriched life-world into which he or she is born to the discovery of scientific theory, we are still left in doubt as to how the life-world came to acquire the scientific enrichments it has that make possible the rediscovery or retrieve of theory by each new generation of children. Surely, there were not always rulers and compasses, thermometers, electron tubes, microscopes, mass spectrographs, and so on! These enrichments had a beginning in human culture. How such genuine and novel artefacts—"readable technologies,"[34] I call them—came to be established in human culture for the first time is not a question for Husserl. In so far as he considers it at all, he seems to assume that there is always to be found in human culture a precedent for theory, that is, some antecedent praxis the perfecting of which leads to scientific theory.[35]

While it is plausible that some modern scientific measurement practices derive from ancient practices such as those of surveying land or of measuring pitch by the length of a vibrating string, it is inconceivable that such practices were themselves primordial or that all current experimental practices have such ancestors. Some scientific entities, such as, for example, electrons, just did not have a sensible pretheoretical presence in the life-world before modern science. Experimental practice related to electrons, for example, has first to produce the electrons that are to be studied. This is done by a standardized theoretically controlled process called "preparation of state." Are then electrons real particulars of a new scientific kind, new scientific phenomena of a life-world enriched by a scientific process of "preparation of state"? Since there is no pretheoretical inductive praxis in regard to them, many phenomenologists—and others—conclude that they cannot be real phenomena like trees and stars but are merely theoretical artefacts invented for the control of nature.

Even though for the majority of people, pure scientific phenomena are about as familiar to them as countries they have never visited or famous people they have never met, still it is well to review the evidence in favor of the view that, say, electrons, electron beams, etc., are truly perceptual phenomena to those who have experimental competence, even though they are (in necessary part) products of scientific

34. For *readable technologies*, see Heelan (1983a), chap. 11.
35. See my forthcoming paper, "Husserl's Later Philosophy of Science."

theory making. Although electrons are not sensible to the unaided senses, they serve as manipulable components of thousands of technologies—both within and outside scientific laboratories—and the reason they can so serve is that they exhibit stable, predictable profiles, both active and passive, to competent observers—usually experimental scientists skilled in the use of standard laboratory apparatus. If any procedure from which one can get or produce information about a scientific state can be called a measurement process (in the broadest sense), then every process that serves to manipulate electrons in predictable ways to produce sensible outcomes is a measurement process. All experimental inquiry then falls under measurement (in the broadest sense), and the final accomplishment of measurement is such control as provides competence to sample at will the active and passive profiles of scientific entities such as electrons.

I suppose that today most scientific entities, such as DNA, synaptic potentials, gluons, etc., are just not usefully thought of outside of the laboratory as related to pretheoretical inductive praxis of any sort. Nevertheless, each entity has the potentiality not merely of making its specific presence felt in the life-world through standard instruments and technologies, but of acquiring a stable, even apodictic, set of profiles with respect to suitably equipped and competent human subjects. Such profiles, as I have said, can often be sampled even by theoretically illiterate observers.

The question as to whether every scientific process of measurement implies a historically antecedent pretheoretical praxis of measurement must then be answered negatively. This answer, however, has to be qualified. Once a new scientific phenomenon is embodied in material structures of the environment, and once these structures become part of the cultural tradition of the pretheoretical life-world of a community, then the "soil" is prepared as "originary" for the retrieve, by each new generation of students, of the theory for such phenomena by perhaps a more complex process than (what Husserl calls) induction.

8. *Should we accept the uncritical assumption made by Husserl, Hilbert, and the physicists of his time that sensible quality X and measured quality X are denotationally the same differing only in their connotation or Sinn?*

No! Each, I argue, is constituted by a different material praxis and a different set of hermeneutical interests. The association between the two—though real—is then only partial and deeply affected by biology, history and culture. If the realities of science are phenomena in the life-world, and if the phenomena of the life-world—whether scientific or nonscientific—are shaped by the bodily and experimental "kinestheses" through which they are explored and in which in turn are fulfilled the meaning of those actions, then it is clear that sensible X cannot be the same as measured X. For, despite the use of a common name "X," sensible X is explored by a set of actions systematically different from those used to explore measured X, for the former do not depend for their essence on families of technologies while the latter do so depend. In addition, the predominantly biological meaning of sensible X is different from the more general and predominantly non-biological meaning attached to measured X, for the former serve the interests of a non-technologically transformed culture, while the latter serve the interests of a technologically transformed culture.[36]

9. *Does Husserl's account not suggest the need for development in the direction of a hermeneutic phenomenology, both with respect to the way phenomena come to be understood through theory and with respect to the creation of new scientific phenomena through instrumentally assisted perception?*
I have already argued that this is so and I offer the following three theses as summarizing the development that is called for[37]: (a) the ideality of theory is not in general relative to infinitely perfectible measuring processes but relative to the purposefulness of the living body (*Leib*); (b) perception is intrinsically governed by bodily kinestheses and essentially hermeneutical in relation to the purposefulness of *Leib;* and (c) the living body, *Leib,* can use technological extensions within its perceptual praxis. None of these theses was actually formulated by Husserl. The first thesis is the contribution of this essay to a critique of the *Crisis.* The second is implicit in Heidegger's *Being and Time* and is also much discussed today by others.[38] The third thesis was taken up by Merleau-Ponty in his posthumous work *The Visible and the Invisible* and is being actively explored today.[39] It is not difficult to see

36. See Heelan (1983a), chap. 10 on "Horizonal Realism."
37. These are the conclusions of Heelan (1987). A more interdisciplinary account of the positive aspects of these conclusions is found in Heelan (1988).
38. For work on a hermeneutical theory of perception, see, for example, Heelan (1983a), (1983b), and (1983c), and Nicholson (1984). Outside the phenomenological tradition, cf. the work of C. S. Peirce and Michael Polanyi. For Heidegger's relevance for the philosophy of science, see, for example, Kisiel (1977), (1973), Kockelmans (1985), Seigfried (1980), and the copious bibliography referenced in these works.
39. See, for example, Merleau-Ponty (1962) and (1968), Heelan (1983a). Hermann Weyl was the first to use phenomenology in a philosophy of the natural sciences, see Weyl (1963, orig. 1949) and Van Dalen (1984), but he was aware that physical conceptions are explored, as he says, by "another type of experience and imagination than those of the mathematician" (Hilbert [1932–1935], III, p. 653). An interest in a phenomenological interpretation of measurement as a praxis began with Heelan's study of

in retrospect that none of these theses is totally foreign to the dynamic of Husserl's later thought.

---

the quantum theory, Heelan (1965). Notable also is the work of Zucker (1982). For the phenomenology of scientific technology and its influence on perception, see, for example, Ihde (1979), Heelan (1975) and (1983a).

REFERENCES

Becker, Oscar (1970). "Contributions towards the Phenomenological Foundation of Geometry and its Physical Applications," pp. 119–146 in Kockelmans and Kisiel (1970).

Boehm, Rudolf (1964). "*Les sciences exactes et l'idèal Husserlien d'un savoir rigoureux,*" *Archives de Philosophie,* 27:424–438.

Carr, David (1974). *Phenomenology and the Problem of History.* Evanston, Ill.: Northwestern University Press.

Courant, Richard, and Hilbert, David (1924). *Methoden der Mathematischen Physik.* Berlin: Springer.

Einstein, Albert (1949). "Autobiographical Notes," pp. 1–96 in *Albert Einstein: Philosopher-Scientist.* Ed. by P. Schilpp. New York: Library of Living Philosophers.

———(1954). "Physics and Reality" (orig. 1935), pp. 283–315 in *Ideas and Opinions.* New York: Dell.

Elliston, F., and McCormick, P. (eds.) (1977) *Husserl: Expositions and Appraisals.* Notre Dame: Notre Dame University Press.

Fang, J. (1970). *Hilbert: Toward a Philosophy of Modern Mathematics.* II. Hauppauge, NY: Paideia.

Gurwitsch, Aaron (1966). "The Last Work of Husserl," pp. 397–447, in his *Studies in Phenomenology and Psychology.* Evanston: Northwestern University Press.

Heelan, Patrick (1965). *Quantum Mechanics and Objectivity.* The Hague: Nijhoff.

———(1983a). *Space-Perception and the Philosophy of Science.* Berkeley and Los Angeles: University of California Press.

———(1983b). "Natural science as a hermeneutic of instrumentation," *The Philosophy of Science,* 50:181–204.

———(1983c). "Perception as a hermeneutical act," *Review of Metaphysics,* 37:61–75.

———(1987). "Husserl's Later Philosophy of Science," *Philosophy of Science,* 54:368–390.

Heidegger, Martin (1962). *Being and Time.* Trans. J. Macquarrie and E. Robinson. London: SCM Press.

———(1988). "A Heideggerian Meditation on Science and Art," pp. 257–275, in *Hermeneutic Phenomenology,* ed. Joseph J. Kockelmans. Washington, D.C. and Pittsburgh: University Press of America and CARP, 1988.

Heisenberg, Werner (1952). *Philosophic Problems of Nuclear Science.* London: Faber and Faber.

Hilbert, David (1932–1935). *David Hilbert Gesammelte Abhandlungen*. Berlin: Springer (also New York: Chelsea, 1965).
———. (1938). *The Foundations of Geometry* (orig. Ger. pub. in 1901). La Salle, Ill.: Open Court.
——— (1970). "Axiomatic Thinking," pp. 187–198 in Fang (1970). Orig. pub. in *Math. Annalen*, 78 (1918), pp. 405–415 and republished in Hilbert (1932–1935), III, pp. 146–156.
Hooker, Clifford (1986). *A Realist Theory of Science*. Albany: SUNY Press.
Husserl, Edmund. (1900–01). *Logische Untersuchungen*. I und II. (2nd rev. ed. 1913). Halle: Niemeyer. English trans. *Logical Investigations*, 2 Vols. Trans. by J. Findlay. London: Routledge and Kegan Paul, 1970.
———. (1929). *Formale und Transzendentale Logik*. Halle: Niemeyer. English Trans. *Formal and Transcendental Logic*. Trans. Dorian Cairns. The Hague: Nijhoff, 1969.
——— (1954). *Erfahrung und Urteil*. Ed. L. Landgrebe. Hamburg: Claasen. English trans. *Experience and Judgment*. Trans. J. Churchill and K. Ameriks. Evanston, Ill.: Northwestern University Press, 1973.
——— (1950). *Ideen zu einer reinen Phänomenologie und phänomenologische Philosophie*. Volume I. Ed. Walter Biemel. *Husserliana* III. The Hague: Nijhoff.
——— (1952a). *Ideen zu einer reinen Phänomenologie und phänomenologische Philosophie*. Volume II. Ed. Marly Biemel. *Husserliana* IV. The Hague: Nijhoff.
——— (1952b). *Ideen zu einer reinen Phänomenologie und phänomenologische Philosophie*. Volume III. Ed. Marly Biemel. *Husserliana* V. The Hague: Nijhoff.
——— (1954). *Die Krisis der europäischen Wissenschaften und die transzendentale Phänomenologie*. Ed. Walter Biemel. *Husserliana* VI. The Hague: Nijhoff. English trans. *The Crisis of European Sciences and Transcendental Phenomenology*. Trans. D. Carr. Evanston, Ill.: Northwestern University Press, 1970.
——— (1970). *Philosophie der Arithmetik (und Abhandlungen)*. Ed. Lothar Eley. *Husserliana* XII. The Hague: Nijhoff.
Ihde, Don. 1979. *Technics and Praxis*. Dordrecht and Boston: Reidel.
Kisiel, Theodore (1970a). "Phenomenology as the Science of Science," pp. 5–44 in Kockelmans and Kisiel, eds. (1970).
——— (1970b). "Husserl on the History of Science," pp. 68–92 in Kockelmans and Kisiel, eds. (1970).
———. (1973). "On the Dimensions of a Phenomenology of Science in Husserl and the Young Dr. Heidegger." *Jour. Brit. Society for Phenomenology*, 4: 217–234.
——— (1977). "Heidegger and the New Image of Science." In *Research in Phenomenology*, 7: 162–181.
Klein, Felix (1932–1939). *Elementary Mathematics from an Advanced Standpoint*. Trans. E. R. Hedrick and C. A. Noble. New York: Macmillan.
Kockelmans, Joseph (1970). "The Mathematization of Nature in Husserl's Last Publication," pp. 45–67 in Kockelmans and Kisiel, eds. (1970).
——— (1985). *Heidegger and Science*. Lanham, Md.: University Press of America and Center for Advanced Research in Phenomenology.
——— and Kisiel, Theodore (1970). *Phenomenology and the Natural Sciences*. Evanston, Ill.: Northwestern University Press.
Koyré, Alexandre (1978) (orig. 1939). *Galileo Studies*. Trans. John Mepham. Atlantic Highlands, N.J.: Humanities Press.

Ladrière, Jean (1970). "Mathematics in a Philosophy of the Sciences," pp. 443–465 in Kockelmans and Kisiel, eds. (1970).

Landgrebe, Ludwig (1977). "Phenomenology as Transcendental Theory of History," pp. 101–113 in Elliston and McCormick (1977).

—— (1981). *The Phenomenology of Edmund Husserl: Six Essays.* Ed. and Intro. D. Welton. Ithaca and London: Cornell University Press.

Mahnke, Dietrich (1966). "From Hilbert to Husserl: First Introduction to Phenomenology, Especially that of Formal Mathematics" (orig. 1923). Trans. David Boyer, *Studies in Hist. and Philos. of Science,* 8 (1966): 71–84.

Merleau-Ponty, Maurice (1962). *The Phenomenology of Perception.* Trans. Colin Smith. London: Routledge and Kegan Paul.

—— (1968). *The Visible and the Invisible.* Trans. A. Lingis. Evanston, Ill.: Northwestern University Press.

Miller, J. Philip (1982). *Numbers in Presence and Absence: A Study of Husserl's Philosophy of Mathematics.* The Hague and Boston: Nijhoff.

Mohanty, J. N. (1969). *Edmund Husserl's Theory of Meaning.* The Hague: Nijhoff.

—— (1974). "Life-World and A Priori in Husserl's Later Thought," in *Analecta Husserliana,* 3 : 46–65.

—— (1977). "On Husserl's Theory of Meaning," pp. 18–37 in Elliston and McCormick (1977).

—— (1982). *Husserl and Frege.* Bloomington: Indiana University Press.

Natanson, Maurice (1964). "The 'Lebenswelt'," pp. 75–93 in Strauss, ed. (1964).

Nicholson, Graeme (1984). *Seeing and Reading.* Atlantic Highlands, N.J.: Humanities Press.

Peirce, Charles Sanders (1931–1958). *Collected Papers of Charles Sanders Peirce,* 8 vols.; vols. 1–6 ed. Charles Hartshorne and Paul Weiss, vols. 7–8 ed. A. Burks. Cambridge, Mass.: Harvard University Press.

Reid, Constance (1970). *Hilbert.* New York and Berlin: Springer.

—— (1974). *Courant in Göttingen and New York.* New York and Berlin: Springer.

Schmit, Roger (1981). *Husserls Philosophie der Mathematik: Platonische und Konstruktivistische Momente in Husserls Mathematikbegriff.* Bonn: Bouvier.

Seigfried, Hans (1980). "Scientific Realism and Phenomenology," *Zeit. f. Philosophische Forschung,* 34, pp. 395–404.

Sellars, Wilfred (1963). *Science, Perception, and Reality.* London: Routledge and Kegan Paul.

Sokolowski, Robert (1964). *The Formation of Husserl's Concept of Constitution.* The Hague: Nijhoff.

Stevens, Richard (1974). *James and Husserl.* The Hague: Nijhoff.

—— (1975). "Spatial and Temporal Models in Husserl's *Ideas II,*" *Cultural Hermeneutics,* 3 : 105–116.

Ströker, Elizabeth, ed. (1979). *Lebenswelt und Wissenschaft in der Philosophie Edmund Husserls.* Frankfurt am Main: Klosterman.

Van Dalen, D. (1984). "Four letters from Edmund Husserl to Hermann Weyl," *Husserl Studies,* 1, pp. 1–12.

Von Neumann, John (1955). *Mathematical Foundations of Quantum Mechanics.* Trans. R. Beyer. Princeton: Princeton University Press.

Welton, Donn (1983). *The Origins of Meaning: A Critical Study of the Thresholds of Husserlian Phenomenology.* The Hague: Nijhoff.

Weyl, Hermann (1963). *Philosophy of Mathematics and Natural Science* (orig. pub. in 1949). New York: Atheneum.

Wigner, Eugene (1967). *Reflections and Symmetries.* Indiana University Press.

Zucker, Francis J. (1982). "Phenomenological evidence and the 'Idea' of physics," pp. 269–290 in Bruzina, R., and Wiltshire, B., eds. *Phenomenology Dialogues and Bridges.* Albany: SUNY Press.

9   Husserlian Transcendental Phenomenology: Some Aspects

J. N. MOHANTY

There are various ways in which the uniqueness of Husserl's phenomenology as a transcendental philosophy can be brought out. I will
not, in this article, go into all of them.[1] After a few preliminary remarks about the most important amongst them, I will single out one
problem which every transcendental philosophy has to face: namely,
the problem of relativism, and hope to be able to show that Husserl's
phenomenological transcendental philosophy has the power, which
the other varieties of transcendental philosophy lack, to confront, accommodate and overcome relativism. At the end, I will briefly deal
with one major difficulty with the Husserlian philosophy. To these
three tasks shall correspond the three parts of this article.

I

Transcendental philosophies differ (a) as regards the constitut*ed*
domain which one may be wanting to account for; (b) as regards the
nature of the constitut*ing* subjectivity, and (c) as regards the account
they give of the constituting activity. There is a close relation between
the choice one makes with regard to (a) and the choice regarding (b)
and (c). In other words, one's account of the constitut*ing* subjectivity
and of the nature of the constitution process largely depends upon
what it is one is seeking to account for, i.e., what constitut*ed* domain
one is starting one's enquiry with. Thus, one may want to account for
the possibility of a given body of knowledge that is taken to be true. In
Kant's case, such a body of knowledge was Newtonian physics along
with Euclidean geometry. There is no reason why one may not, as a

---

1. For more on this topic, see my book, *The Possibility of Transcendental Philosophy*,
The Hague: Nijhoff, 1985.

transcendental philosopher, reject this Kantian starting point and begin with the more contemporary picture of the world in terms of quantum mechanics and relativity physics (along with the non-euclidean geometries). In any case, one would be starting with commitment to a historically accomplished body of knowledge as a privileged representation of the world. While this is a genuine, viable route to follow, there is a more fundamental concern, overlooked but in a certain sense presupposed by the Kantian enterprise. This is the route from the *theories* back to the perceived and lived world which underlies all such theories as their foundation and ground from which they take off. One may then raise the transcendental question with regard to this perceived and lived world: how is such a world constituted? The question about the possibility of this world was never raised by Kant, who began at a much higher level of intellectual accomplishment, namely, mathematical physics so that even when he appears to be giving a theory of perception, perception, for him, is continuous with physics. The perceived world, as Kant thematises it, is nature as it is organized by the human intellect, not the pre-theoretical, pre-objective lived world. This is why Kant's theory of perception is a theory of perceptual judgment which on the one hand rests on the formal-logical theory of judgment, and on the other, merges into a theory of physics.

Should one, following Kant, focus upon a given body of knowledge such as physics and enquire into the constitut*ing* acts which make it possible, one inevitably is led to recognize, again not unlike Kant, a highly delimited constituting domain. Recall the Kantian table of categories as a model. But should one, following Husserl, focus upon the perceived world precisely as it is perceived, and enquire into its constituting origins, one is led to recognize a constituting domain which is open-ended and only minimally structured.

Hence the distinction between two kinds of transcendental philosophy. One kind, closer to Kant, construes the constituting domain as a structure that is the source of formal-logical *principles*. The other kind, of which Husserl is a protagonist, construes the constituting domain as experiential subjectivity which is the source of all *evidence*. The former sort, the *prinzipien-theoretisch* transcendental philosophy, provides the principles which determine knowledge, principles which also function as critical norms. The latter sort, the *evidenz-theoretisch*, grounds knowledge in experiential evidence but lacks the principles which organize knowledge into system. What transcendental philosophy needs is to combine a minimally structured set of principles with an evidence-providing experiential subjectivity and a critically operative normative element. In a sense, Husserlian thinking shows us the way to achieve this goal.

I have, on another occasion, distinguished between the Kantian transcendental philosophy which enquires into the conditions of possibility of the *truth* of a body of knowledge (such as Newtonian physics), and the Husserlian transcendental philosophy which enquires into the conditions of the possibility of *meanings* (propositions, theories). The connection between this distinction and the distinction as formulated in the just preceding paragraph is not immediately clear. In fact, the two distinctions are not identical. For the present, I will say this much in order to clarify the situation. There are three levels of enquiry: first, committed to the *truth* of a certain theory such as Newtonian physics, one may ask how is it possible for such a theory to be true of the world. Second, recognizing that there is no "privileged representation of the world," that there are alternate theories each making claim to be true, one may put these truth-claims under bracket and regard the theories as theories, i.e., as meaning-structures, and enquire into the conditions of their possibility, i.e., into those intentional acts which constitute such a meaning-structure. Third, one may go beyond such theories and focus on the pre-theoretical everyday perceived world which is the basis on which theoretical acts come into play, and then look for the pre-theoretical intentional acts—perceptual, actional and emotional—which constitute this life-world.

In the light of these remarks, one may safely say that the distinguishing features of Husserlian transcendental philosophy consist in: (a) an open-ended concept of the constitut*ed;* (b) an enriched concept of the constituting, transcendental subjectivity, which is not merely a source of logical principles but is also the concrete on-going experiencing-of-the-world, and so incorporates into its own structure historicity, temporality, corporeality and linguisticality; (c) a notion of constitution which encompasses both active and passive constitution. To these, I should also add: (d) a notion of *criticism* that is, in the long run, dependent on the idea of evidence rather than on the application of logical principles; and (e) a certain *neutrality* as between metaphysical realism and metaphysical idealism.

II

Now to come to the problem of relativism. Since Husserlian phenomenology aims at an absolute, i.e., non-relative, grounding of human knowledge, it has to come to terms with relativism which denies precisely the possibility of such grounding. At first, it appeared as though by refuting psychologism, and by implication all forms of relativism, Husserl had, in the *Prolegomena to a pure logic*, demonstrated the possibility of non-relative, essential truths about all domains of human experience. But the spectre of relativism tends to appear from within phenomenology, as the concern with essences is replaced by the concern with meanings. The possibility of very different, often radically different, interpretations of the same hyletic data, and so of the constitution of incommensurable objectivities, comes to the fore. The transition to the relativism of alternate conceptual framework did not require a long step. The idea of life-world was no more immune to relativistic onslaught: for the cultural relativist, there are in fact radically different life-worlds; the idea of one life-world meant to provide the rock bottom foundation for all theoretical enterprise was but a philosophers' dream. In the face of such relativistic challenges, the early *refutation* of relativism appeared too empty and formalistic to carry conviction—in fact, as has been suspected by many, may be question-begging in so far as it presupposes a non-relativistic concept of logical principles used in the alleged refutation.

I propose that if relativism has to be overcome, one cannot just begin by "refuting" it. One must be able to "go through" it as far as one can, and then go beyond it. In the rest of this article, I will, in a brief outline, show how transcendental phenomenology can, with its own conceptual resources, traverse this long and arduous path towards overcoming relativism while coming to terms with it. In doing this, I will *not* be simply re-stating the typically Husserlian argument which depends upon (a) the idea of logic as formal ontology laying bare the form of any world whatsoever; (b) the essentialism which discovers invariant features through contingent, contextual variations; and (c) the experienceability of any possible world by *me* as the primal ego. I will not use these strategies, because (a) delivers, at most, a formal universality; and (b) and (c) would appear to the relativist as begging the issue.

However, I will make use of two Husserlian principles: the principle of noesis—noema correlation and the principle of *constitution* of identity through a congruence of overlapping noemata. With these two principles in mind, we can begin by taking one modest step: let us "suspend," "neutralize" our concern with *truth* (or with the question "Which of the theories, world-views, religious beliefs, is true?") and make a shift to a concern with *meanings*. What I propose is to formulate relativism, not as concerning truth, but as concerning meanings. Ian Hacking proposes a similar transformation: he wants to replace concern with truths by consideration of truth-or-falsehood, of the *sense*.[2] Once this shift takes place, what we have are "belief systems," "noematic structures" or "theories."

Once this level of discourse is reached, I propose two moves with a view to "overcoming" relativism. One is to connect each meaning-structure, belief-system or theory to an appropriate interpretive act or nexus of acts, "style of reasoning" (Hacking), act of believing, con-structive proof procedure (Putnam) or verification procedure (Dummett). Once we establish this correlation, we, as a matter of fact, re-trieve a non-relativistic structure, a noesis–noema correlation. This structure is relational but not relativistic; it was not available at the first order level of beliefs, truth-claims, theory-constructions. The "bracketing" enables us to focus upon the belief-system, the theory as such, and to correlate it to the acts which go with it.

The next step may be briefly described thus: just as the identity of an object is constituted by the system of noemata through which "one and the same" object is presented, so also in the case under considera-tion the one world—not in the sense of the totality of all worlds, but in the sense of that whose versions they all are—may be looked upon as that regulative concept which not only orders the various quasi-incommensurable worlds, but also delineates the path that shall lead us out of a possibly hopeless chaos towards communication and understanding.

Let W and W* be two world-noemata such that they are furthest removed from each other in the sense that any communication be-tween them seems impossible. In such a case I postulate that there will always be a series of Ws such that (i) every succeeding member of the series overlaps the preceding member, and (ii) the first member will overlap W and the final member overlap W*. Nothing in this guaran-tees that there is only one such series. There may in fact be many dif-ferent ways of linking W and W*. But in any case the result would be the same: there would be in principle a way of establishing communi-cation between W and W*, and so of translatability. In the sense in

2. Ian Hacking, "Language, Truth and Reason," in Hollis and Lukes (eds.), *Rational-ity and Relativism* (Cambridge, Mass.: M.I.T. Press, 1982), esp. p. 49.

which I am arguing for translatability, as a language L is translated into another language L¹, the two languages undergo transformation. Translation changes both the languages. Languages have to grow towards mutual translatability.

What this method of overcoming relativism, even in its barest outlines, shows is that relativism cannot be overcome by that violent act which posits one validity-claim as imperiously superseding all others—be it science or any particular religious belief, for example. What is needed rather is that gentle and tolerant view which recognizes that unity is always in the process of being achieved by communication and understanding, and is just too fragile to be sustained by violence. To elevate any world to the status of absolute is to fall into the trap of relativistic arguments: the "other" would remain unconvinced and communication will be cut off. The world-in-itself is rather a regulative ideal that guides communication and translation.

For transcendental philosophy, the lesson is this. It need *not* be committed, as Kant was, to a favored representation of the world. It should rather be open to different theories of the world and their historical (and logical) process of constitution in the historically developing life of consciousness.

III

In this concluding part of the article, I will briefly turn to a Heideggerean point which Bert Dreyfus has made as against transcendental phenomenology. Dreyfus insists that one's cultural understanding of reality is not a picture, not a belief-system or a theory—in short, not a representation. It rather consists in a "socialized" set of practices. Being "habitual," it cannot be objectified. Such practices and skills have no "abstractable intentional content," no *noema.* To a member of a community, such practices as distance-preserving practices are simply learnt and inherited; they do not have a noematic content whose constitution transcendental philosophy could possibly retrace. Cultural worlds therefore refuse to be grounded in a constituting subjectivity.

Now, I agree that this "practical" understanding which permeates one's being-in-the-world is the result of habitualization and is "inherited" rather than "originarily instituted" by any particular member of a community. But the Heideggerean objection overstates its case by overlooking two things. In the first place, an actor does not simply perform a ritual, he also interprets himself as doing such and such thing; he has a certain understanding of what he is doing and why he is doing it. His self-understanding may not be the community's best interpretation available, nor is it located by any sundry actor within a theory. But there is nevertheless a self-understanding. In preserving an appropriate distance from an elder, he knows—however obscurely, implicitly and non-cognitively—that he has to show respect to his addressee. Secondly, it is precisely the task of the interpretive social scientist to make explicit the most satisfactory (second order) interpretation of the (first order) self-interpretations of the members of the community. In this process, the noematic sense gets articulated, and transcendental phenomenology regains the foothold it seemed it had lost.

Where in all this does the 'transcendental ego' come in? I want to understand by the 'transcendental ego' that stance which is the condition of the possibility not only of objectifying and critiquing my own culture (my own world), but also placing it side by side with many other possibilities, of contemplating them—these other relativistic structures, along with mine—as equal possibilities.

10   "The Strangeness *In* the Strangeness": Phenomenology and the Mundane

MAURICE NATANSON

Papers on Husserl and his phenomenology tend to fall into well-ordered categories: programmatic utterances, manifestoes, far-reaching outlines of work done and still more to be accomplished; there are papers which are largely exegetical in character, which take up various themes and concepts in Husserlian thought and which endeavor to elucidate them; there are papers which might broadly be called comparative, which contrast some feature of Husserl's philosophy with a resonant notion in some other thinker's work; there are interior treatments of phenomenology which show, to imagine an illustration, how topics Husserl takes up in his *Logical Investigations* find fresh but related employment in *The Crisis of European Sciences and Transcendental Phenomenology;* there are what might be called text-bound papers, those which restrict themselves to Husserl's writings and which, however sympathetic or critical they may be, try to get Husserl right by getting him from himself: pure Husserl; there are immanent criticisms and examinations of Husserlianism and, of course, external critiques; there are papers which argue that intentionality is already to be found in earlier thinkers than Husserl and papers which attempt to show that phenomenology is redeemable, in parts at least, if only its language is rescued from its formulator and translated into the vocabulary of non-phenomenological or even anti-phenomenological positions; and there are Yeatsian papers whose message is: On Husserl, on phenomenology, cast a cold eye; Philosopher, pass by.

Symposia and meetings on Husserl, these days, are not uncommon, but it was not always so. It is worth remembering that in 1950, Dorion Cairns concluded an article by saying: "So far, [phenomenology] continues to be an exotic."[1] In that year I applied for my first job teaching philosophy. I had just received my Ph.D. Interviews were scarce in that time, but I did manage to have an audience with one chairman of a department. He told me—and I believe that he was quite sincere—that he was well impressed with my credentials but that I simply would not do for the position which he was going to fill. "You see," he told me, "we have no opening for a mystic." I remain convinced that had there been room for a mystic, I would have at least been a contender! But my list of categories is incomplete. I must add what is perhaps one of the more welcome kinds of phenomenological papers to many audiences: those which carry out phenomenological investigations without making a great fuss about the history of Husserl's thought and without lapsing into phenomenological rhetoric. Had I not a personal aversion to the expression, I would say that these are the papers "which do" phenomenology. Such efforts tend less to description than to argumentation. To some ears, they come to philosophy "clean." Although I know in which categories my paper does not fit, I am less sure about whether it meets the requirements of any of the classifications which I have named. To be safe, let us check that little box marked "other."

I

The mundane world—the world in which we live our everyday lives—is, for the most part, a straightforward realm. We rely on daily life always to "be there," waiting for us to catch up with, join its ranks, swallow that last gulp of coffee as we move into the work of the day. It is not clear what would be meant by saying: "Suppose, one morning, daily life disappointed us, failed to show"—as they say at the workplace—played ontological hookey. Husserl's idea that there is what might be called a "believingness" which underlies the Natural Attitude—an idea manifested in the tacit assumption that the world in which we live is real, real for Others as well as for ourselves, consequential, obdurate, rewarding, and thieving. "Thieving?" the dormant attender may be roused to exclaim. "Where did Husserl ever say, 'thieving?'" He didn't; I did. And this is as good a moment as any to indicate the limits of responsibility in what I have to say. Without the work of Husserl, I might not be speechless, but I would be bereft of many of my adjectives and naked in my nouns. In many respects,

---

1. Dorion Cairns, "Phenomenology," in *A History of Philosophical Systems* (edited by Vergelius Ferm), New York: Philosophical Library, 1950, p. 363.

this paper is "about" Husserl; it is certainly indebted to Husserl; still more assuredly, it is mediated by the influence of other phenomenologists—Alfred Schutz, chief among them—but it is, finally, not only my own responsibility, but *mine. I* am saying all these things; blame me. Well, then, not only does the mundane world depend on "believingness" being gratified by the tacit object of its desire—the everyday world—but all of us, as comers and goers in daily life, expect things—the "states of affairs" of everyday existence—to continue much as they have in the past. Mundanity, in these terms, is permanently stabilized.

In the first volume of his *Ideas,* without abandoning, as Husserl says, "the ground of the natural standpoint,"[2] he views, for the moment of our quotation, individual consciousness as "interwoven with the natural world. . . ."[3] The natural attitude, we may say, does not "lose out" in phenomenological procedure; to the contrary, it is given its due. And it is given its due in such a way that nothing respecting the "natural world" is disregarded or altered during the time of phenomenological inspection. That dual mode of attention is one of the most difficult aspects of Husserl's method to appreciate fully. At the moment I abstain from taking the world as existent, real, historical, value-laden, intersubjectively shared, "ours"—at that very moment I, as a phenomenologist, intend or *mean* the world as phenomenon, mean it as it presents itself as a correlate to "my" acts of intending it. "Abstention" does not signify or imply disregard. Straightforward acceptance is modified, but such modification does not make the ordinary current of experience with its objects and with its events and with its fellow human beings anything less than "real" simply in virtue of the phenomenologist taking a special and curious interest in what is "real." For some critics of Husserl it comes to having one's dessert and eating it too; for some partisans of Husserl—and here I count myself among them—it comes to controlled but splendiferous seeing. In "olden" days—say, forty to fifty years ago—some philosophers— "sense-data men" they were then called—claimed to have "seen" a sense datum. All I can say is that I once shook the hand of a man who claimed to have seen a sense datum. I wanted to ask him what it was like—that kind of seeing, not what he saw; but there was, so it appeared to me, a look on his face of "How could you possibly understand!" and I never pursued the matter. Now I seem to have inherited his place if not his doctrine. What is it like to abstain from seeing the

---

2. Edmund Husserl, *Ideas: General Introduction to Pure Phenomenology* (translated by W. R. Boyce Gibson), London: George Allen and Unwin, 1931, p. 126 (section 39).
3. *Ibid.*

object perceived as existent and yet at the same time to *intend* it as
"existent?" No matter what kind of look is on my face, I hasten to
quote Husserl. In *Cartesian Meditations* he writes:

the world experienced in this reflectively grasped life goes on being for me (in
a certain manner) "experienced" as before, and with just the content it has at
any particular time. It goes on appearing, as it appeared before; the only difference is that I, as reflecting philosophically, no longer keep in effect (no
longer accept) the natural believing in existence involved in experiencing the
world—though that believing too is still there and grasped by my noticing
regard.[4]

We have conflated two moments of phenomenological noticing. Obviously, Husserl is concerned with advancing his own method; he is
also profoundly interested in understanding the Natural Attitude as
the Natural Attitude, that is, on its own philosophical terms. Going
back to his book *Ideas* and to his claim that "individual consciousness is
interwoven with the *natural world*. . . ," we may now observe that the
context in which that assertion is made involved an attempt to trace
out the root of what Husserl calls the "general thesis" of the Natural
Standpoint. He writes:

let us seek out the ultimate sources whence the general thesis of the world
which I adopt when taking up the natural standpoint draws its nourishment,
thereby enabling me as a conscious being to discover ever against me an existing world of things, to ascribe to myself in this world a body, and to find for
myself within this world a proper place. This ultimate source is obviously *sensory experience*. For our purpose, however, it is sufficient to consider *sensory perception*, which in a certain proper sense plays among experiencing acts the
part of an original experience, whence all other experiencing acts draw a
chief part of their power to serve as a ground.[5]

It would appear that this passage owes more to *Logical Investigations*
than to the advanced (or radical shift) which Husserl made in *Ideas*
from a non-egological theory of consciousness, as it has come to be
called, to the location of the transcendental ego as the absolute clue to
transcendental phenomenology. Before the General Thesis of the
Natural Standpoint (here I was going to compare the source of the
Natural Standpoint to the source of the Nile, but I couldn't remember
what *was* the source of the Nile; after consulting a 1967 edition of the
Encyclopaedia Britannica, I learned that Lake Tanganyika, Lake Vic-
toria, and Lake Albert are all mentioned as source-related bodies of
water feeding the Nile, but that there are also various rivers and

---

4. Edmund Husserl, *Cartesian Meditations: An Introduction to Phenomenology* (translated by Dorion Cairns), Martinus Nijhoff, 1960, pp. 19–20 (section 8).
5. *Ideas*, pp. 126–127 (section 39).

mountains which may be still deeper suppliers of water for the great River. At the moment, I am prepared to abandon my comparison with the Natural Standpoint, but to stand by the statement that the source of the Nile is not Lake Titicaca, which I know to be in South America)—before the General Thesis of the Natural Standpoint can be traced to its transcendental origin, it appears that Husserl emphasizes the immediate—everyday—presence of the subject perceiving and the object perceived. Indeed, in the starkness of perception, a distinction between perceiver and perceived seems premature. Sensory perception, Husserl maintains, makes it possible for the "objectness" of the object to become manifest and for the embodiment of the self to come to realization. He writes:

I meditate first as would the man "in the street." I see and grasp the thing itself in its bodily reality. It is true that I sometimes deceive myself, and not only in respect of the perceived constitution of the thing, but also in respect of its being there at all. I am subject to an illusion or hallucination. The perception is not then "genuine." But if it is, if, that is, we can "confirm" its presence in the actual context of experience, eventually with the help of correct empirical thinking, then the perceived thing *is real* and itself really given, and that bodily in perception. Here perceiving considered simply as consciousness, and apart from the body and the bodily organs, appears as something in itself essenceless, an empty looking of an empty "Ego" towards the object itself which comes into contact with it in some astonishing way.[6]

The last part of that statement is haunting: "an empty looking of an empty 'Ego' towards the object itself which comes into contact with it in some astonishing way." The description seems to be that of the kind of "seeing" which occurs in some dreams—at least as they are remembered. Is the "astonishment" that the "empty looking of an empty 'Ego'" is consciousness unembodied? Perhaps, but I have another alternative to recommend for consideration. In what I have called the straightforwardness of daily life, the embodiment of the perceiver is taken for granted along with that of the perceived. "Elvira!," I shout to a very old acquaintance, someone I haven't seen for eight or ten years. "Give me a hug," I continue, "let me look at you." "Dear, dear," I say to myself, "the years have taken their toll. How fortunate I am in having remained exactly the same." Was that a crack I heard coming from Elvira's ribs when we embraced? "Can't we sit down?" Elvira says. "I'm afraid you've dropped your cane." So that was the "crack." Not Elvira; me. But in the initial instant of recognition, before assessments and without recollections, it was simply *Elvira*—not even "Elvira recognized" but just *Elvira*. "How long have you been using a cane?"

6. *Ibid.*, p. 127 (section 39).

Elvira asks. "Oh, it's not mine," I reply—gallant to older days—"I'm just carrying it for a friend." The astonishment comes to me in a twinkle, just a bare second before "Why, there's Elvira!" But the matter at issue is not temporal. Seeing Elvira is the finely honed edge of perception, not the cutting edge but the edge brilliantly prepared to cut. Myself and my friend: my "sighting" coming not from the "me" who undergoes an act of recognition but Husserl's "empty" Ego already-there, "memoried" but at the instant "memoryless," bodyless, caneless. Yet the central fact of the encounter is that the "sighting" is "recognitionful" before the larger sense of identification has been made. It is not a matter of giving a name to a face but of a face "naming."

There may be some objections to my notion of "straightforward-ness." "Does he think daily life is all that simple, all that directly *given?*" I can imagine someone asking of me. Certainly not! I have spent prac-tically my entire life opposing such a view. To think of me as holding a simplistic view of everyday life would be like accusing a conscientious objector of having war fever. "Straightforwardness," as I intend it to be understood, is not a characterization of daily life but a feature of how the individual in the midst of daily life perceives his world. The characterization is not psychological: I am not saying that each of us sees things "directly." Rather, I am concerned with the bitterness of intending. We do not see things, fellow-men, or events "straightfor-wardly"; we see them contextually, in situation, "contexted," I am tempted to say. But in that "contexted" seeing, there are epistemic layers of complexity. Seeing Elvira is a piece of cake! Yes, but a more cautious examination of that delight reveals not only a sugary surface, softer insides, but strata of textures and ingredients, a complexity of pungence. Simply stated: the commonsense world of daily life con-ceals as much or more than it reveals; daily life may "work" for prac-tical purposes but that hardly means that its opaque aspects are inno-cent; daily life is not a goody-goody, nor do we need Céline to teach us that. What does "straightforward" mean then? That what is meant, as it is meant, *acts* "before" the Ego enters the perceptual fray. At bot-tom, my "sighting" of the Other is free of the familiarity of the Natu-ral Attitude, more hectic than perceptual habituality, *itself-there*, itself-there all at once, possessing so sly a glance that there is hardly time to surprise either perceiver or perceived.

II

Now we can proceed in one of two ways; either we can take a closer look at what Husserl might have meant by the "astonishment" of an "empty 'Ego'" caught at the moment of its "looking" or we can turn to an illustration of what I think is phenomenologically at issue. The advantage of the first way is that reference to Husserl's texts gives us a kind of philosophical *Droit de passage*. Although I anticipate some striking disadvantages to the other way, it is the one I choose to follow. My way will be the way of literature.

The illustration of the astonishment of an empty Ego which I have selected is that of John Marcher who, with May Bartram, is the protagonist of Henry James's story, "The Beast in the Jungle." I have no intention of "telling" the story. It will be enough for present purposes to say that for its hero, "The Beast" is a definitive, very likely horrible manifestation which will confound if not destroy him. Early on, he has imparted his dread to a friend, May Bartram, who promises to "watch with him." For years that watch is kept; a secret vigil is held by the two—a vigil of disturbing differences. In condensed form: May says to John:

You said you had had from your earliest time, as the deepest thing within you, the sense of being kept for something rare and strange, possibly prodigious and terrible, that was sooner or later to happen to you, that you had in your bones the foreboding and the conviction of, and that would perhaps overwhelm you.[7]

"It's to be something," May Bartram continues a bit later, "you're merely to suffer?" And John Marcher replies: "Well, say to wait for—to have to meet, to face, to see suddenly break out in my life; possibly destroying all further consciousness, possibly annihilating me; possibly, on the other hand, only altering everything, striking at the root of all my world and leaving me to the consequences, however they shape themselves." And May responds: "Isn't what you describe perhaps but the expectation—or at any rate the sense of danger, familiar to so many people—of falling in love?"[8]

Marcher does not think it's love. Whether or not he has been in love, the experience which might qualify as some sort of test case was not "overwhelming" to him. "Then it hasn't been love," said May Bartram. "Well, I at least thought it was." And then he goes on to say: "I took it for that—I've taken it till now. It was agreeable, it was de-

7. Henry James, "The Beast in the Jungle," in *The Novels and Tales of Henry James,* Vol. XVII (New York Edition), New York: Charles Scribner's Sons, 1922, p. 71.

8. *Ibid.,* pp. 71–72.

lightful, it was miserable. . . . But it wasn't strange. It wasn't what *my* affair's to be."[9] May continues to watch with John until she becomes ill to death, and even then she keeps her vigil. It would appear that the two have gone as far as they can without Marcher comprehending what his friend knows but cannot tell him to know. Marcher is convinced that May knows the secret but will not venture far enough to disclose it. *Not far enough* is at once Marcher's complaint and his ambush. James writes:

He had to admit, however, what she said. "Oh yes, there were times when we did go far." He caught himself in the act of speaking as if it all were over. Well, he wished it were; and the consummation depended for him clearly more and more on his friend.

But she had now a soft smile. "Do you mean you're prepared to go further?"

She was frail and ancient and charming as she continued to look at him, yet it was rather as if she had lost the thread. "Do you consider that we went far?"

"Why I thought it the point you were just making—that we *had* looked most things in the face."

"Including each other?"[10]

I wonder, by the way, if Jean-Paul Sartre ever read "The Beast in the Jungle." Perhaps someone will catch me out and show that he did. It wouldn't embarrass me; indeed, I would be grateful. But I would be left with some strong questions about how the passage I just cited could be interpreted in terms of what Sartre says about "The Look." But that must properly be left by the way. Our path is clear: the story turns on May Bartram's question. Did John Marcher ever look May Bartram in the face? The answer is no measure of the question. The answer is "obviously not." But the question generated by May Bartram's question is: Into whose face *did* he look? Not: was there someone else? But: What fatal incapacity, what perverse choice marked John Marcher when he looked into his friend's face, not without seeing, not without all want of delicacy but without even the mother wit to recognize—not his friend's love—his own rapture for waiting. That rapture never leaves him; it transforms itself. After May's death, Marcher is tormented by the void failed consciousness has left him— "the lost stuff of consciousness," James calls it.[11] Marcher is now alone, not because his friend has died and not even because the *spring* of the Beast is recognized by Marcher to be its genius, but because, as James tells us, "the Jungle had been threshed to vacancy" and "the Beast had stolen away."[12]

9. *Ibid.*, p. 73.
10. *Ibid.*, p. 101.
11. *Ibid.*, p. 117.
12. *Ibid.*, p. 116.

It is difficult to believe that John Marcher never really *looked* at May Bartram. It would be easier and seemingly more acceptable to say that he never appreciated her, never looked at her as she was and as he was, never *ventured* her. And it might seem that James permits other readings: "Oh how he looked at her!," James (or the narrator) says of Marcher in a scene which launched my title. At the time of this conversation, May Bartram was already dying. But, as James writes,

She showed how she wished to leave their business in order. "I'm not sure you understood. You've nothing to wait for more. It *has* come."
Oh how he looked at her! "Really?"
"Really."
"The thing that, as you said, *was* to?"
"The thing that we began in our youth to watch for."
Face to face with her once more he believed her; it was a claim to which he had so abjectly little to oppose. "You mean that it has come as a positive definite occurrence, with a name and a date?"
"Positive. Definite. I don't know about the 'name,' but oh with a date!"
He found himself again too helplessly at sea. "But come in the night—come and passed me by?"
May Bartram had her strange faint smile. "Oh no, it hasn't passed you by!"
"But if I haven't been aware of it and it hasn't touched me—?"
"Ah your not being aware of it"—and she seemed to hesitate an instant to deal with this—"your not being aware of it is the strangeness *in* the strangeness. It's the wonder *of* the wonder." [13]

"Oh how he looked at her!" *Did* he? That Marcher stared at May Bartram we can easily accept; but the stare, in that case, was merely the sign of his amazement at the announcement that "it" *had* come. And in between the early years in their association when they looked at each other, what did John Marcher see in May Bartram's face? As a "self," we might say, Marcher saw the face of the vigil-keeper, saw not the watcher but the watch; as an "Ego," in Husserl's sense, as we have presented it, Marcher is empty. Empty of what? Of the face which cries: "Look at me!" Such dodges as "perhaps Marcher never realized that May loved him" leave us nowhere. "Live!," says Henry James; "Wait!," says John Marcher. Nor, I believe, will psychological explanations of Marcher's reticence do much for us. The stare of the empty Ego will never become the look of the living man. It is not a question of withdrawal. Marcher has gone out to his friend, he has sought her aid. It is her presence over the years which never rouses Marcher from his rapturous slumber. Whatever May says to him, John hears only his own question: "Will you watch with me?" Even that cry, which, despite everything I have said, *must* somehow have made itself heard

13. *Ibid.*, pp. 109–110.

before the "stuff of consciousness" was lost, is treated by John Marcher with a brave but futile gesture, like an Alpinist who hears a distant cry of distress and dispatches a St. Bernard—with an empty cask.

III

Whatever advance which we may have made in understanding the astonishing way in which the empty Ego comes into contact with its object, some questions remain about using literary examples for philosophical purposes. Let me turn then in a different direction. Sometime after the Second World War, as I recall—or at least twenty to twenty-five years ago—*Life* magazine ran a feature story, with photographs, of course, built artificially on the idea of bringing together for two or three hours one afternoon a group of very distinguished adults and—how should one say it?—a group of children, four- or five-year-old children. They were strangers to each other and they did not meet as a group. Rather, adults and children were paired off to spend part of an afternoon together—just to see what would come of it. I forget almost all of the details, but they can just as well be imaginatively reconstructed: an architect, a scientist, an artist, and—this is the one detail I *do* remember, quite precisely, in fact—a philosopher (at least a well-known professor of philosophy). Each pair was left free to do what they wanted. *Life* simply followed after, wrote it up, did the pictures. On the whole, the excursion seemed to work out rather well for almost all of the adventurers. Some went to the circus, some to the zoo, some boarded the Staten Island Ferry. The conversations, at least as they were written up, also went well—rather interesting, not just cute, conversations. Alas, the sole exception was the jaunt led by the philosopher. He said something like this to the reporter at the end of his excursion: "I endeavored to engage young William"—four years old—"in a discussion of Kant's Third Critique, but he was unforthcoming. Then . . ."—but why bother to fill it in. I doubt that William even got an ice cream cone out of the venture. Had the reporter—and he didn't—said "Professor, what do you think of children?" the answer would have been "They are nasty, brutish, and short."

It is common enough to encounter an adult who doesn't understand children, who simply has no interest in young children, who prefers company other than that of four-year-olds. Why, then, did the professor agree to the outing? Was the occasion misrepresented? Did he say, "Oh well, why not give it a try?" I am hardly in search of an answer because I think such questions—at least in some cases—are misposed. Why did he agree? I don't know and I don't think that it matters. The professor may have suffered from misopaedia or he may have been given advanced standing as an adult and been permitted to skip childhood. It makes no difference to this discussion. Is the empty Ego also empty during childhood? Phenomenology seems to be such an adult affair. But, then, what would be missing in the child? At first glance, the child would seem to be phenomenologically closer to the "object" than someone older; but such a view tends to equate "direct-ness" with naiveté—something alien to phenomenology and some-thing certainly foreign to the claim I have made on behalf of Husserl that "nothing respecting the 'natural world' is disregarded or altered during the time of phenomenological inspection." The astonishment of the empty ego is not that of the blind person who miraculously *sees* for the first time; the astonishment is that there is perception at all, that consciousness is "thing-bringing," the epiphanous presence of mundanity, the miracle of the commonplace.

Something not only new but startling appears to be given when the empty Ego moves from its initial lowly estate to a fuller existence as an empirical ego—the other guy present at the feast of intersubjectivity. Just as literary examples are to some people nervous-making, so chil-dren examples may occasion some displeasure. It is so hard to help! That is, it is hazardous to choose the right illustrations. Let me turn, then, to a different sort of case. For years, I have met with the follow-ing story, offered up in discussions by vigorous advocates, each of whom seems to be convinced that the story was *his.* Suppose an acci-dent occurs and a horrific gash in your neighbor's wrist instead of splashing gore reveals wires in place of blood or tendons or nerves. Not an artificial limb but an artificial man. I am aware that this illus-tration is dated, that not even freshmen are interested in it—they had it on their SATs. Still, it may do us some little service. I, for one, was never surprised by this story. Barring the odd short circuit, I am at ease with wired people, having spent much of my life with them. And I know something of their history. They once tried to baptize Kierke-gaard but all that came of it was a blackout. Well then, has the wired man a wired Ego? What, finally, is the emptiness and the astonish-ment of which Husserl speaks? If my several examples have been of any use, it amounts to this: In perceiving, the ego—the individual, let us say—is at once both bare and clothed. I look at another person and see *another;* I also, at the same time, recognize my friend or observe a stranger. As John Marcher, I see May Bartram betrayingly, and the betrayal is in the strange circumstance that any notion of "betrayal" would be incomprehensible to me: that is "the strangeness *in* the strangeness." As the professor, I did my best to sound out William on

Kant; was it my fault that the child turned sullen? "May I offer you my acetylene torch?" I inquired of my wired neighbor. What more could anyone desire? Yet I fear—and from past experience, I know—that this account of one aspect of the phenomenology of perception is unlikely to satisfy everyone and least likely to find pleasure in those who are—not sense-data men—habeas corpus men; they want the emptiness produced. They leave me feeling "protestful," like a disgruntled patron taking the cure at Baden-Baden who unfurls a Sartrean banner: "Slime is the agony of water."[14] I am a disgrace to the calibrated world.

IV

There has been a restlessness in these pages. Although Husserl and James are both artists of consciousness and masters of the "irreal," there seems to remain a distance between the "empty 'Ego'" of the one and the *wait* described by the other. Our various illustrations have reflected that distance but not overcome it. But one must not expect too much from philosophy. Going into philosophy is somewhat like marrying into a *very* extended family, one with even more extended quarrels. Everything ends with an accusatory question: What about Husserl? What about Heidegger? What about Sartre? What about Merleau-Ponty? Or: What about Lévi-Strauss? What about Foucault? What about Lacan? What about Derrida? Somehow, I think of this sort of question as having its grandest expression in the Christmas dinner scene in *A Portrait of the Artist as a Young Man:* What about Parnell? The distance between philosophy and fiction remains; but it remains an instructive distance. It would be false of me to leave you with the impression that because I recognize a distance, I believe distance to imply a qualitative difference. I do not believe that in the end philosophy remains philosophy and literature remains literature. I do not believe in "the end"; I am a partisan of in-between. And in-between we may at least endeavor to move from James to Husserl by a different source for illustration—that of memory, not memory as a chapter in philosophical psychology but memory which we livingly *are*. I remember the "empty 'Ego'" as a sound I was familiar with, which I knew was there during a certain season of the year, but a sound which was too distant to carry the few miles further it needed to go if I were to hear it as, in Husserl's terms, "itself-given." I went to high school in New

14. Jean-Paul Sartre, *Being and Nothingness: An Essay on Phenomenological Ontology* (translated with an introduction by Hazel E. Barnes), New York: Philosophical Library, 1956, p. 607.

York, in Brighton Beach—or near enough to call it that—now nick-named "Little Odessa" because of the relatively large concentration of Soviet Jews who have immigrated to New York and settled there. But when I was attending high school in the late thirties, which were just peeking through a crack in the ajar door of the forties, I thought of the place as the tag end of Coney Island. That was not strictly true geographically, but I was close. And what made me think of Coney Island was not its proximity but the sound, to be heard during the season—the sound of the laughing clown-machine of the Coney Island Fun House. Whether in season or not, that sound could not be heard in my high school; but I heard it there. Among other things, it provided a needed undercurrent to the animated arguments among us "advanced students" about the latest schism in the already ferociously splintered Socialist Workers Party. I never thought of Brighton Beach as "Odessa"—big or little—and I never thought of Brighton Beach as Brighton Beach; it was Brooklyn. The "empty 'Ego'" delivers me homeward. I can hear the voice of the barker, well into his spiel: "For the price of ta-wenty five cents, my friends, just one quarter, two dimes and a nickel . . ." while the laughing clown-machine produced his screaky howl and doubled over in geared glee. That gateway sound—the mockery of laughter—was the visa which granted leave from everydayness as well as the passport which guaranteed safe return to mundanity.

11   Heidegger, Early and Late, and Aquinas

THOMAS PRUFER

PREFACE

This lecture is about some relationships among several themes in Heidegger's early course lectures given in Marburg in the Winter Semester of 1925/6 and in the Summer Semester of 1927, in *Being and Time*, which was published in 1927, and in his later development. That later development can be fairly represented by his last two sets of course lectures, given in Freiburg in the Summer Semesters of 1943 and 1944 on Heraclitus; by his last public lecture, called "Time and Being," given in 1962; by a seminar on that lecture, also in 1962; and by four further seminars, held in 1966, 1968, 1969 and 1973. Heidegger died in 1976 at the age of eighty-six.

My lecture today suffers from two kinds of zig-zag. Ideally an understanding of the several themes themselves would be assumed, permitting the exposition to focus on the relationships among them. But in fact, considering the occasion, the lecture has to zig-zag back and forth between a summary exposition of the themes themselves and a summary exposition of the relationships among them. That is the first zig-zag.

The second zig-zag results from the fact that it is impossible to talk about Heidegger without using some of the key words he uses, and these key words are German and Greek (the relationship between German and Greek is a theme which runs through Heidegger's work from beginning to end). The lecture has to zig-zag back and forth between using the words which Heidegger himself uses and trying to explain those words accurately in English. Besides these extreme alternatives of using the German and the Greek words themselves and explaining those words in English, there are the alternatives of awkward translation and short paraphrase.

I hope that you will bear with these two zig-zaggings, the one between themes and their relationships and the other between German and Greek words and English words. The result of these compromises between trying to do justice to Heidegger's complexity and also trying to consider the occasion is no doubt, first, some simplification of Heidegger and, second, offering a little to everybody and not much to anybody.

I began by saying that this lecture is about some relationships among several themes in Heidegger. A theme can be related to another theme in various ways, among other ways by suppression of one theme by another, by reduction of one theme to another, by reversal of a theme, and by transposition of a theme into a new context. Heidegger weaves a complex web of suppressions and reductions, of reversals and transpositions.

The publication of course lectures given by Heidegger in Marburg in the 1920s, as well as an account given by him in 1963 called "My Way to Phenomenology," confirm the importance of Aristotle and Husserl for the early Heidegger. A great deal of my lecture has to do with ambivalence and misinterpretation in Heidegger's relation to Aristotle and Husserl. Only toward the end does the lecture come to the comparison and contrast of Heidegger and Aquinas.

Both Heidegger and Aquinas distinguish "to be" from "beings" and "being." Likenesses and differences in the ways in which they take this distinction suggest another web, a web of comparison and contrast between Heidegger and Aquinas concerning the common theme of "to be," the most obscure of themes.

Suppression, reduction, reversal, transposition; ambivalence and misinterpretation; comparison and contrast—we will try to thread our way through this thicket in the hope of reaching a clearing.

INTRODUCTION

Heidegger has been persistently guilty of three misinterpretations. There may be others as well, but I wish to consider only the following three:

(1) The first misinterpretation is the reduction of Plato to the theme of *eidos* or form. Further themes in Plato, themes such as the *otherness* of kind to kind and the weaving together and carding apart of kinds, and, beyond that, the themes of both a unity beyond kinds, a unity which binds kinds together, and a *"not"* which is beyond the "not" of one kind not being another kind—to central themes in Plato such as these Heidegger seems blind.[1]

1. See Hans-Georg Gadamer, *Gesammelte Werke* (Tübingen: Mohr, 1985ff.) VI, pp. 129–153; II, p. 12; *Heideggers Wege* (Tübingen: Mohr, 1983), pp. 70–80, esp.

(2) The second misinterpretation is the reduction of creation as a theme in medieval thought to making or production and, closely related to that, the reduction of the difference between essence and existence to the issue of making "ideas" "real," to the producing of the "real" out of "ideas" or out of the possible. Idea as possibility-to-be-made-real is thus successor to *eidos* or form in the context of an apotheosis of making. Heidegger seems blind to the difference between being "out of possibility" and being "out of nothing," a difference central to the specificity of creation, which is not *ex possibili* but *ex nihilo*.

(3) The third misinterpretation is the reduction of the deepest theme in Husserl's thought to the theme of reflexivity or the objectification of subjectivity to itself. Heidegger seems blind to Husserl's deepest theme, the theme of the interplay of the presencing and absencing of presence and absence themselves as distinguished from that-which-is-present and that-which-is-absent.

Presence is not simply the same as that-which-is-present because that-which-is-present could be absent too and still be the same. That which can be either present or absent is the same, but presence and absence themselves are not the same, neither the same as each other nor taken together the same as that which is both present and absent. But presence and absence are not simply psychological either; they are too at one with that-which-*is*(-present) and that-which-*is*(-absent). To have been taken by this difference-in-unity between presence and that-which-is-present is to have presenced the presence itself of that-which-is-present.

We will return to this triple: presencing, presence, that-which-is-present. For the moment, however, note that presence is ambiguous. It is both presence of that-which-is-present and also itself, insofar as it itself is presenced, somehow a that-which-is-present.

Heidegger denies any indebtedness to Husserl's analysis of time.[2] Perhaps the reason for Heidegger's blindness to this theme in Husserl is that this theme is so crucial for Heidegger himself, but Heidegger transposes it into a very different way of speaking. Perhaps Heidegger occluded this theme in Husserl because Heidegger was searching for a more suitable way to speak about the theme, a way not still embedded, as it was for Husserl, despite Husserl's attempts at purification, in a matrix of terms redolent of psychology.

78–80; 134–135. See Heidegger, *Gesamtausgabe* (Frankfurt am Main: Klostermann, 1975ff.), Vol. 26, §11(b).

2. "Über das Zeitverständnis in der Phänomenologie und im Denken der Seinsfrage," in *Phänomenologie—lebendig oder tot?*, herausgegeben von Helmut Gehrig (Karlsruhe: Badenia Verlag, 1969), p. 47; Gadamer, *Heideggers Wege*, p. 106.

Husserl made a central issue of the difference between the psychological and the transcendental, and, further, he moved beyond the object-act-ego display of the transcendental. In connection with this difference and this move, he anticipated Heidegger's shift to the primacy of manifestation and hiddenness over the one to whom what-is-manifest and what-is-hidden is manifested and hidden. Husserl anticipated Heidegger's shift to the primacy of manifestation itself over the dative of manifestation, over the *mihi*, the "to me," the "to me" which seems to be a declination from the *ego*, the "I," but which Husserl himself reverses to the status of that out of which the ego comes about, the ego as the center of responsibility and as the recipient of objectifications. Manifestation has primacy over "to me," and "to me" has primacy over "I."

In retrospect, in looking back at Husserl from Heidegger, we can see that Husserl himself deconstructed the terminology of psychology, and to some extent also the terminology of the transcendental, from within, that is, by using it to say something strictly beyond its means.

Husserl's deepest theme, the theme of so-called "inner time-consciousness," is finally neither "inner" nor "temporal" nor "consciousness."[3] It is not "inner" because it is beyond the distinction between immanent and transcendent, for example, beyond the distinction between the act of seeing a white horse (the act is immanent) and the seen white horse itself (the object is transcendent). It is not "temporal" because it is beyond the object or the act which is present or absent and which therefore can be timed as "now" or "no longer" or "not yet." It is not "consciousness" because it is beyond the distinction between act and object, for example, beyond the distinction between an act of remembering and its object, which is the act of having seen a white horse, and also beyond the distinction between this act of having seen a white horse and its object, the seen white horse itself.

In Husserl's terminology, so-called "inner time-consciousness" is the unity articulated into primary showing (*Urimpression*) together with retention and protention,[4] and this unity is not an act-object unity, although act-object unity is the usual sense of intentionality.

3. See, for example, *Husserliana* X, p. 333, lines 21–22; p. 371, line 16; p. 382, line 22.

4. Retention is *not* an *act* of remembering; protention is *not* an *act* of anticipating.

On "inner time-consciousness" in Husserl, see the following: Robert Sokolowski, *Husserlian Meditations* (Evanston: Northwestern University Press, 1974), §52–§63, pp. 132–167; John Brough, "The Emergence of an Absolute Consciousness in Husserl's Early Writings on Time Consciousness," *Man and World* V (1972), pp. 298–326; Rudolf Bernet, "Is the Present Ever Present? Phenomenology and the Metaphysics of

The primary showing is not an *act* which intends as its *objects* acts of retention and protention, and one articulated unit of the unity primary-showing-together-with-retention-and-protention intends other whole units in retention and in protention, but not as an *act* intends an *object* (Husserl calls this unusual intending *Längsintentionalität*). Primal presencing, primary showing, whatever *act* it may present or show (in *Querintentionalität*), is always also absencing into a presencing absénted or cleared out in retention and into a new primal presencing which itself has another presencing yet to come but still absent in protention. For Husserl this clearing out (in retention) and accepting (in protention) is more basic than any act-object achievement of the transcendental ego; it lets that ego living in such achievements come about.

This distention, Husserl's so-called "inner time-consciousness," the primary showing together with retention and protention, is in the last analysis the primal presencing/absencing of the presence/absence of that-which-is-present/absent. But to say this is to translate what Husserl said into a language we learn not from Husserl but from Heidegger. Husserl worked his analysis out using a psychology of the perception of tones and melodies; Heidegger, on the other hand, presents his analysis in *Being and Time* using themes like tools and death. The means of persuasion and demonstration are different. But what Husserl calls "the appearance of the flow to itself" is beyond the object-act-ego display, and so Heidegger's reduction of Husserl to the self-objectification of transcendental subjectivity is a misinterpretation.

On the other hand, we can see in retrospect why Heidegger braced himself against the terminology which Husserl still used. Gadamer recalls[5] that Heidegger made his Aristotle strong in his very opposition to Aristotle; but perhaps Heidegger was so close to Husserl, in contrast to his distance from Aristotle, that he made Husserl weak in order to free himself from the matrix in which Husserl was still to some extent entangled, the matrix of the language of acts and their objects, especially the objects which acts themselves become when they are reflected on by other acts.

These, then, are misinterpretations of which Heidegger is persistently guilty: (1) he reduces Plato to the theme of *eidos* or form; (2) he reduces creation to an apotheosis of making as realization out of possi-

---

Presence," *Research in Phenomenology* X (1982), pp. 85–112, and the German version, "Die ungegenwärtige Gegenwart. Anwesenheit und Abwesenheit in Husserls Analyse des Zeitbewußtseins," *Phänomenologische Forschungen* XIV (Freiburg/Munich: Karl Alber, 1983), pp. 16–57.

5. Gadamer, *Heideggers Wege*, pp. 31–32; *Gesammelte Werke* II, pp. 485–486; *Philosophische Lehrjahre* (Frankfurt am Main: Klostermann, 1977), p. 36.

bility; and (3) he reduces Husserl's last word to the self-objectification of transcendental subjectivity.

In addition to considering these three misinterpretations, I wish to add consideration of an issue of ambiguity and an issue of comparison and contrast:

(4) The ambiguity is in Heidegger's use of a crucial term, *Lichtung,* a term which is ambiguous because Heidegger uses it to mean both clearing up or bringing to light or making clear, on the one hand, and, on the other hand, he also and finally uses it to mean clearing away or lightening or opening up: *etwas lichten, etwas frei und offen machen.*[6]

(5) The comparison and contrast are between *Sein* for Heidegger and *esse* for Aquinas. Both terms are accurately and awkwardly translated "to be" as distinguished from "beings" and "being." (*Sein* is to *Seiendes* as *esse* is to *ens.*) Comparison is suggested because both Heidegger and Aquinas make strong claims for "to be" as distinguished from "beings" and "being." But contrast is suggested because Aquinas sets *esse* against a foil of essence, essence as the principle which receives *esse* and in receiving *esse* limits it, *esse* of itself "being," so to speak, unlimited. Heidegger, on the other hand, sets *Sein* as the interplay of presence/absence themselves (or itself) against the foil of that-which-is(-present/absent). Recall the triple: presencing of the presence of that-which-is(-present), a triple which distinguishes from one another pre*sencing* of the pre*sence* of the pre*sent.* And note that "pre*sencing*" is a participle with both verbal and nominal senses (cf. "Forgetting your umbrella is a nuisance."), "pre*sence*" is a noun, and "pre*sent*" is both an adjective and a noun. So we come to *grammatica speculativa,* the mirroring of the highest themes in grammatical forms.

EXPLANATORY NOTE ON *SEIN-DASEIN-SEIENDES* AND *ALĒTHEIA*

A.

In English we use the infinitive as a noun ("To err is human, to forgive divine."), but we do not use the definite article with the infinitive used as a noun; we do not say "*the* to-err" or "*the* to-be"; we have no

---

6. *Zur Sache des Denkens* (Tübingen: Max Niemeyer, 1969), p. 72; Martin Heidegger—Eugen Fink, *Heraklit* (Frankfurt am Main: Klostermann, 1970), p. 260; *Zur Frage nach der Bestimmung der Sache des Denkens* (St. Gallen: Erker, 1984), p. 17. In these three late texts (made public between 1964 and 1966) Heidegger is emphatic about the difference between *Lichtung* and light in the sense of bright-dark. *Lichtung* is *Gewährnis des*

articular infinitive. German, however, can use the neuter definite article (*das*) with the infinitive, which is then capitalized because it is used as a noun (all German nouns are capitalized). The German infinitive *sein* means "to be." Using it as a noun, capitalized, and with the neuter definite article, gives the form *das Sein:* "the to-be."

The present participle of *sein*, which is the infinitive of the verb "to be," is in its verbal or adjectival form *seiend* and in its neuter singular nominal form *Seiendes* or, with the neuter definite article, *das Seiende*. As the nominal form, it is capitalized. For Heidegger it means "being(s) as distinguished from 'the to-be' or from *das Sein*." The translation of the title of Heidegger's book *Sein und Zeit* as *Being and Time* blurs this distinction.

da is an adverb meaning the one root-meaning common to both "here" and "there." Using it as a prefix with the infinitive *sein* and taking the compound as a noun, and so capitalizing it, gives the form *Dasein*, which means something like "the availability (in withdrawnness) of 'to-be' as such." *Dasein* is the central term of Heidegger's book *To Be and Time*, and it is wisely left untranslated.

The perfect passive participle of the infinitive *sein* is *gewesen*, a form related to an infinitive form of the verb "to be" which is no longer used: *wesan* or *wesen*. However, this old form of the infinitive "to be" still occurs in compounds: *anwesen, abwesen:* "to be present (to . . .)" and "to be absent (from . . .)" or "to be presenced (to . . .)" and "to be absenced (from . . .)."

The *-sens* root of the Latin forms *praesens, absens* derives from *sant,* the present participle of the Sanskrit verb "to be," *as. prae* means "in front (of)"; the idiom *prae se ferre* means "to show, exhibit, discover, manifest." *ab* means "away (from)."

Dasein can thus be translated as something like "the availability (in withdrawnness) of the interplay of presence to . . . / absence from . . ." or "the availability (in withdrawnness) of the interplay of (to be) available to . . . / (to be) withdrawn from . . ."

In summary form:

sein:	to be
da:	here/there
Dasein:	to be available(here)/withdrawn (there)

Freien für Anwesen und Verweilen von Anwesendem and *das Offene für alles An- und Abwesende:* the granting of the space free and open for the interplay of presencing/absencing and the presenced/the absenced. Cf. *Sein und Zeit*, 14. Auflage, p. 133 (a, b, c: p. 442), pp. 350–351. See note 13 below.

wesen:	to be
an/ab:	to/from
anwesen/abwesen:	to be (present) to/(absent) from
sens:	being
prae/ab:	in front of/away from
praesens/absens:	being in front of/away from

Presence/absence taken as such or *das Sein* is to be distinguished from that-which-is(-present/absent) or from *das Seiende.* Heidegger calls this difference "the ontological difference." This difference is formulated in §2 of *To Be and Time:* "The to-be of being(s) 'is' not itself a being."[7]

For Heidegger the ". . ." of the "to . . . / from . . ." of "presence to . . . / absence from . . ." is a reversal away from subjectivity without being thereby a reversal toward objectivity. *Das Sein* appropriates (as) *Dasein* or avails itself (*braucht:* "needs"/"uses") of or through *Dasein.* *Das Sein* needs or uses a being among beings, the being to whom and from whom beings-which-are are manifest and hidden. Presence/absence brings about the *who,* so to speak, for its *to* whom/*from* whom. Only because *das Sein* "is" the interplay of presence/absence can there "be" human beings who can represent things to themselves and manipulate things for themselves in the derivative and reduced senses of *logos* and *technē.*

B.

alētheia is a Greek compound with three elements.

As the center part of the compound, *lēthē* means something like "forgotten, covered (over), concealed, veiled, inevident, hidden, obscure."

With a prefix *a-* for "not" and a suffix *-ia* for "-ness" or "-th" or "-ty," *lēthē* is the root of the word *alētheia,* "truth" or "verity" understood as "*un*coveredness, *un*concealedness, *un*hiddenness." If *lēthē* is thought of as the *un*articulated and the *in*evident, then, through a double reversal, *alētheia,* as the *not-un-*articulated and the *not-in-*evident, would be the root of the articulation and the evidencing in *logos:* truth and "logic" somehow go together.

EPIGRAPH

"*Logos* und *technē* aber sind, ganz weit genommen, diejenigen Verhaltungen, in denen sich das Seiende überhaupt zunächst offenbart,

---

7. See p. 195 and pp. 248–252 of Volume 26 of the Complete Edition.

so zwar, daß in diesem Horizont die Idee des Seins zunächst sich aus-
bildet." Complete Edition, Volume 26 (Course Lectures given in the
Summer Semester of 1928, Marburg), p. 146.

"But *logos* and *technē*, taken in the widest sense, are those involve-
ments in which being(s) as such first come(s) to light, so that it is within
this horizon that the idea of to-be itself is first formed."

TWO SUMMARIES

A. *logos*

Summary of Course Lectures given in the Winter Semester of
1925/6, Marburg; §11-§12-§13-§14 in the context of §10, Volume 21,
Complete Edition.

According to Heidegger's 1925/6 lectures, the primary synthesis is
the unthematic synthesis of something together with whatever we
take it *as* (being) *for*. Concern is the context of this primary synthesis,
the synthesis called the interpretative *as*. This primary unthematic
synthesis can, through a shift to a secondary concern, be suppressed
and replaced by the thematic predicative synthesis: saying something
as (being) a characteristic *of* something: S is articulated as *being* P; P is
said to be *true* of S. When this synthesis of predication is itself evidenced or verified, then there is a third synthesis, a synthesis of merely
saying P to be true of S ("empty intention") together with indeed *seeing*
P to be true of S ("filling intention"). When in turn and finally this
synthesis, the synthesis of evidence or verification, is itself thematized
and evidenced, then we focus on the *is* or *to be* itself as *being-truth* or
on *being as truthing* (cf. Husserl, *Logical Investigations* VI, §36–§39).

B. *technē*

Summary of Courses Lectures given in the Summer Semester of
1927, Marburg; §10-§11-§12 in the context of §9(b)(c), Volume 24,
Complete Edition.

According to Heidegger's 1927 lectures, the genealogy of existence
as different from essence is the achievedness of the finished product
insofar as the product is brought to a stand over against the producer
and over against the producer's "mere idea" of the product to be
produced: *existentia* is understood as *extra causam stare*. As so achieved,
the product is there in the context of primary concern, there to be
used, and it is brought about out of material which has not been
produced, out of nature as the limit of production. What is placed or
set up as standing there over against for use can then, through a shift

to a secondary concern, the theoretical concern, be taken as something there for contemplation to gaze on as *being true*.

PART I

Heidegger uses Husserl (especially *Logical Investigations* VI, §36–§39) for an exposition of Aristotle's analysis of *logos* (especially in *Metaphysics* Book IX, Chapter 10): declaration is both characterization (or predicational synthesis) and verification (or evidential synthesis). Heidegger then criticizes Aristotle's analysis of *logos* for having suppressed the roots of declaration in use, use flowing from concern. Gazing is secondary to using. Heidegger shows the roots of *logos* in *technē*, that is, in *technē* as producing products to be used. The predicative truth of something characterized as being *so* is secondary to and rooted in the prepredicative good of something taken as being useful *for*.

Heidegger also criticizes an understanding of the articulation of being into a difference between essence and existence in the context of creation *ex nihilo* by reducing that articulation back to roots in Aristotle's analysis of *technē*, that is, in *technē* as producing products by bringing them to a stand over against the producer. Heidegger suppresses the importance of creation *ex nihilo* by assimilating it to producing understood as bringing to be the real out of the possible, producing understood as translation of an essence from the status of possibility to the status or stand of reality. Heidegger suppresses creation *ex nihilo*, as contrasted with making *ex possibili*, as a context for understanding the articulation of being into essence and existence. Creation is reduced to *making* "ideas" or possible beings into "real" beings, to *making* "real" beings out of the material of possible beings or out of "ideas."

Heidegger also suppresses the context of Aristotle's analysis of *technē*, that is, Heidegger suppresses nature and contemplation. More precisely, he suppresses nature as *more* than just the limit of production, that out of which products are produced. He suppresses nature as being for contemplation, and he suppresses nature as suspended (1072b13–14) from that contemplation which is *best* because it is unity without articulation and presence without absence: *noēsis* beyond *logos*. (Heidegger analyzes *Metaphysics* Theta 10 in §9 of Volume 31 of the Complete Edition.)

In *To Be and Time* Heidegger introduces a non-Aristotelian context for his analysis of *technē*: death as the limit of presencing out of absence. Each one's death cannot be presenced for each one out of its absence, but each one is always already in anticipation his necessarily still absent death. Death is the limit of *Dasein, Dasein* which is concern (*Sorge*), oscillating between presence and absence.[8] Concern, in turn, is the context of use, use which is the context of produced products, which are brought to a stand over against the producer.

These three criticisms, namely,

(1) the criticism of *logos* because *logos* obscures our primary access to the world through use flowing from concern;

(2) the criticism of creation as an apotheosis of making;

(3) the criticism of *noēsis* as unity without articulation and presence without absence;

and these three suppressions, namely,

(4) the suppression of the roots of *logos* in *technē*, a suppression which Heidegger criticizes [(4) corresponds to (1)];

(5) Heidegger's own suppression of creation *ex nihilo*, in favor of making *ex possibili*, as a context for understanding the articulation of being into essence and existence, a suppression of creation *ex nihilo* by reducing it to roots in *technē*, to an apotheosis of making [(5) corresponds to (2)];

(6) Heidegger's own suppression of nature *for* contemplation and of nature in the highest sense *as* contemplation as contexts for *logos* and *technē* [(6) corresponds to (3)];

—all these criticisms and suppressions are placed by Heidegger in the service of an understanding of *Sein* and *alētheia*, an understanding which parallels both Husserl's treatment of empty intentions and of retention (paralleled by *lēthē* in Heidegger) and Husserl's treatment of transcendental subjectivity at its core, "the appearance of the flow to itself" or so-called "inner time-consciousness" (paralleled by *Sein* in Heidegger). Heidegger's understanding of *Sein* and *alētheia* can be formulated as the presencing/absencing (taken as such) *of* the presence/absence (taken as such) *of* the present/absent, that is, of that-which-is(-present/absent). What is the sense of this triple: the presencing *of* the presence *of* the present?

The white horse is not yet here; the white horse is still absent.

The white horse appears on the scene; the white horse, which was at first absent, although expected, is now present.

8. This oscillation is the *formal* ontological structure of *phronēsis*, spanning *hexis* and the possible, with the agent as *archē* "between" them; see Aristotle, *Nicomachean Ethics*, 1140b27–30. Gadamer confirms the importance of Heidegger's analysis of *phronēsis* in the 1920s. See note 5 above.

The presence of the white horse is to be distinguished from the white horse itself, which is present, because the same white horse which is present was absent too, and its presence is not its absence. So the absence too of the white horse is to be distinguished from the white horse itself, which is now present after first having been absent.

The same white horse can be both present and absent, and presence and absence are not each other. Neither the presence alone of the white horse nor the absence alone of the white horse can be the same as the white horse itself. And both together, united in their difference, are not the white horse either; the white horse is not the same as its presence/absence. But neither is the white horse without its presence/absence, just as they are not without it. What would presence or absence be without the presence of . . . and the absence of . . . ? And what would a being be without presence/absence? The presence/absence of the white horse, to be the being the white horse, is not on the same line as the white of the white horse or as the horse of the white horse. Yet the white and the horse are that-which-*is*(-present/absent). And if to be the being the white horse absorbed or exhausted "to be," then there could not be the being a red rose as well as the being a white horse. But can we ever take "to be" *only* as "to be" and *not* as "the to-be" *of* being(s),[9] *of* white horses and red roses?

We in our analysis have just been presencing for ourselves the presence itself and taken as such of the white horse, which is present. Soon this presencing of the presence of the white horse will itself be absenced, forgotten, even though the white horse itself may still be present. We will forget to discriminate the white horse present from its presence itself, a presence which we in our analysis have just been presencing because we were taken by the difference between presence and that which is present.

We in our analysis have been engaged in an act or an achieving, a philosophical act, which can be initiated and stopped and which can be forgotten and remembered (and controverted). But the primal presencing with absencings, the primal showing together with retention and protention, cannot be gained or lost by us, cannot be begun or ended by us. Inexorably and gratuitously it presences and absences the whole network of presencing and absencing *acts* or achievings and their presenced and absenced *objects* or themes, and out of it comes about what we call "I" as the center of responsibility which initiates and as the recipient of objectifications which are displayed. We cannot ⁻

9. For a time Heidegger used an old spelling, *Seyn*, for "to be" only as "to be." Heidegger's *Seyn* and Aquinas's *esse commune* are *in this sense* similar: both mean "to be" only as "to be" and as distinguished but not separated from "the to-be" *of* being(s).

represent or manipulate the bringing about of us, we who can represent or manipulate beings only because we are caught up in the web woven by the interplay of primal presencing/absencing happily beyond our control.

In 1909/11 (according to Bernet's dating of crucial manuscripts, revising Boehm's dating) Husserl, in thinking about what he called "inner time-consciousness," clarified a distinction between acts or achievements of presencing (for example, acts of seeing the white horse and acts of remembering having seen the white horse), on the one hand, and, on the other hand, a flowing-away-and-gathering-together which is the presencing/absencing *of* those very acts or achievements of presencing, but *not* in the same space as they. Husserl saw that this flowing-and-gathering is *not* in the same space as acts or achievements of seeing and of remembering having seen the white horse. This space of acts of seeing the white horse and of remembering having seen the white horse is the space where reflexivity takes place, the space where I can think myself having thought. Even *my act* (as an owned achieving), my *philosophical* act of presencing the presence itself of the white horse is within this space open to reflexivity. But the flowing-and-gathering itself, the primal interplay of the presencings and absencings *of* all presencing *acts* (precisely as having this genitive "*of . . . acts*," it is called by Husserl *Querintentionalität*), even *of* my philosophical *act* of presencing presence itself, this flowing-and-gathering itself is a space different from and beyond the whole space where reflexivity takes place. It is beyond the *cogitatum-cogitatio-ego cogitans* and the *ego cogito me cogitantem cogitatum*, that is, beyond the subject-object distinction and beyond the objectification of subjectivity to itself. For Husserl the flowing-and-gathering, primal distention and interplay, primal presencing absencing as retention and protention, and thus presencing itself presenced as absénted in retention and absent in protention, all this is beyond and different from presenced and presencing *acts,* whether perceptual, memorial, or philosophical.[10]

It is true that Husserl spoke of this space of flowing-and-gathering using terms of the language of psychology and of transcendental subjectivity as the unifying pole of acts achieving the presentation of objects as well as of acts achieving objectifying presentation of those acts which achieve the presentation of objects. But then Heidegger too

---

10. The distinction between the philosophical act of presencing the presence of that-which-is(-present) and the primal interplay of presencing/absencing corresponds roughly to the distinction Heidegger makes between *Seinsverständnis* and *Seinsgeschehnis* in "Zur Kritik der Vorlesung," *Einführung in die Metaphysik,* Volume 40 of the Complete Edition, p. 219.

had to struggle to free a language of "to be" itself and taken as such from the language used to speak about beings. Both Husserl and Heidegger struggled to free the *significatum* from the inappropriate *modus significandi*. Heidegger freed himself from the language of what he calls "metaphysics," which according to Heidegger understands "to be" only as "*of* beings" and not by itself and taken as such, but he freed himself from this language by recapitulating it. Perhaps Husserl freed himself less from the language of reflexivity, the language of the objectification of subjectivity to itself. But Heidegger paid a heavy price for his greater freedom from an inappropriate language: Heidegger's twists or tropes of his base language sometimes carry him to the very edge of that communication without which there is no language at all.

PART II

Heidegger later transposes the analysis of *logos* into a context of *Sein* and *alētheia* in his interpretation of *logos* in Heraclitus[11] as the collectedness in which presence/absence comes about, and he later transposes the analysis of *technē* into the context of *Sein* and *alētheia* in his interpretation of technology (*Technik*) in terms of *Ge-stell:* the produced is brought forth and set up, set up in being clear or in standing forth as being manifest. The apotheosis of *making* products leads by way of *making clear* to an obscuring of nature by representation and manipulation.

In these interpretations of Heraclitus and of technology, Heraclitus early and technology late, linked by the theme of making clear or bringing to manifestness, Heidegger reverses his early suppression of nature and contemplation as the context of *logos* and *technē* by recovering *logos* and *technē* in the context of nature and contemplation, themselves now recovered in the light of *Sein* and *alētheia*.

Heidegger now understands nature as the interplay of presence/absence or of manifestation/hiddenness, and he understands contemplation as taking or accepting both the coming about of the difference (*Austrag*) in the interplay itself and the difference between the interplay and that which it needs/uses: that-which-*is* as now standing out as made clear to. . . .

Heidegger speaks of an obscuring of *Sein* (*Seinsvergessenheit*), an absencing of the interplay of presence/absence itself in favor of that-

11. See §8 of the course lectures of the Summer Semester of 1943 and §8 of the course lectures of the Summer Semester of 1944, both in Volume 55 of the Complete Edition. These last Freiburg lectures rejoin the early Marburg lectures by way of a reversal and recovery in a new context.

which-is(-present/absent). The presencing of presence/absence itself almost necessarily turns presence/absence itself into a that-which-is(-*now*-)(-present). The reversal of this necessity of turning presence into something present in the present, the reversal of this necessity of favoring that-which-is(-*now*-)(-present) over presence/absence itself, this reversal Heidegger calls "the other beginning."

The other beginning is a recapitulation of the first beginning, the beginning with Anaximander, Parmenides and Heraclitus. This other beginning is the recapitulation which comes at the end of what was begun by the first beginning. The first beginning lived in *physis* and *logos* and *alētheia* as the interplay of presence/absence or manifestness/hiddenness, and it also lived in the pull toward turning presence/absence or manifestness/hiddenness into a that-which-is (-present/absent) or that-which-is (-manifest/hidden). The first beginning lived in the pull toward favoring making clear that-which-is. The first beginning ended with technology. The other beginning recapitulates that first beginning with a reversal favoring the presencing of the interplay of presence/absence or manifestness/hiddenness itself as distinguished from its fall into that-which-is(-present or -manifest).

The first beginning lived in the manifestness of that-which-is(-manifest), but that manifestness itself and as such remained withdrawn in obscurity. The other beginning overcomes that withdrawnness into obscurity and brings the manifestness itself of that-which-is(-manifest) to clarity or manifestation out of obscurity. *And it tries to do this without falling under the sway of the necessity to turn this manifested manifestness itself into another something among others which has now been made clear to. . . .*

PART III

Heidegger later moves beyond his theme of *Sein* and *alētheia* toward what he calls *Lichtung*, which finally means not so much a clearing up out of obscurity or a clarification or a lighting up as rather a clearing away or a lightening up, leaving room or space beyond the interplay of presencing/absencing. The theme of *Lichtung* goes beyond both Aristotle and Husserl. It goes beyond Heidegger's recapitulation and deconstruction of Aristotle's *logos* and *technē* and beyond Husserl's so-called "inner time-consciousness." But it does not go as far as an understanding of the articulation of being into essence and existence in the context of creation, the gift of *esse ex nihilo*.

Although *Lichtung* is beyond the interplay of presencing/absencing, it is almost impossible to speak of it except in terms of absencing (*Abwesen*), withdrawal (*Entzug*), reserve (*Vorenthalt*), hiddenness (*lēthē*).

Like Husserl before him, Heidegger has to use inappropriate language to speak about something which is strange (*atopon*) because it is so simple. He has to borrow language which is appropriate to what is more familiar because it is less simple. This expropriated and troped language strains to bring to speech what is beyond its resources.

Before the move beyond the interplay of presencing/absencing into *Lichtung* as clearing away, there is a shift of accent within that interplay itself: truthing or clearing up out of obscurity or presencing out of absence is not just a working *against* absence or withdrawal or obscurity. Rather it is just as much *letting* obscurity and withdrawal and absence *be* as that out of which clarity and availability and presence come forth: hiding (*Verbergung*) is protecting (*Bergung*), protecting from the excessive demand for making clear, the demand for exhaustive clarity, a demand which pushes toward manipulation of the represented.

CONCLUSION

The *subsistens* of Aquinas's creator God, *esse subsistens*, means, in contrast to *esse commune,* in contrast to *esse completum* ("full") *et simplex sed non subsistens* (*De potentia Dei* I, 1), self-sufficiency, non-receivability in an other. *esse commune*, in contrast to *esse subsistens*, is *componendum alteri:* it is to be received in an other, in an essence as other to *esse*. Although *esse* as *esse commune* is considered or taken without that other with which it is to be composed, nevertheless it has a unity not reducible to the unity owed merely to considering it without that other with which it is composed. For Aquinas the foil to *esse* is the limiting essence with which the *esse* is composed, such that the compound, the *ens* as the unity of *esse* and essence, has subsistence or self-sufficiency, which neither *esse* nor essence can enjoy alone. For Heidegger, on the other hand, the foil to *Sein* as the interplay of presence/absence itself is that-which-is(-present/absent): the to-be is the to-be *of* beings.

Although Heidegger's *Sein* as the interplay of presence/absence is prior to its "to . . . / from . . . ," it is nevertheless bound back into the "to . . . / from . . . ." In this way too Heidegger's *Sein*, like Aquinas's *esse*, is *componendum alteri*, to be together with an other. Just as Aquinas's *esse*, if it is not *subsistens*, needs or uses essence if there is to be *ens subsistens*, that is, if *esse* is to be "the to-be" *of* being(s), so Heidegger's interplay of presence/absence needs or uses (*braucht*) its dative of manifestation/hiddenness. It needs or uses its "manifest *to* . . . / hidden *from* . . ."; it needs or uses a being among beings, the being to whom and from whom beings-which-are are manifest and hidden. And although Heidegger exhorts us to think "the to-be," *das Sein,* by taking it as itself and not only as "the to-be" *of* being(s), and although this genitive, "*of* being(s)," can be suppressed or occluded, so to speak, in order to focus on "the to-be" itself and taken as such, yet the "*of* being(s)" cannot be done away with, any more than for Aquinas the essence *in* which created *esse* is received (in order that there be beings) or *with* which it is composed and *by* which it is limited can be done away with or reduced to nothing at all.

Heidegger takes presence/absence as "the to-be" itself and as such of beings, "the to-be" to which we, as datives of manifestation and as coming to represent and to manipulate beings, are subsidiary, although never superfluous. Heidegger in the end goes beyond *Sein* as the interplay of presence/absence. And he goes beyond the presencing/absencing itself of this presence/absence of that-which-is(-present/absent). But of this beyond, this *Lichtung,* this clearing away beyond all presencing/absencing, he can only say that it is the context for the interplay of presencing/absencing, a context both cleared of that interplay and yet readable only as translated into the text of that interplay, a translation which always reduces and thus traduces. This context beyond the interplay, this context of which we almost have to be silent or of which we can speak only inappropriately or in bad translation, is the proper sense of *Lichtung,* a sense reached only through and beyond, first, distinguishing presencing/absencing from the presence/absence which is presenced/absenced, and, second, understanding absencing as more a protection (*Bergung*) of presencing, a protection protecting presencing from the tendency to separate itself off from the absencing over which its solitary splendor would then triumph. Absencing is more a protection of presencing than an obstacle which presencing fights against in order to overcome it by translating it into nothing but presence.

Lichtung beyond all interplay of presencing/absencing, even beyond the interplay in which absencing protects presencing, this proper sense of *Lichtung* cannot itself "be," and above all it cannot "be" as closed to *esse subsistens,* but thereof Heidegger is silent.

It seems that we have come to the end without having spoken about a central theme in the later Heidegger: *Ereignis.*[12] However, "itself, taken as such and distinguished from . . . ; proper, appropriate" are words which have been often used, and they are the meaning of the

---

12. See the account of the 1962 seminar on the 1962 lecture "Time and To Be" (*Zur Sache des Denkens,* pp. 27–60).

DIAGRAMS

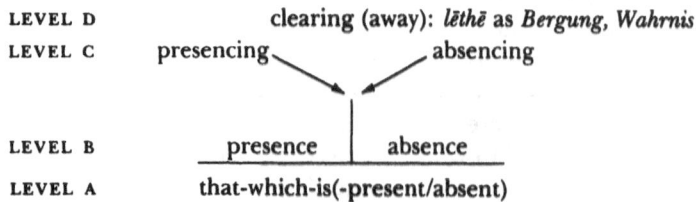

LEVEL D clearing (away): *lēthē* as *Bergung, Wahrnis*
LEVEL C presencing absencing

LEVEL B presence | absence
LEVEL A that-which-is(-present/absent)

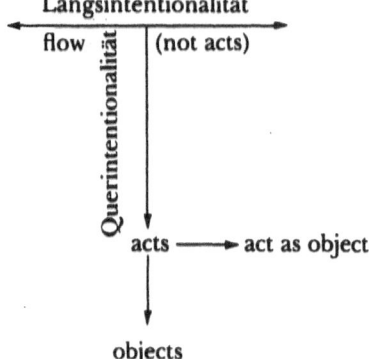

Längsintentionalität
flow (not acts)

Querintentionalität

acts ⟶ act as object

objects

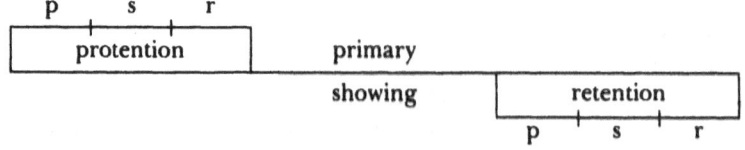

p   s   r
protention   primary
                    showing   retention
                              p   s   r

word *eigen*,[13] a word which Heidegger hears in *Ereignis*. So in the end saying "clearing away the inappropriate" (*Lichtung*) says "letting come into its own" (*Ereignis*).

13. *eigen* as in *eigens, eignen, eigentlich, eigentümlich. Ereignis* has the same root as *Auge*, "eye." Just as *Lichtung* has the ambiguity *Licht/leicht (leukós/elakús)*, so *Ereignis* has for Heidegger the ambiguity *Auge/eigen*. As "bright" is to "eye," so "cleared away" is to "appropriate." Heidegger says in the essay "Die Kehre": *"Ereignis ist eignende Eräugnis."* See *Die Technik und die Kehre* (Pfullingen: Neske, 1962), p. 44.

The "four further seminars" referred to in the first paragraph of the Preface are published as *Vier Seminare* (Frankfurt am Main: Klostermann, 1977).

§7(a) of the Appendix to Volume 45 (Freiburg Course Lectures of the Winter Semester 1937/38), pp. 209–211, moves within the whole complex of (1) the interplay of (a) presencing/absencing of (b) the presenced/the absenced; (2) withdrawal (*Entzug*) as protection (*Bergung*); and (3) *Lichtung* as both (a) bound into brightness (*Helle*) and (b) openness for the interplay of manifesting/hiding and the manifest/the hidden.

In 1937/38 (Vol. 45, p. 209) Heidegger says: "Wir sprechen von einer Waldlichtung, einer freien, hellen Stelle." In the passages referred to above in note 6, passages made public almost thirty years later, he says: "Das Lichte im Sinne des Freien und Offenen hat weder sprachlich noch in der Sache etwas mit dem Adjektivum 'licht' gemeinsam, das 'hell' bedeutet." "Haben Lichtung und Licht überhaupt etwas miteinander zu tun? Offenbar nicht." "Das Lichte in der Bedeutung des Hellen und das Lichte der Lichtung sind nicht nur in der Sache, sondern auch im Wort verschieden."

See also in the Complete Edition: Vol. 29/30, §67, pp. 405–406, and §76, pp. 530–531; Vol. 33, §14(b) and §20, pp. 201–203, 206.

Aquinas distinguishes *esse divinum, cui additio non fit et non fieri potest* from *esse commune, cui additio non fit sed fieri potest.* Not only is the *additio* (= *coarctatio*: limitation by essence) possible, it is necessary if there be beings. See *Summa theologiae* I 3, 4, ad 1, and *De potentia Dei* I 2, and 6.

Husserl's *Ideas* and the Natural Concept of the World

JOHN SCANLON

"What is the stars, Joxer? . . .
What is the stars?"

Sean O'Casey
Juno and the Paycock

APPROACHES TO THE QUESTION

The natural concept of the world plays a pivotal role in Husserl's overall view of the enterprise of phenomenological philosophy. Pursued in one direction, an investigation of the sense of the natural concept of the world is meant to provide a philosophically neutral ground from which to explore the experiential basis for diverse experiential sciences. Within that orientation, the study of the natural concept of the world develops as a general ontology of the experiential world and discloses both universal eidetic structures of the experiential world as such and specific eidetic structures of materially differentiated regions of the experiential world. The clearest example of such a study is probably the one contained in Husserl's *Phenomenological Psychology*.[1] The particular interest there lies in differentiating the field appropriate to a phenomenological psychology. Hence, the natural concept of the world is analyzed only to the extent required to show how the region of psychic life can be delimited from within the scope of the experiential world.

The advantage of this approach to the natural concept of the world is its relative ease of access. The natural concept of the world is tacitly identified with the concept of the pre-theoretical, experiential world. And since the experiential world, from this perspective, is explored as

1. Edmund Husserl, *Phenomenological Psychology: Lectures, Summer Session, 1925*, translated by John Scanlon (The Hague: Nijhoff, 1977).

fundamental to all senseful experiential sciences, the question of the origin of diverse sciences reaches back only to the world as found in experience. Within that context, no questions arise concerning the origin of the sense of the experiential world itself, which is simply to be taken as given. And the direction to pursue in filling in the natural concept of the world seems at least to be sufficiently predelineated by the contrast between the various possible domains of possible experiential sciences on the one hand and the all-encompassing world of experience on the other. Whatever pertains to experience itself taken in its all-encompassing scope belongs to the natural concept of the world.

Pursued in the opposite direction, as in *Ideas I*,[2] the analysis of the sense of the natural concept of the world is only a preliminary stage in a movement which does not rest with the experiential world but attempts to disclose its origin or grounds of sense in a dimension of being which is not itself included within the experiential world and which accordingly is not accessible to the pervasive attitude[3] which pertains distinctively to the natural concept of the world. This approach, though more familiar to students of Husserl's phenomenology, is clearly much more difficult to follow through than the previous one. And since this approach eventually challenges the claim to comprehensiveness of a concept which is taken at first, provisionally, as all-encompassing,[4] the inherent difficulties of that movement tend to appear utterly paradoxical.

To mention one apparent paradox in Husserl's presentation of that issue in *Ideas I*, the transcendental phenomenological attitude has to be understood as founded upon the natural attitude, as a modification of the natural attitude.[5] Hence, one must be able to understand the natural attitude first in order to understand just what is being modified and how that modification transforms the original, natural,

2. Edmund Husserl, *Ideas Pertaining to a Pure Phenomenology and to a Phenomenological Philosophy. First Book: General Introduction to a Pure Phenomenology*, trans. F. Kersten (The Hague: Nijhoff, 1982).

3. The explicit connection of the natural attitude with the natural concept of the world is made in Husserl's lectures, "Grundprobleme der Phänomenologie," Winter Semester 1910/11. Chapter 1 of those lectures is entitled "Die natürliche Einstellung und der natürliche Weltbegriff." The lectures have been published in Edmund Husserl, *Zur Phänomenologie der Intersubjektivität. Erster Teil: 1905–20*, ed. Iso Kern (The Hague: Nijhoff, 1973), pp. 111–94.

4. Natural cognition begins with experience and remains *within* experience. In the theoretical attitude which we call the *"natural" [theoretical attitude]* the collective horizon is therefore designated with *one* word: It is the *world* . . . and, as long as it is the exclusively dominant [theoretical attitude], the concepts 'true being,' 'actual being,' that is, real being and—since everything real joins together to make up the unity of the world—'being in the world' coincide." *Ideas I*, p. 5.

5. *Ibid.*, p. 57.

attitude. But when one is told to begin by reflecting upon the world of natural life, the world of the natural attitude, one might well look in perplexity for some contrast to direct one's understanding: natural as opposed to what? Are we to think, perhaps, of natural life in so-called primitive societies as opposed to the unnatural life of more developed technological civilizations?[6] Should we consider, for example, life in a village of straw huts as natural, but not life on Three Mile Island? Life on a sailboat made of reeds, but not life on a nuclear submarine?

We learn, eventually, that all such contrasts are irrelevant because in each case both poles of the opposition belong equally within the world of the natural attitude, fall within the scope of the natural concept of the world. However, we can know that and show that only by contrasting the natural attitude, in its at first apparently all-encompassing scope, with the transcendental attitude. But that contrast is not available from the beginning, since the clarification of the transcendental attitude requires as its prior condition a clarification of the natural attitude itself, from which it originates as its modification. How can one be at all clear as to one's beginning stance, if the natural attitude, as basic to the natural concept of the world, can be fully clarified only in contrast to the transcendental attitude, which in turn can be understood only with reference to the natural attitude which it modifies?

THE PRECEDENT IN AVENARIUS' TREATMENT OF THE NATURAL CONCEPT OF THE WORLD

The facility and directness with which Husserl introduces his analysis of the natural attitude (as a transitional step toward a disclosure of the transcendental attitude) suggests that the German philosophical reader of 1913 would already be familiar with the "natural concept of the world," and would readily understand the concept of "the natural attitude" in reference to it. By contrast, the situation has so changed that today's readers might readily credit Husserl with an original move in thus introducing the concept of "the natural attitude" as a first step toward fundamental philosophical considerations. In that context, it would be easy to think that the only philosophical function exercised by the natural attitude is that of an obstacle to be overcome on the way to the genuinely philosophical, transcendental attitude. Since that historically naive assumption provides no ready escape from the appar-

---

6. That such a line of questioning is readily associated with this concept is suggested, e.g., by Heidegger's explicit rejection thereof in his reference to the "Natural Conception of the World." See Martin Heidegger, *Being and Time*, trans. John Macquarrie and Edward Robinson (New York: Harper and Row), p. 76.

ent paradox mentioned above, it may be helpful to reconstruct, at least partially, the direct source of the concept that Husserl appeals to. Fortunately, Husserl has identified that source explicitly (in posthumously published writings and in unpublished manuscripts) as Avenarius' doctrine of the natural concept of the world.[7] Thus, incidentally, the empirio-criticism of Avenarius[8]—an otherwise all-but-forgotten episode in the history of philosophy[9]—is one vital link between the multifaceted phenomenology of Husserl and that richly diversified source of problems and inspirations all too loosely gathered under the vague title, "the philosophical tradition."

Avenarius' discussion of the natural concept of the world involves three main questions: what is involved in that concept, how philosophy has strayed from it, and how it can be restored.[10]

The natural concept of the world, on Avenarius' account, is that general concept we all have about the world in its entirety before any exposure to philosophy and its possible deviations from that concept. Philosophy asks, "What is everything?" But, before philosophizing, we have all formed a general concept of the world, based on experience. That concept is not logically clear and precise; it is merged with a living intuition rather than distinctly articulated. Assuming that such a concept is natural, each of us can recall and articulate the rudiments of that concept as we held it before we began to philosophize.

It takes the experienced world to be whatever is posited as found. Basically, I find myself with all my thoughts and feelings in the midst of an environment. That environment contains many components, among them other human beings. They stand out from the rest of my environment because, besides acting upon and being affected by other component parts of my environment, they also, like me, express by certain distinctive sounds and movements their purposes, needs, desires, reasons, and the like.

Intrinsic to the natural concept of the world is the unshaken belief that all the component parts of my environment exist and develop,

---

7. "My original formulation of the question [was] suggested by Avenarius' *positivistic doctrine of the natural concept of the world:* the scientific description of the world purely as world of experience. . . ." Husserl, Ms. A VII 20, 47a.

8. "Whatever position one may take regarding the particular theories of this 'empirio-criticism,' an ingenious instinct is displayed in its beginning with the natural concept of the world." Husserl, Ms. K III 27, 2b.

9. Familiar, however, to students of Lenin's works as the object of his scathing critique: V. I. Lenin, *Materialism and Empirio-Criticism: Critical Comments on a Reactionary Philosophy* (Moscow: Foreign Press Publishing House, 1952).

10. The following exposition is based on Richard Avenarius, *Der menschliche Weltbegriff*, Third Ed. (Leipzig: Reisland, 1912).

change or remain constant, in interaction with one another, in some form of stable regularity, all independently of my observing them or not observing them, thinking about them or not, referring to them linguistically or not. The apple tree in my neighbor's yard, for example, was growing there when I moved into my house. And it goes through its regular seasonal changes year after year, regardless of whether or not I notice it, think about it, or mention it.

Modern philosophy, Avenarius notes, has strayed from the natural concept of the world. Instead of accepting what in the experience of natural life I find as an environment in which I find myself included, it interprets the world as included in me: "the world" being the general name for whatever is experienced, whatever is posited as found. According to the modern philosophical concept, whatever is experienced must be mere impressions and ideas: immediate data of consciousness (the subjective idealist version) or images in the brain (the skeptical materialist version).

According to Avenarius, various forms of psychosis might also lead to such a disruption of the natural concept of the world, but the disruption which interests him is the result of prevalent trends in modern philosophy. Consequently, his strategy is to treat the dominant position of modern philosophy as, in effect, the product of an "unconscious"[11] delusional process and to present a sort of proto-psychoanalytic therapy, by which the unconscious motivations of the delusion can become consciously recognized and consciously rejected as delusional. Further, he treats this deviation from the natural concept of the world not as a privately held belief but as a historically conditioned conception embedded in philosophical language. "Introjection," the source of the deviation, has taken place in our distant past history,[12] was unconscious in its origin, and has been perpetuated in our common philosophical language.[13] Liberation from introjection— the restoration of the natural concept of the world—requires a regression into our archaic past, a plausible account of the unconscious motivation underlying introjection, and the rigorous excision from our philosophical language of all traces of the resulting delusion.

Introjection has taken various specific forms under various specific

---

11. Avenarius characterizes the disruptive process that he calls "introjection" as taking place *"unwissentlich, unwillentlich, und unterschiedslos,"* p. 27.

12. "Wir beginnen mit derjenigen niederen Stufe der Kultur, die man als ihre Anfänge bezeichnet hat," p. 32. . . . "Die Doppelseitigkeit des Individuums T, zu welcher die Introjektion führt, ist durch die Doppelerfahrung der niederen Kultur zum Doppelindividuum geworden," p. 34.

13. P. 26.

motivations. But generally it is an unconscious thought process that, minimally, attributes to an individual human being a mind or soul that contains images or ideas as an internal duplicate of external reality—thus doubling the one world of the natural concept into an external world and an internal world—and at its most advanced stage introjects the entire world itself into my consciousness or into my brain—thus reversing entirely the natural concept of the world.

Avenarius' clarification of the natural concept of the world involves a clarification of the character of the concept itself and a clarification of the world as represented by it. Further, his discussion is an illustration of a philosophical approach to a purportedly pre-philosophical concept.

The concept is characterized as: having been formed prior to philosophizing, based upon experience, accessible to memory, taking the experienced world to be whatever is posited as found, merged with a living intuition, and lacking logical clarity and precision.

Its particular content, what is actually posited as found in the world, is not stable but historically and culturally variable. Hence, each philosopher recounts his or her own contents of experience.[14] For example, at the stage of so-called primitive animism, spirits were found virtually everywhere, in rocks, streams, and fountains. Later, spirits were no longer found speaking from rocks and fountains. Such spirits were not to be found in the environment of a late nineteenth-century empirical philosopher, even before he began to philosophize.

As opposed to the variable contents of experience, the constant, invariant structure of experience inherent in the natural concept of the world is that of an environment: component parts are always structured in a "principle coordination" involving a central member and its opposite members.[15] This structure of principle coordination Avenarius sees as the root of the philosophical misconception which construes the central member of the coordination to be a mind or soul and constructs the notorious subject–object dichotomy. That construal he views as an introjective falsification of the natural coordination of component parts of the environment with the central nervous system of an organism in its environment. The component parts of the world, though otherwise variable, constantly include myself (or

14. Likewise, we find Husserl stipulating, "What that signifies we shall make clear in simple meditations which can best be carried out in the first person singular," *Ideas I*, p. 51. Note 2 on the same page specified further, "We do not stand now in an eidetic attitude; rather, let each say *I* for himself and state with me what he finds quite individually."

15. Avenarius, *op. cit.*, p. 149.

whoever is performing the reflective analysis) and others like me who, besides acting upon and being affected by other component parts of the environment, also express their purposes, reasons, wishes, etc., by certain distinctive movements and sounds.

The world of the natural concept is one world: the same for me and for other human beings, and containing within it myself and other human beings, myself with all my thoughts and feelings, others with all their thoughts and feelings, as component parts—each as the central member of a principle coordination in which others are also, along with other component parts, structured as opposite members.

The world of the natural concept is taken as existing in itself: its component parts come into being, develop variously, and sometimes pass out of existence, all independently of my observing them or thinking about them.

Some points of Avenarius' philosophical approach to the natural concept of the world are consequences of the character of that concept; others are contingent features of Avenarius' philosophical perspective. To begin with the former, the project is essentially a philosophical attempt to recover a pre-philosophical concept. Consequently, it involves an attempt to present a logical clarification of an already formed concept that would otherwise remain implicit, inarticulate, and vague. On that score, the apparent paradox raised earlier can be seen to be specious. Since the appeal to the natural concept of the world is part of a philosophical attempt to recover a pre-philosophical concept, we do not need to wait until the transcendental attitude is clarified in order to understand, by contrast, the natural attitude. Rather, we already have the natural concept of the world available to us. It has been formed automatically, as the very sense of our experience. That sense can be explicated. And it is understood as natural in opposition to all philosophical theory, especially to modern philosophy with its deviations from the natural concept.

However, the project does involve its own peculiar difficulties. Although the natural concept of the world in its pre-philosophical, inchoate state may well function as a vital safeguard against the lures of deviant philosophical theory, it can be of positive theoretical value only to the extent that it is made explicit, articulate, clear, and precise. And, of course, it does not clarify itself. The work of conceptual clarification is the contribution of the philosophical self-analyst. And what passes for mere logical clarification can incorporate basic theoretical prejudices. That point can be clearly illustrated in the case of Avenarius by contrasting his general description of the content of the natural concept of the world with his logical analysis of the same concept.

Avenarius describes the constant content of the natural concept of the world thus:

> I with all my thoughts and feelings found myself in the midst of an environment. This environment was composed of various component parts which stood in various relations of dependence to one another. To the environment belonged also fellow human beings with various assertions; and what they said was also usually in a relation of dependence to the environment. For the rest the fellow human beings spoke and acted like me: they answered my questions, as I did theirs; they sought after or avoided the various component parts of the environment; and they designated with words whatever they did or did not do and explained their reasons and purposes for their deeds and omissions. Everything as in my own case: and thus I thought nothing else but that fellow human beings were creatures like me—I myself a creature like them.[16]

The basic points of the foregoing description seem broad enough and innocuous enough to serve as a preliminary point of departure for a discussion as to whether philosophical theory ought to adjust itself to the natural concept of the world, efface itself before it, revise and correct it critically, abandon it, or accept it but clarify its unquestioned grounds.

However, Avenarius' next step is to introduce a logical distinction into that descriptive account. Avenarius claims that it is necessary to distinguish two unequal values mingled in the account: in formal-logical terms, an *experience* and a *hypothesis*. Strictly speaking, "the experience—the found—includes myself and my environment with its component parts (to which the fellow human beings also belong), and certain dependencies belonging to them."[17] The hypothesis, which goes beyond what is strictly experienced, involves the interpretation of certain movements and sounds made by fellow human beings as being assertions, as having sense; the hypothetical element of the natural concept of the world consists in assuming that such movements and sounds have "a not merely mechanical significance."[18] Avenarius recommends adopting that hypothesis, for various reasons. But it remains forever a mere hypothesis. What is strictly experienced, beyond my own thoughts and feelings, falls strictly within the scope of a mechanical system of interaction in which I am inserted as an organism in its environment.

Clearly, that evaluation of the different contents of the natural con-

16. *Ibid.*, pp. 4–5.
17. *Ibid.*, p. 7.
18. *Ibid.*, p. 9.

cept of the world is imposed upon it for theoretical reasons, and not simply derived from it. As described, experience in its natural functioning does not make that distinction. And the distinction can not be justified on purely formal-logical grounds: the description proposed was categorical throughout with no mixture of hypothetical statements. The basis for making such a distinction must lie in an unspoken theoretical decision as to what *can be experienced,* strictly speaking. And, for a reader who does not share that prior theoretical commitment, it stands out clearly as a form of naturalistic mechanism. Though it may be argued that we form some general ontological concept of the world prior to actively philosophizing, it does not follow that our clarification of that concept will remain philosophically neutral. Rather, the situation involves the inherent danger that in clarifying the natural concept of the world we may end up expressing directly or indirectly some fundamental philosophical position.

What Avenarius "restores" in the face of deviations favored by other philosophical positions is not merely a philosophically neutral, natural concept of the world, but his own philosophical interpretation of it. In proposing a cure for the delusions of subjective idealism and skeptical materialism, the therapeutic process never questions the unexpressed motivations for mechanistic naturalism. The cure, if accepted, would repress subjectivity so completely as to leave us with a world from which we are effectively alienated in favor of a mechanical process involving a principle coordination of a central nervous system with its environment as all that can be experienced, strictly speaking. The eeriest indication of that self-alienation lies in what Avenarius recommends in place of traditional reflection or psychological introspection: by opening up my skull and arranging mirrors properly, I can observe the functioning of my own central nervous system just as I could anyone else's.[19]

The return to Avenarius' treatment of the natural concept of the world seems desirable as a means of filling in the context for understanding Husserl's discussion of the natural attitude. That return serves to dispel the air of apparent paradox involved in interpreting the natural attitude before being able to contrast it with the transcendental attitude. However, Avenarius' procedure also highlighted some inherent difficulties and dangers in such an appeal to the natural concept of the world. Husserl, like Avenarius, wants to begin on grounds which precede philosophy and, even more generally, which precede all theory:

19. *Ibid.,* p. 20.

What we presented as a characterization of the givenness belonging to the natural attitude, and therefore as a characterization of that attitude itself, was a piece of pure description *prior to any "theory"*. In these investigations, we keep theories—here the word designates preconceived opinions of every sort—strictly at a distance.[20]

Avenarius' treatment of the natural concept of the world showed clearly the inherent risk of reading back into that concept unnoticed theoretical prejudices that have become so habitual as to appear natural to the philosopher who is appealing to that allegedly neutral concept. Avenarius' recourse to that concept was motivated by his disappointment with the prevailing philosophical deviations from it—his disappointment with the conceptions of the world represented by subjective idealism and materialistic skepticism. And his enterprise involved a form of therapy: a logical analysis of the natural concept of the world had to be supplemented with a persuasive account of the specious unconscious motivations that had led to the prevalent philosophical deviation from that natural concept of the world. Thus, implicitly, his position was that modern philosophy was, as it were, a neurosis to be cured by a peculiar form of philosophical analysis. The risk instantiated by Avenarius' approach is that the analysis will remain one-sided: self-analysis will be lacking or incomplete.

IDEAS I AND THE NATURAL ATTITUDE

Avenarius' example arouses suspicion. If it is, necessarily, a philosopher who appeals to the natural concept of the world and who makes distinctions and clarifications in its regard, the possibility of complete philosophical neutrality appears highly questionable. Without attempting to take up that general philosophical question here, we can look to Husserl's *Ideas* to discover whether his discussion of the natural concept of the world is similarly slanted.

Husserl, of course, does not end up in naturalism, mechanistic or otherwise. But it is possible to discern in *Ideas I* a movement by which he surpasses naturalism only in virtue of the transcendental reduction, in a way that seems to involve a virtual surrender of the world of the natural attitude itself to a naturalism that, though not philosophically ultimate, is apparently granted a position of accuracy with regard to the world of natural experience itself.

Husserl does not employ the same distinction as Avenarius does,

20. *Ideas I*, p. 56.

namely, between a description of the world of the natural attitude and a logical analysis of the concept involved. Nor does he employ the explicit language of naturalism. However, a shift in his treatment of the world of the natural attitude is clearly discernible in "The Considerations Fundamental to Phenomenology."[21] The preliminary descriptive passages include, as did Avenarius', other human beings as clearly part of the world, as communicating with me in various ways, shaking hands with me, expressing what they feel, think, and wish.[22] And Husserl's description goes beyond Avenarius' by explicitly taking note of the inclusion of use-objects, value-objects, and practical objects in the world of experience, found *with the same immediacy* as that with which mere things can be found.[23]

However, as the fundamental considerations proceed, that rich human concept of the world of the natural attitude, including persons and cultural objects as immediately given, gets attenuated to a web of material things displayed in space and time. Again and again, the demonstration focuses attention upon "the physical things" as given to perception. The purpose becomes to

> look for the ultimate source which feeds the general positing of the world effected by me in the natural attitude, the source which, therefore, makes it possible that I consciously find a factually existing world of physical things confronting me and that I ascribe to myself a body in that world and now am able to assign myself a place there.[24]

The quest for such a source exceeds and contradicts Avenarius' approach. But the *world of the natural attitude* itself, as Husserl's considerations proceed, becomes *the natural world*. Eventually, it is considered as a fundamentally material nature from which, apparently, subjectivity has been repressed as effectively as it was in the case of Avenarius: once again, the work of philosophical clarification seems to yield a world quite alien to the experiencing human being.

> To what extent, in the first place, is the *material world* something of an essentially different kind excluded from the *essentiality proper of mental processes?* And if that is true of the material world, if the material world stands in contrast to all consciousness, and to the own-essentiality of consciousness, as "*something alien,*" the "otherness," then how *can* consciousness become involved with it—with the *material* world and consequently with the *whole* world other than consciousness? For one is easily persuaded that the material world is not just

21. *Ibid.*, pp. 51–143.
22. *Ibid.*, p. 51.
23. *Ibid.*, p. 53.
24. *Ibid.*, p. 82.

any part, but rather the fundamental stratum of the natural world to which all other real being is *essentially* related.[25]

What has happened to the friend reaching out to shake my hand? He now has to be regarded as a "psychophysical unity" composed of material being and (founded upon it) its alien, mental life. But whence comes the easy persuasion that the material world is "the fundamental stratum of the natural world to which all other real being is *essentially* related?" Are we faced with a situation parallel to that of Avenarius? This easy persuasion surely cannot come from a descriptive charac- terization of the world of the natural attitude, for which friends, ene- mies, superiors, servants, glasses, pianos are all encountered as imme- diately as any merely physical things. Does that easy persuasion, then, arise once more from theoretical convictions too habitual and too ob- vious to take into account, to question, or to set aside?

The parallel, indeed, seems complete—with one essential differ- ence. Avenarius stands doggedly by his mechanistic reformulation of the natural concept of the world. He yields no ground to subjectivity in any form. Faced with Husserl's basically naturalistic reformulation of the world of the natural attitude in *Ideas I*, repressed subjectivity returns, it seems, with a vengeance. Unable to find itself at home in the alien world of nature, subjectivity asserts itself as beyond nature, beyond the world, transmundane, transcendental.

IDEAS II AND NATURAL ATTITUDES

But that one essential difference makes all the difference in the world. Husserl has not arbitrarily posited a repressed subjectivity to compensate for the one-sidedness of Avenarius' naturalistic miscon- strual of the natural conception of the world. He has developed a method for turning reflective observation upon experience as it func- tions (anonymously) in natural experience. Consequently, the sense of experience need not remain something dogmatically upheld in the face of philosophical theories that deviate from it. And it does not have to be articulated and refined from the perspective of psycho- physical naturalism.

By way of the phenomenological reduction, Husserl opens up to descriptive articulation the theme of the correlation between func- tioning experience and the world of experience, as its inseparable sense. The subjectivity affirmed as transcendental is not a subjectivity disconnected from the world of experience but that subjectivity in re-

25. *Ibid.*, pp. 81–82.

lation to which and by virtue of which the world is experienced and posited as existing in its own transcendent, spatio-temporal context of observable causal regularity. That same subjectivity that functions unnoticed in the natural attitude can be reflectively observed by way of the phenomenological attitude. Its invariant structures can then be elicited with no less justification than structures of experienced objectivity.

Once the sense of the natural attitude is made a theme for descriptive articulation, the movement of *Ideas I* can be understood without paradox and without involving an unacceptable dichotomy in interpreting the beginning and end points of that movement. And the "easy persuasion" mentioned for convenience in that context can become in *Ideas II* a topic for hard-won insight.

The beginning description, we recall, included human beings and nonhuman animals as well as inanimate objects as "immediately there for me: I look up; I see them; I hear their approach; I grasp their hands; talking with them I understand immediately what they objectivate and think, what feelings stir within them, what they wish or will." [26] "Moreover," the descriptive account continued, "this world is there for me not only as a world of mere things, but also with the same immediacy as a *world of objects with values, a world of goods, a practical world*." [27] At the end of the movement of analysis, by contrast, "I consciously find a factually existing world of physical things confronting me." [28]

Do we have to choose between two conflicting descriptions of the sense of the world as there for me in natural experience? Can we reconcile the two different descriptions as both accurate in spite of their differences? If so, how can we move from one to the other and still remain true to experience throughout, still remain within an analysis of the natural conception of the world?

To accept both descriptions as accurate requires that we relativize and limit each, take each as true within a distinct context of experience. Generally speaking, the natural attitude of experience takes what is found as actually existing in the world. But within that general attitude, different specific attitudes, different specific contexts of apperception, can be distinguished by careful analysis. Husserl calls attention in this regard to a liberating function and an educating function of the phenomenological reduction. By disclosing a sphere of reflective observation not accessible within the natural attitude, the re-

26. *Ibid.*, p. 51.
27. *Ibid.*, p. 53.
28. *Ibid.*, p. 82.

duction points up the limits and relativity of the sense and validity of natural experience, limits not noticed by an observer who remains immersed in that attitude. By thus liberating phenomenological philosophers from those limits, the reduction also brings to light the general lesson of the fundamental significance of changes of attitudes. Thus instructed, we can discern essentially different attitudes within the overall natural attitude, each with its appropriate apperceptive categories.[29]

The movement mentioned above with reference to *Ideas I* is painstakingly analyzed in *Ideas II* as basic to the discovery of an observable realm of nature in the modern sense (nature as correlate of modern, mechanistic, natural science). It is a movement within experience that involves two shifts of attitude: a shift from non-theoretical to theoretically interested experience, and, within the theoretical attitude, an exclusive focus upon those abstractively distinguishable features of experienced objects that are of interest to purely naturalistic observation.[30]

Briefly stated, ordinary experience is, for the most part, not focused upon purely theoretical interests. It presents the world, not as it would exist for a purely disinterested spectator, but as it does exist for an interested, involved participant. Hence, it presents objects, events, and situations as meaningful, as value-laden, and as having practical significance. But I can deliberately adopt the stance of a "disinterested spectator." I can assume a stance in which I am, temporarily or habitually, disinterested in those aspects of experienced objects that refer, explicitly or implicitly, to my personal value-preferences and my personal practical projects. I do so in order to focus attention exclusively upon the purely theoretical aspects of experience, those that disclose what objects are and how they are, regardless of how I feel about them or how I might be prompted to respond to them practically.

To clarify that shift of attitude within natural experience, Husserl employs the metaphor of layers of experience and layers of experienced objects. Full-fledged, concrete experience can be analyzed as involving three such layers, ordinarily merged into a unity: a merely objectifying layer, a feeling layer, and a practically oriented layer. For example, as I am driving a car into an intersection, I see a speeding truck approaching rapidly from the road off to my right. That is *what* I observe (the merely objectifying dimension of experience), but the experience is hardly a disinterested one. The truck is experienced *as* highly threatening to life and limb (the valuative dimension of the experience, in reference to how I feel about it). And it is experienced *as*

29. Edmund Husserl, *Ideen zu einer reinen Phänomenologie und Phänomenologischen Philosophie, Zweites Buch.* (The Hague: Nijhoff, 1952), p. 179.
30. *Ibid.*, pp. 1–90.

calling for evasive action from me (the practical dimension of experience, in reference to doings or sufferings on my part). And all those aspects, analytically distinguishable for reflection, are experienced as the one complete sense of the experienced object in a non-theoretical context, within the natural attitude.

The shift to the theoretical attitude (obviously not recommended while driving a car into an intersection) can be seen as involving a deliberate disregard for those aspects of the experienced object that are constituted by the valuative and practical strata of experience, in order to bring to light just what something is, independently of my individual feelings and practical concerns. The disregarded strata of experience continue to function, but they are not taken into consideration as presenting data for theoretically interested observation.

However, the shift to the purely theoretical attitude is not sufficient to delineate the sense of naturalistic observation. A disinterested spectator can observe events having valuative or practical characteristics, without relating those characteristics to his or her individual feelings or practical concerns. For example, a literary critic can report on the merits of a work of fiction without being immersed in it as a naive reader would be, can appreciate such merits even in a work not to his own liking, by adopting the disciplined stance of the professional critic. And a political commentator can report on strategies and counter-strategies in a legislative debate over a proposed bill without being personally involved in the struggle, and without reference to her own practical preferences, by exercising the restraint of the trained reporter. In neither case will the descriptive account present a purely mechanical succession of changes in a purely objective nature. And in both cases, the reports will be true or false of the observed objects.

The second phase of the movement involved is a focus of attention within the theoretical attitude upon the above-mentioned "fundamental stratum of the natural world to which all other real being is *essentially* related."[31] The basic insight that gives rise to naturalistic observation is that, regardless not only of the observer's values and practical concerns but of anyone's at all, in order for something to count for experience as a component part of the real world, it must present itself to experience as located in objective space and time and as interacting regularly with its environment. That basic insight gives rise to a theoretical focus of observation upon aspects of experienced objects that can be described in purely objective, spatio-temporal and causal categories. The naturalistic observer goes on experiencing things in a

31. *Ideas I*, p. 82.

fully personal context, like anyone else, but counts as data for theoretical purposes only what can be categorized in purely objective, impersonal terms.

At that point, for official theoretical purposes, the observation records nothing but physical bodies in motion interacting with one another in a manner that can subsequently be subjected to precise measurement and explained in idealized mathematical formulas. This is the end point of the movement mentioned above with reference to the treatment of the natural attitude in *Ideas I*. This is the entrance into the specialized, restricted, and disciplined sort of experience that counts as naturalistic observation.

Husserl characterizes that last move as a sort of reduction:

> We accordingly perform a sort of "reduction." We put into parentheses, as it were, all our feeling-intentions and all apperceptions stemming from the intentionality of feelings, by virtue of which the spatio-temporal objects appear constantly to us, prior to all thought, in immediate intuitiveness, as endowed with certain value-characters and practical characters—all characters that surpass the layer of mere materiality. Therefore, in the "pure" or purified theoretical attitude, we no longer experience houses, tables, or streets; we experience only material things, and concerning such value-laden things, only their layer of spatio-temporal materiality—and also with regard to human beings and human societies, only the layer of psychic "nature" connected with their spatio-temporal "bodies."[32]

On the basis of Husserl's intentional analysis of the development of naturalistic observation out of pre-theoretical experience, it becomes evident that neither the non-theoretical, personally rich experience of a value-saturated and practically involving world, nor the theoretically purified region of naturalistic observation, nor, for that matter, the theoretically purified region of human-scientific observation, is to be absolutized or simply equated with the natural attitude of experience. Rather, "experience" has to be taken as a general term for various sorts of presentations of something as actually existing, having many dimensions of sense, and always occurring in an apperceptive context that relates being and sense within some specific domain.

CONCLUSION

The natural attitude, derived from Avenarius' account of the natural conception of the world, as world for experience, is ambiguously natural. It is natural in the sense that it pertains to the nature of experience itself, prior to and independent of any philosophical theoriz-

32. *Ibid.*, p. 25.

ing. But it is also natural in the sense that (at least in its modern, theoretically influenced version) it is predisposed to view the world in its entirety as a merely natural environment and to view nature itself as a purely objective mechanical system of physical energy.

Husserl's detailed analysis of the sense of the natural conception of the world, with its characteristic natural attitude, provides a persuasively argued basis for accepting that natural attitude as pertaining to the nature of any experience of the world without accepting the naturalistic bias with which it is readily identified. Phenomenologically clarified, experience is seen to present a world permeated with values and references to purposes that can be understood only by reference to persons living and working in various forms of social and cultural contexts. "Purely objective nature," ironically enough, turns out to be the title for the product of a very sophisticated form of highly disciplined observation guided by an ingenious insight into a fundamental layer of reality. Accordingly, it is fully intelligible only with reference to such self-disciplined, insightful subjectivity.

13　　　　　　　　　　　　　　　Moral Thinking
ROBERT SOKOLOWSKI

I

There have been many philosophical attempts to clarify what makes
a human act to be morally good or bad, and to clarify what makes human behavior to be a moral action at all. I suggest 'that most of these
attempts, at least in the forms they have taken in the past few centuries, can be divided into two kinds of theories, two kinds of moral
philosophies. I further suggest that each of the two kinds of moral
theory is determined by the kind of categoriality that the theory appeals to in explaining what moral action is. Each kind of theory tries
to explain the being of moral action by claiming, implicitly, that a certain kind of thinking makes up the substance of a moral performance.
And finally I claim that these two kinds of moral theory fail to provide
a sufficient account of moral thinking, and that we must turn to another, to a third kind of moral categoriality for a more adequate philosophical description of moral thinking and moral behavior.

I use the term "categoriality" in the way that Husserl uses the term
in *Logical Investigations;* it refers to logical structure or logical form,
but to logical form as it is realized in states of affairs or in articulated
things. For example, a car's being blue is more than just a car and
blue; as a fact or a state of affairs, it is permeated with the syntax or
the logical and ontological form of S's being p. Husserl claims that we
do not discover such categorial forms just in the internal working of
the mind; he insists that they modify the presentation and the being
of things as such. In a profound opposition to the Kantian tradition in
philosophy, he shows that there is such a thing as categorial intuition:
we can intuit not only simple things or sensory givens, but states of
affairs, groups, universals, and other categorial objects as well.

I claim that categorial forms are also to be found in the moral domain, and that they play a strategic role in determining the morality
of human behavior. I begin my analysis by saying that there are two

kinds of moral theory, and that each kind appeals to a special type of categoriality as the substance of moral behavior.

(1) The first kind of theory appeals to what I want to call the categoriality of *judgment*. In a moral judgment, we subsume an individual action under a moral category. Deontological and axiological ethical theories appeal to such judgmental categoriality when they try to explain what makes a human action moral. According to such theories, an action is moral and it is good or bad because it is identifiable as an instance of, say, generosity or greed, courage or murder, or because it obeys or violates a rule of behavior, or because it serves and instantiates a moral value. The particular action comes under, it is subsumed by, the moral category, rule, or value; the particular action is judged according to that category, rule, or value. Its being judged in that way makes it to be a moral action and not merely nonmoral human behavior.

However the categories, rules, obligations, and values are themselves not derived from anything more ultimate; they are not judged by anything beyond themselves. Nor are they established by empirical induction. They have a kind of irreducibility, a presentation and force of their own. Somehow or other they must be grasped on their own as obligations and as values. But once grasped, they have to be applied, and the kind of thinking that goes on when they are applied is judgmental thinking. It is this sort of thinking, according to the moral theories we are now describing, that constitutes human action as moral.

(2) The second kind of moral theory I wish to distinguish turns to the categoriality of *relation:* an action is said to be moral, and morally good or bad, because it is related to another action or to some other state of affairs which follows from it. In this group we have teleological, utilitarian, and consequentialist moral theories, those that explain the goodness or badness of an action by appealing to that in view of which the act is done, or to that which is the outcome of the action. This kind of moral theory would claim that the moral character of a behavior is constituted by the categorial form of relation rather than that of judgment. One action is good because it leads to, or is done in view of, greater happiness or greater relief of distress; another action is bad because it leads to, or is done in view of, some unhappiness or displeasure or some undesirable condition.

In summary, then, there are two kinds of moral theories, the judgmental and the relational. Each of them locates the substance of moral behavior in a categoriality that informs human behavior. The judgmental moral theories, the deontological and the axiological, claim that an action is first constituted as moral when it becomes involved in a moral judgment: this or that action is judged to be an instance of this or that moral category, or it is judged to be in accordance with or in violation of this or that moral rule. The relational moral theories, the teleological, utilitarian, and consequentialist, claim that an action is first constituted as moral by its reference to the goal or the outcome in view of which it is done.

The categoriality in question, whether judgmental or relational, is articulated by the moral agent or by the moral evaluator, not by the moral theorist. The moral theorist points òut what it is in the action itself that makes the action to be moral. The moral theorist is not the one who first introduces moral categorialities; he merely describes and clarifies them. He points out the thinking at work in the minds and actions of those who are engaged in the moral performance. It is the categorial form, the moral thinking, that establishes a human performance as a moral action.

Now each of the two kinds of moral theory I have described has a serious problem associated with it. (1) The first, the judgmental kind of theory, cannot show where the moral categories, rules, and values come from. Although we can make inferences and applications once the categories and rules and values are there, we do not seem able to establish them themselves. It means that we can be rational *within* the context of the categories, rules, and values, but that we cannot be rational *about* the categories, rules, and values themselves. We seem to be forced to appeal to moral intuitions, to custom and social convention, or to a simple perception of values. (2) The second kind of moral theory, the relational, cannot explain the moral goodness or badness of the goals or the outcomes of the actions, nor can it show how such goals and outcomes can generate moral obligations. It cannot explain how a moral point of view is introduced into human life by the fact that certain desirable goods issue from what we do.

I suggest that these difficulties arise because the nature of moral thinking is not adequately clarified by the two kinds of moral theories we have distinguished. Moral categorialities are not exhausted by the two forms we have described, by moral judgment and moral relation. These two forms have a place in moral action, but they are not basic enough to explain what moral action is. We must introduce another kind of moral thinking. And because Husserl has done so much to clarify the nature of categoriality in general, I think he can.help us in supplying what is needed to give a more adequate account of moral thinking.

As Husserl shows in *Logical Investigations*, we articulate what we experience into various categorial objects: into states of affairs, facts, relations, collections, universals and their instances, and the like. Husserl observes that we can intuit such articulated categorial objects. Thinking is not merely a rearrangement of concepts in our minds but a registration of the various states and relations in which things can be presented and intended by us. We can, for example, register and present the "being together" of the house and the tree, when we say "the house and the tree," and we can register and present the "being red" of the car when we say, "The car is red." When we do this, when we accomplish categorial intuitions, we do not simply absorb sensuously what is around us; we do absorb, but we also articulate. We differentiate and identify.

The culminating part of *Logical Investigations*, Section 2 of Investigation VI, deals with the categorial form of predication, of articulating an object into subject and predicate. But Husserl also provides an analysis of a more simple identification. He describes what happens when we simply recognize, say, Hans as Hans or Berlin as Berlin. This is less than the achievement of predication, but it is nevertheless a form of thinking. In fact the more articulated categoriality of predication is rooted in this simpler form of thinking, the kind that occurs when we just identify or recognize an object *as* itself. This kind of thinking is simple identification, and Husserl explores it in his analysis of empty intention and fulfillment in Section 1 of Investigation VI.

Now I would suggest that the moral categorialities we have discussed above, the categorialities of judgment and of relation, can also be grounded upon a more elementary form of moral thinking, on a type of fundamental moral identification. When the categorialities of moral judgment and relation are thus based on this more fundamental kind of thinking, they receive a philosophical clarification that resolves the difficulties that seem endemic to them. The categories, rules, values, goals, and outcomes will no longer seem to dangle from nowhere, they will no longer seem to be unexplained, simply given, and almost arbitrary. Thus I want to use the philosophical resources Husserl has given us to provide an escape from the bad alternative of either deontologism or teleology that has marked recent ethical theory.

III

I maintain that what makes human behavior into moral action is a special kind of thoughtful identification. It can be described as follows. I perform a moral transaction when I do something that is good or bad for you, and identify it, *insofar as it is good or bad for you*, as my good or bad. In other words, I perform a moral transaction when I want and do *this* precisely insofar as it is good or bad for you; or when I avoid *that* precisely insofar as it is good or bad for you. For example, you are hungry and I give you some food. Being fed, as being good for you, is identified and brought about as my good. It is not just that you are being fed; it is also not just that your being fed is somehow beneficial for me; it is that *as* being good for you, your being fed becomes good for me. I want and bring about your being fed insofar as it is good for you. There is, so to speak, a kind of laminated identification that occurs here. I recognize this activity as good for you, and *as such* I want it and recognize it as good for me. Your good, *as* your good, becomes *my* good. Or, in another kind of moral transaction, I may want and recognize a bad that I do for you as being, as such, good for me: your losing your job, *as* bad for you, is wanted, achieved, and recognized by me as good for me. In such a case I am being cruel or harmful to you. In either case, whether I am being kind or cruel, whether I am doing good to my friend or harming my enemy, it is the thoughtful dimension, the complex identification, that provides the categorial form that turns mere behavior into moral transaction. This categorial form is what establishes the difference between a nonmoral human performance and a moral action.

A moral action therefore is made into a moral action by two things: by a behavior of some sort, which works as a substrate; and by the categorial identification that I have described, which works as the form. To be moral agents we must initiate a performance, but we must also understand and identify the performance in a certain way. The identificational form, this special pattern of recognition, is more basic in what we could call "moral ontology" than are the categorial forms of judgment and relation that, in other moral theories, are said to constitute the substance of a moral performance. Indeed the judgmental and relational forms presuppose this identificational categoriality.

IV

I would like to amplify my description of a moral transaction. The recognitional form I have introduced—my doing and taking what is good or bad for you, as such, as my good or bad—is a categoriality that permeates a concrete performance. It is not a mere mental intention. Something has to be done. To be moral agents, we have to initiate something, we have to crease the world. The categoriality modifies how something worldly is presented to us. The categoriality is placed outside, it is not just somehow in the mind. In this respect the moral categoriality resembles the categorialities Husserl describes in *Logical Investigations*. They too are not just forms or categories in the mind, but articulations and structures that permeate the objects we experience and that modify how these objects are presented and intended. The approach I have provided thus makes moral behavior more of a public, manifest phenomenon, not something accomplished in an intention or in an interior act of willing.

Furthermore my analysis shows that moral behavior is essentially interpersonal, that it is a transaction, since I as a moral agent take the good of someone else formally as my good. My actions are first made to be moral by virtue of this intersubjective identificational structure, not by virtue of conforming or disconforming to a rule, value, moral category, or goal. Even the virtues and vices that seem to be purely personal or self-directed, such as temperance and intemperance, or fortitude and cowardice, are established as moral by this structure, since in such actions we become related to our own selves—our present and our future selves—in a moral way. If we act temperately we perform an action that is good for us, and as such, we take it as our good; we want and we do the action as good for ourselves if we are indeed acting out of the virtue of temperance. In these self-regarding virtues and vices, in temperance and intemperance, fortitude and cowardice, there is a kind of reflexivity that is analogous to our relationships with other persons. We act toward ourselves as toward another, and we become either friends or enemies to ourselves.

My claim therefore is that a human performance is made to be not merely a nonmoral event but a moral transaction by the special categoriality that informs it. I not only hand some food over to you; this handing over becomes kindness because as good for you it is taken as my good. I not only bump into you; this bumping becomes an insult or a cruelty because as bad for you it is taken as good for me. Only when this moral form is present does a moral relationship between you and me become established or adjusted. Only through this form am I established as generous or cruel, are you established as a beneficiary or as someone who has been harmed, and are you justified in being grateful or resentful for what has happened.

In the case of malevolent moral actions, the primary instance is the one in which I accomplish what is bad for you and do so directly as good for me. This occurs in acts of cruelty, insult, revenge, ridicule, and the like. These are the paradigm cases of malevolent moral transaction. Very many cases of doing injury, however, are not as direct as this; often harm is done not out of direct malevolence but because the action in question is somehow useful for me: I assault you not because I hate you but because I want your money; I calumniate you not out of revenge but in order to get your job. But even in such cases of utilitarian malice, the form we have described is what makes the action moral, because your bad still becomes good for me: not directly, but as a means to some benefit that I want. My transaction is still malevolent, but in a different way.

And in a more positive vein, gifts are an instance of a special kind of benevolence. Most good actions are prompted by needs that emerge in our situations. Someone is hungry, confused, tired, saddened, or wounded. The urgent substrate calls for a form of benevolence and if our character as agents is good we will respond appropriately. But giving a gift is not controlled by a necessary good. It is not prompted by what is needed. It is a form of benevolence that searches for a substrate in which it can realize and express itself. The form, not the substrate, comes first.

The introduction of the form of moral identity opens up for us the possibility of a moral life. There are countless different ways in which I can take your good or bad formally as my own, and in which you and others can do the same for me. Acts of gratitude and revenge, generosity and envy, loyalty, betrayal and forgiveness, reconciliation and hatred, are only some of the structural variations possible in this interaction. What happens in this domain—what we do and what is done to us—are the most important things in our lives with one another. It is through the human actions constituted by the form of moral thinking that we establish, confirm, and change the human relationships without which we could not be what we are, and there is no human happiness or grief more arresting than the kind that occurs in this domain.

V

Let us then suppose that the recognitional form that I have described is indeed the element that makes an action to be moral, that it is what changes nonmoral behavior into a moral transaction. We can now ask the question of how this categorial form is related to the two other categorialities we discussed earlier, the categoriality of moral

judgment and the categoriality of practical relation, of doing one
thing in view of another. I have claimed that these two forms of practical thinking are grounded on the form of a moral transaction; how is
this the case?

The structure of a moral transaction—identifying the good or bad
of another, as such, as my own good or bad—is analogous to the
structure of a perceptual recognition. And just as simple perception
does not engage the issue of meaning as forcefully as do the articulations that are built upon perception, so too the moral transaction does
not yet raise the question of what exactly I am doing in taking this
good or bad as my own. The form of a moral transaction moves my
behavior into the domain of morals, but it does not itself classify what
I am doing and does not articulate whether I am acting rightly or
wrongly, whether what I am doing is praiseworthy or blameworthy.
To draw the analogy with the case of cognition, perception alone is
not fully elevated into the kind of meaning and the kind of justification that is reached in the further categorial articulations of predication, collection, measurement, and the like.

In other words, the moral transaction needs to be evaluated, and it
is evaluated in the further categorialities of judgment and relationship. These two categorialities bring out the meaning of the moral
performance. For example if in a particular circumstance I take this
good of yours, as such, as my good, then I, you, and the others will all
go on to judge my action in the light of the moral maxims, categories,
rules, exemplars, and exhortations that our moral tradition provides.
We will say, for example, that it was a cowardly action, or a generous
act with a touch of envy, or an ambitious action, or one worthy of an
Achilles, or a Napoleonic action. These judgmental categories have
themselves originally issued from countless moral transactions in the
past; they are the moral memory of our world; they are there to help
us bring out the meaning of our actions and to make our moral actions truly good. But our actions can be so evaluated only "after" they
are first made to be moral and good or bad not by this deontological
judgment, but by the recognitional form of moral thinking. The judgment articulates what the actions already are.

Moral relativity, the fact that moral values, categories, emphases,
and paradigms can differ from one culture to another, appears more
pronounced when we focus on the categories used in moral judgments and neglect the concrete moral performance, the action that is
constituted as moral by the form of a moral transaction. Cultural differences in ethics appear to be almost unbridgeable if we remain only
with the abstract formulations of moral traditions (and this, of course,

is what academic and anthropological analyses of cultures tend to do).
If we go beyond moral abstractions toward the concrete moral performance, toward the substantial moral action, there is a far greater possibility of appreciating, even across cultural lines, the goodness or the
badness of what is being done by one agent to another.

Furthermore, in contrast to moral abstractions, the concrete moral
transaction is always individualized and situated, but it does not become arbitrary. To understand how I as agent can be taking your
good or bad as such as my own good or bad, one must comprehend
the particular circumstances at the moment of action, the alternative
courses of action that, realistically, might have been followed, who the
agent is and who the target is, what has gone on before between them,
and so on. Only then can one tell how and why this is a good or a bad
for both the agent and the target. And yet, despite this situatedness,
the good or bad is objective and not arbitrary; it is what is indeed possible here and now, it is what is called for by this situation at this time
and place. The form of a moral transaction thus accounts for both the
individualizing and the objectifying of a moral performance. Just as
Husserl's account of perception and thinking clarifies both the objective and the subjective dimensions of knowledge and experience, so
this form accounts for the objective and subjective aspects of moral
experience and recognition.

We have shown how the deontological form, the form of moral
judgment, can be grounded on the form of a moral transaction. The
relational form, the kind that is the center of emphasis in teleological
or utilitarian moral theories, also brings out the meaning of a moral
transaction. It is a further articulation that registers what has occurred in a moral performance. However, it works by exploiting the
peculiar temporal structure of moral action: when we act, we do not
always simply do what we are doing now. We are not exhausted in the
present of our behavior. Instead of just doing *this*, we may be doing
this for the sake of *that*. And what follows later will often shed light on
what we are doing now; it will let our present action show up more
vividly for what it is in itself. The scope of our action can be so ex-
panded that a kind of duality emerges that is peculiar to human behavior. *This* and *that*, what is done *now* and what will follow *then*, the
action and its purpose or the action and its consequences are distinguished and yet joined in the unity of a complex performance, and
the full meaning of what we are doing now, the full meaning of *this*,
can only be seen in relation to *that*, to what will follow then. These are
possibilities inherent in human performance. Therefore another way
of evaluating what we are doing is to see what it is done for and what

issues from it. The purpose and consequences can reveal the character of what we have done. This relational form of moral thinking, along with the deontological form of moral judgment, is another way of showing the ethical meaning of what we are doing; but again the teleological form presupposes that the action in question has already been constituted as a moral transaction. The relational form merely brings out what has already been accomplished. It does not originally establish the action as moral.

Therefore, just as the forms of predication and relation are founded upon simple identifications, so also are the forms of moral judgment and of moral relatedness founded upon what we have described as the simple form of a moral transaction. It is this simple form—the categorial form of taking what is good for you, as such, as being good for me—that moves us into the domain of morals; it is the kind of thinking that first introduces reason into desire and aversion, that allows us to see goods and bads not only as they seem to us, but as they are for others, and that allows us to begin asking whether what seems to be good for me is really good or not.

If we recognize this moral categoriality as the substance of moral action, it becomes clear that there never is a serious problem about whether and how a human being needs to be persuaded to adopt the moral point of view. We have no choice about adopting the moral point of view. We exist morally not by virtue of a decision, but by virtue of the fact that we share a world with other agents, and that what seems good to us will usually also show up as good or bad to others, that as good or bad for others it can be good or bad for us, that there can consequently be both conflicts and harmonies in the intersection of our goods and bads, and that we as agents can appreciate the intersection of our goods and bads with those of others. That space of intersection is the space in which we act. There is no more a problem about how we enter into the moral point of view than there is a problem about how what I perceive from this angle can also be perceived from another angle by someone else. That is the way things are, and that is the way we are. The moral point of view is simply another expression of our ability to think and to identify things and goods across various perspectives. It is an expression of our rational being and of our being with others. We can, of course, be mistaken about the various goods and bads and about how they intersect. Things that are bad may seem good to us, and things that are good may seem bad. There is always the problem of distinguishing the real meaning from the mere appearance in morals, and moral education consists in being helped to become insightful in such matters. But to be or not to be moral is not itself a matter of choice; we are moral by the way we exist with others.

VI

We have distinguished and discussed two levels of thinking in moral conduct. The first level involves the simple form of moral identification. The agent takes the good or bad of the target, as such, as his own good or bad. This categoriality makes conduct to be moral as opposed to nonmoral. The second level of moral thinking contains the categorialities of judgment and relation, which bring out the meaning of the moral action. In them we determine what kind of action is going on. On this second level we bring the categories, rules, and paradigms of our moral tradition to bear on what has transpired between agent and target, and we consider what the purposes and outcomes of the action have been. By using judgmental and relational forms, we articulate whether the action was moral or immoral, praiseworthy or blameworthy. But we can move on toward a third level of moral thinking. We can go beyond meaning and introduce a question of truth. This issue will have repercussions on what we accomplish on the first two levels of moral categoriality.

The question of truth can be raised in two different ways. (a) When an evaluation, a moral description, of an action has been made, we can go on to ask whether that evaluation was correct or not, whether the attribution of this or that meaning to the act was true or false. Someone draws another person into dubious financial practices and declares, "I'm only loosening him up, getting him to look out a bit for himself, to make a profit here and there;" but a more perceptive commentator might say, "No, you're making him dishonest." The meaning given to the action by the agent is rejected as false. His judgment about the action is denied and said to be not true. In other cases, of course, the original assessment may be confirmed as true. The point is that one is not just attributing a sense to the action and evaluating it, but discussing the truth or the falsity of the attribution and evaluation. The issue of truth is raised.

(b) But we can also ask whether the category our moral tradition gives us is itself truly good or bad. We can question the truth not of the application of a category, but of the category itself. If cannibalism is practiced in a particular society, the moral tradition may have a category for it as praiseworthy such as, "eating your enemy to absorb his strength," and this category will be applied to particular performances to express their meaning. But a question can be raised whether this is a moral term for the *truly* praiseworthy. Here the question of truth is not about the correctness of a particular application of a term, but about the term itself as a moral category. Is this term the expression of something truly morally good or bad, as we have taken it to be? Is this custom or law, this way of behaving, truly good or bad, as we have taken it to be? Is this moral category, is this practice genuinely good or bad?

This issue of the moral truth or falsity of a moral category is the issue of the difference between nature and convention in morals. At this point there arises the distinction between what is good or bad by custom, convention, or law, and what is good or bad by nature. Sometimes the inherited moral category will become manifest as unnatural or against nature, but sometimes it will be confirmed as true, as in accordance with nature and the morally genuine. But the issue of its truth or falsity has been raised and the distinction between nature and convention has been drawn. This distinction introduces a further set of moral categorialities that supplement and penetrate those we have seen on the first two levels of moral categoriality, the level of moral transaction and the level of moral characterization.

Furthermore, although the distinction between nature and convention occurs in regard to a moral term, the distinction is triggered by the application of that term to particular cases. It is in "living out," say, cannibalism that human agents begin to appreciate that the practice is not in conformity with the beings and relationships involved in it. They begin to appreciate that this is no way for people to be related to one another. Something in the thing asserts itself as not subsumable under this practice and this moral category; the category does not fit what it is supposed to fit. The distinction between nature and convention does not arise through a kind of abstract description of alternative ways of acting, but through thoughtful action itself and the identifiability and differentiation that arise in action. The distinction between nature and convention is made when we go back to actual moral transactions, to concrete cases of an agent's taking the good or bad of another as such as his own good or bad, when we go back to a moral transaction that has been shaped by the practices of our moral tradition and evaluated by its categories. The meaning of the action has been articulated, but now the truth of that meaning gets called into question: the action itself calls the convention into question. The action may ultimately confirm the convention, but it also may show that the convention is against nature. Such a questioning and denial of a convention occurs when someone disobeys a law he considers unjust, as a way of showing the injustice of the law; he appeals to nature against convention not by abstract argument but by action, by using the action to show the incoherence of the convention.

Thus the contrast between nature and convention does not emerge in a comparison of two abstractions called "nature" and "convention," nor in the comparison of two abstract descriptions of behavior, one of which would give the natural features of the action while the other would provide the conventional characteristics. The contrast arises rather in a concrete performance, when a convention is blended with a moral transaction, but when the blend does not "take," when the action refuses to be described as the convention describes it, and when the action shows the convention to be morally incoherent. Thus the actual moral transaction is the place in which a contrast between nature and convention is first made. The moral transaction, constituted by the categorial form we have described, is the origin even for the difference between the natural and the conventional.

In summary, (1) the form of a moral transaction establishes a human performance as moral as opposed to nonmoral; (2) the forms of judgment and relation bring out the meaning of the moral performance and allow us to distinguish between the moral and the immoral, the praiseworthy and the blameworthy; and (3) we can go on to ask (a) whether the moral category or moral meaning attributed to the action has been correctly attributed, whether the attribution is true or not, and (b) whether the category or meaning itself is a moral category of the truly good or bad, whether as a moral convention it is or is not according to nature. These three levels in moral thinking are analogous to three levels that can be distinguished in cognition: (1) the level of perceptual identification or recognition; (2) the level of predication, relation, and other categorialities, the level of articulated meaning; (3) the level of the truth of the categorialities articulated in (2).

In closing, I would like to point out a limitation in what we have done in this paper. A philosophical analysis such as the one we have carried out, a study of the form of manifestation and the form of being of moral behavior, does not as such make us morally good or bad. Only our actions, only what we do makes us into a particular kind of agent. But our philosophical analysis can disclose what it is in us that makes us to be moral agents at all; and this understanding, although not strictly a moral good, has another kind of goodness all its own. It is a philosophical good. I hope that in achieving this understanding, if indeed I have succeeded in doing so, I have accomplished not only something good for myself, but something good for you as well. If I have done so, however, my accomplishment will not have been a moral transaction. I will not have acted morally toward you, nor you toward me. Instead, we will have accomplished a philosophical clarification, an activity that neither of us does alone, but that we achieve together.

14   Phenomenology as First Philosophy: Reflections on Husserl

ELISABETH STRÖKER

I

There are many different answers to the question of what Husserl's phenomenology is. It is above all a new philosophical method, as Husserl himself emphasized again and again, expressing his conviction that truly profound accomplishments in philosophy arise principally from innovations in method, rather than from reformulations of earlier doctrines and reinterpretations of philosophical systems from the past.

The Husserlian method claims to be a set of non-constructive, descriptive, and analytical procedures to gain access to what Husserl called "the things themselves." The method was, it is true, originally created for a very particular and limited end. But this method, already inaugurated in its basic features in *Logical Investigations,* held within itself such a latent power of renewal—even of philosophical revolution—that it was able to take on different forms, because of the growing variety and range of those "things" that came into Husserl's focus as he used and refined the methodological instruments.

Thus Husserl's phenomenology could be characterized first as an inquiry into formal logical and mathematical structures as well as into meanings and essences, then as a phenomenological description of consciousness, then as an intentional-constitutive analysis of the transcendental ego and transcendental intersubjectivity, and finally as a phenomenological approach to life-world and history.

All these characterizations, and others as well, each of which was presented by Husserl himself at different stages of his research, can be irritating not only to philosophical laymen, but also to non-phenomenological philosophers, who might have heard about his phenomenology and may want to know at least roughly what it is about. No single answer seems to be given. But an answer can be given, since the diversity we have mentioned does not indicate obscurities or confusions. What may at first sight appear inconsistent in Husserl's work shows itself to be logically related once one follows the guiding thread that remained constant throughout the half-century of his research. There is one and only one goal for his phenomenology, and it remained his goal throughout all his apparently diverse studies. Husserl pursued it incessantly from his *Philosophy of Arithmetic* in 1891 until his very last research manuscripts of 1937. This goal is indicated by the term "foundation," more precisely by "absolute foundation."

But what is it that has to be absolutely founded? What does it mean to be in need of an absolute foundation? What does it mean to claim that phenomenology provides such a foundation?

In the course of his work, Husserl addressed different subjects in his foundational studies. In the *Logical Investigations*, it was to pure logic as well as to epistemology that he wanted to give a "new" foundation, and the novelty turned out to be a non-psychological foundation. It was not accidental that Husserl's early phenomenology gained its main contours from the overcoming of psychologism. The untenable assumptions of psychologism and its false descriptions of the logical as well as of the corresponding epistemological states of affairs initiated Husserl's reflections on objectivity and truth, and on the validity claimed for knowledge in general: he wanted to understand what knowledge is, to clarify what it really means, and above all to get appropriate access to the domain of investigation where such clarification can successfully be brought about.

Questions like these prompted a double preoccupation in Husserl's phenomenology: while searching for new foundations for all knowledge, phenomenology had also to be the analysis of consciousness. It is in consciousness—thanks to its intentionality—that the relations between objectivity and subjectivity occur, and it is only through the analysis of *these relations* that we can expect to gain insight into the true sense of knowledge.

This implies, however, that the problem of foundations is not confined to the mathematical and logical knowledge of ideal objectivities. Rather phenomenology, in opening up the field of consciousness with all its intentional activities, must take up the question of foundation in general. So it must refer to the knowledge of all sciences as well as to the everyday knowledge outside or even beyond science. And finally it has to be concerned with philosophical knowledge and in particular with that of phenomenology itself.

It is in connection with this phenomenological self-reference that we meet Husserl's early conception of first philosophy. Husserl expressed it for the first time in 1913 in his *Ideas I*, saying "that phenomenology, according to its essence, must claim to offer 'first philosophy' and the means which are necessary for the critique of reason; that it therefore requires the most complete presuppositionlessness. . . ." And Husserl remarkably continues that phenomenology needs "in relation to itself absolute reflective insight. It is its own essence to realize ultimate clarity about its own essence and therewith also about the principles of its method." (III/1, 136)[1]

This quotation is not as easy to understand as it might appear at first sight. I propose to prepare the way carefully to get to the concept of "first philosophy" and to grasp it in its very structure, since it will turn out to be, though in only a preliminary form, the very kernel of Husserl's later refined and more deeply reflective understanding of what "first philosophy" is to be.

Let us first pay attention to Husserl's use of the key terms that occur repeatedly in his definitions of phenomenology. In the quotation above Husserl refers to "presuppositionlessness" and "absoluteness"; a further notion significant for that of first philosophy is "rigorous science." These terms have met with misunderstandings, and Husserl might have had a share in causing them, since he made use of several ambiguous formulations. On the other hand certain ambiguities reside necessarily in these terms, and it is not accidental that the ambiguities will have an impact on Husserl's concept of first philosophy.

This holds above all for Husserl's notion of *absoluteness* and its verbal derivations. Without going into too many details, we must distinguish at least three different meanings. But the three meanings are not independent of one another, and they did not remain unmodified in Husserl's philosophy.

I want first of all to focus on a certain radicalization in Husserl's epistemological claim. He asserts that our knowledge of reality—whether the objective knowledge adopted by the sciences or the sub-

---

1. Numbers in the text refer to the critical edition of Edmund Husserl's works, *Husserliana*, volume and page. For this first citation, the German version, III/1, 136 is as follows: "Die phänomenologie hat nicht bloss die Methode zu entwickeln, den neuartigen Sachen neuartige Erkenntnisse abzugewinnen, sie hat über Sinn und Geltung der Methode volkommenste Klarheit zu schaffen, in der sie allen ernstlichen Einwänden standzuhalten vermag.

Dazu kommt—und das ist, weil auf Prinzipielles bezogen, sehr viel wichtiger—dass die Phänomenologie ihrem Wesen nach den Anspruch erheben muss, 'erste Philosophie' und aller zu leistenden Vernunftkritik die Mittel zu bieten; dass sie daher die vollkommenste Voraussetzungslosigkeit und in Beziehung auf sich selbst absolute reflektive Einsicht fordert. Ihr eigenes Wesen ist es, vollkommenste Klarheit über ihr eigenes Wesen zu realisieren und somit auch über die Prinzipien ihrer Methode."

Cf. also E. Husserl, "Entwurf einer 'Vorrede zu den *Logischen Untersuchungen*' (1913)," edited by E. Fink: *Tijdschrift voor Philosophie*, vol. 1 (1939), pp. 106–33, 319–99. Husserl (p. 337f) mentions that phenomenology has the function of being the true "first" philosophy.

jective knowledge of everyday affairs in life—our knowledge is not so much to be defended against any kind of psychologism that would darken its true sense; rather it is to be comprehended by the disclosure of basic assumptions that lie hidden in it. Husserl's often used images—to go back to the origins, to dig down to the roots, to lay open the foundations of knowledge, and, last but not least, to make phenomenology a science of beginnings—indicate what is at stake when he aims at "absolute foundation."

In whatever manner such a foundation may be obtained, and whether or not it can be obtained at all, it is meant to be "absolutely" first in the sense of an *ultimate foundation:* i.e., it is to allow us to recognize that there cannot be a further, still more fundamental basis for knowledge. Also, it is to be understood as absolute in regard to the *absolute givenness* of the foundation in question. This absolute givenness is not to be confused with an absoluteness of validity which phenomenology might claim for its propositions. When Husserl speaks of absolute knowledge he means knowledge of something absolutely given, and not absolute certainty, as though phenomenology would claim to offer unshakeable truth. On the contrary, the Husserlian instruments used to investigate knowledge finally bring to light the fact that unmodifiable certainty is excluded, even in principle, from phenomenological propositions, and they show why this must be so. The propositions in phenomenology are as open to critical discussion as are the propositions of the sciences, and this concession of phenomenology is part of its own scientific claim. When phenomenology even aims to become a rigorous science, it does so precisely in regard to its own sort of givenness, which is different from that of the positive sciences. It works with absolute givenness especially in regard to the ultimate foundations of knowledge.

This absoluteness is, however, not simply a metaphysical qualification of the given, since nothing else is meant by it but an absoluteness of clarity as to the essential features of what is phenomenologically given and to be given. Absoluteness in this sense is a phenomenological norm to be reached by a distinctive method.

This method is commonly known as Husserl's eidetic reduction and eidetic variation. It is a reductive procedure insofar as it leads from the given as an unreflectively presupposed fact to an essence, i.e. to that which belongs to the thing and to its content independently of its accidental features and the qualities it has *hic et nunc.* We get access to essences by what Husserl calls eidetic variation. In it we are to start from the actual experience of a fact and then modify it in our free phantasy; we are to project it into imaginative contexts, into as many as possible; we are to vary its circumstances and even push it into the impossible, in order to see which of its features withstand such a series of variations.

Insight into essence does not, to be sure, serve any knowledge of the real world, since it is not at all concerned with empirical facts, events, and laws. Nor does it contribute to our knowledge of phenomenological matters of fact concerning the intentionality of consciousness, since such matters of fact are to be made subject to a detailed intentional analysis. These limitations are, however, not a defect but the strength of eidetic insight: while eidetic insight does not tell us anything new about the things we learn about in empirical ways, it helps us to find out what such things really are and what it necessarily is we are concerned with in all our empirical knowledge. And as to the knowledge that phenomenology specifically aims at in investigating intentionality, the eidetic reduction enables us to get clear on what it is to refer intentionally to something given. And becoming clear on this is not a marginal accomplishment: getting clear about such matters is the very heart of the phenomenological method itself.

When Husserl regarded the epistemological tradition which had, at least since Descartes, aimed at absolute foundations of knowledge by referring knowledge back to subjectivity, and when he realized that in the past those foundations had never been reached, he drew the conclusion that a completely new philosophical discipline was needed with quite new methods, if it was to get to the foundations. He therefore set his phenomenology off against all tradition.

Hence Husserl initially claimed another kind of absoluteness: only as "freed from" traditional suppositions and all tacit assumptions from the past, only as absolute in a historical sense, would phenomenology become able to arrive at the ultimate foundations of knowledge; and only thus would it be able to show and justify them as being truly, and finally, the ultimate foundations.

Thus another meaning of absoluteness came into play. It was to legitimate the first one: phenomenology, seen historically, had to become an absolutely new philosophy in order to discover the systematically absolute foundations that, in Husserl's view, the traditional epistemologies had missed or failed to find.

This twofold absoluteness (i.e. the systematic and the historical) is implicated in Husserl's early postulate of a presuppositionless phenomenology, which should then be called a rigorous science, if it were actually achieved.

Before turning to this notion of rigorous science in order to see what it implies, we must realize that there is still a further meaning of absoluteness. It is particularly important for Husserl's understanding of first philosophy; it has entered the scene in the passage we quoted above in which Husserl referred to the necessity of the phenomenologist's self-reflection and called for "absolute reflective insight." That is to say, a kind of insight concerning phenomenology itself is needed, and its forms and structures, its norms and standards must not be borrowed from any other field of research, but have to be made available by phenomenology itself.

So the problem seems to be as follows. There are two necessary conditions to putting phenomenology in position to become a new philosophical science: the separation from or even the renunciation of all philosophical tradition, and a new method to get to the ultimate foundations of knowledge and to make them absolutely given in their essential structures. Both these conditions, if fulfilled, would establish phenomenology as a rigorous science.

But this alone would not suffice to make phenomenology into first philosophy. For that, a further condition is needed, and Husserl expressed it when he required an absoluteness of phenomenological self-reflection, in which the essence of phenomenology itself is grasped.

One can see from this that the various conditions for phenomenology as first philosophy are not all of the same sort and are not to be all located at the same categorial level. The two former conditions refer to phenomenological procedure and to the claims on behalf of which phenomenology has to be inaugurated and promoted, but the latter condition, the third, is concerned with reflection upon this procedure, and it must establish phenomenology as the ultimately legitimated phenomenology, worthy of being called philosophy. The conditions of ultimate foundation and absolute givenness would make phenomenology a presuppositionless rigorous science as Husserl had claimed it to be since 1910, but the condition of absolute self-reflection, however it may show up upon closer examination, is supposed to provide the absolutely grounded justification of such a rigorous science, and it is to allow phenomenology to come into its own as first philosophy.

Two different categorial layers of argumentation thus come into play, both as the outcome of Husserl's conception of first philosophy and as the defense of it. This has certain consequences for the formal structure of Husserl's discourse; he himself sometimes described it as a necessary zig-zag movement, i.e. a movement forward to the given in phenomenological analysis and a movement back to reflection on what has been performed, then the beginning of another new analysis, and so on. It also implies that modifications in either one of these conditions will affect the others, since they are closely connected. It is most illuminating to see how they are connected and to follow the modifications that occurred in their mutual relationship during the course of Husserl's work, and to see how they determined Husserl's concept of first philosophy in his later years.

II

After these more or less preliminary considerations I would like to examine the main characteristics of Husserl's first philosophy a bit more thoroughly by looking at Husserl's actual performance of phenomenology.

Husserl claims presuppositionlessness for his procedure. But this does not mean that he tried to get rid of all assumptions and make phenomenology start from nothing. Rather he started, and expressly so, from the pregiven systems of knowledge, and he appreciated very well that they provide knowledge of the real world. Objectivity, truth, validity and knowledge-claims (in every domain except those of formal logic and mathematics) do indeed mean nothing but a relation to real things that shows us precisely how things really are.

However the philosophical problem is how we are to understand *that* things are and that they can be *given* to us. In other words, how are we to understand the basic assumptions that all types of knowledge have in common, namely the assumption of a really existing world as certainly being transcendent to our consciousness and yet given to it?

Questions like these show that Husserl does not only ask how scientific knowledge can be traced back to knowledge in everyday life as to its foundation. Everyday life does function, it is true, as a foundation since scientific knowledge proves to be built upon it. But Husserl goes beyond prescientific knowledge when he asks for the basic suppositions that are always implicated in it. Hence he raises the more radical question of the existence of the world that is normally, and for good reasons, taken for granted. Our unreflective belief in the world's reality—though certainly not working as a premise from which we draw conclusions or as a basic principle from which we deduce other items of knowledge—nevertheless is the all-comprehensive and ultimate presupposition not only of all our knowledge, but also of our concrete life as a whole.

This does not mean that Husserl wanted to do away with this presupposition. Rather the problem of reaching a presuppositionless philosophy amounted to the problem of how to thematize the presupposition itself and to understand it as such. This thematization and this understanding would make his own phenomenology presuppositionless.

In order to appreciate Husserl's treatment of this problem we must look again at his procedure.

Husserl's early description of phenomena had opened a way for him, but it was not able of itself to lead to his goal. Even the theory of essences did not focus on the question of how to comprehend the reality of the world and our objective and true knowledge of it. Since reality and being are totally suspended in eidetic insight, this kind of insight does not claim to give us anything to know about the real world, let alone reality itself. Rather its claim is to help us clarify what we are thinking, doubting, arguing about, and denying, when we deal with the world and its reality.[2]

But the new question is that of finding the place, so to speak, where the thematization of the reality of the world can be performed, and performed in such a way that the new kind of knowledge to which it eventually leads can be shown as ultimately fundamental knowledge and, as such, be brought to absolute givenness.

It is in respect to this problematic that Husserl discovers and introduces the phenomenological reduction which, when fully radicalized, becomes a transcendental reduction. It might at first seem a paradoxical step: in order to show how the existence of the world is to be understood, the world has to be "put into brackets" or "in parentheses"; it has to be "suspended." The belief in its existence has to be "inhibited" or it must get "the coefficient of nullity." The true sense of these and other somewhat misleading Husserlian expressions is not a scepticism or doubt about the existence of the world. Rather the sense is that we no longer attach any validity to the belief in the world's existence in order to make it the object of phenomenological analysis and to investigate which sense might legitimately be attributed to what we unreflectively conceive as being.

Hence by this step every kind of being is retained: not as it is unquestionably given prior to all thinking, but as something that "claims" being, that is now understood as something "meant as being." This is

2. In this respect eidetic insight fulfills the postulate of presuppositionlessness automatically, as it were. Furthermore, it should be kept in mind that no other hidden or tacit assumptions are involved in it, not even the metaphysical assumption of the existence of essences outside and independent of consciousness, as has often been maintained in nominalistic counterarguments. It is true that Husserl did not deny a kind of being for essences. However the being in question is that which is constituted by the procedure of obtaining essences in eidetic and imaginative variation; it is not pregiven in any way prior to that procedure.

what Husserl demands as the phenomenological reduction, which must be performed in order to reduce any kind of being to pure phenomena of being.

When universally performed, this reduction changes the world as a whole into its pure phenomenon, i.e. its real being is changed into a "being-meant-as-real." And this reduction is a transcendental reduction, since the world as such a phenomenon cannot be conceived as a phenomenological object related to our natural, empirical consciousness, which is itself a part of the world. Rather, when consciousness performs this reduction, it establishes itself as transcendental consciousness. Its transcendentality means first of all that it intentionally "contains" all transcendent being, but it contains such being as "being meant to be transcendent," being in its "claim" of being transcendent, something that is to be examined by further analysis.

Nevertheless it is already at this point that Husserl's claim of giving phenomenology the status of rigorous science takes on its contours: phenomenological knowledge is that kind of knowledge that is concerned with the transcendental relations between subject and world; it enables us to understand that every empirical knowledge in whatever sense, including that of our own self, in all its demonstrations and corroborations, is basically founded on the intentionality of consciousness. This knowledge has to be regarded as in principle freed from unquestioned presuppositions; it is absolute knowledge in the sense that there are procedures available to make it absolutely given in its essence, and it is ultimately founded knowledge in the sense that there is certainly no other knowledge prior to it, nothing else to which the transcendental relations between subjectivity and objectivity could be traced back; any assumption of that sort would evidently and necessarily belong to those same relations as well and could thus be treated only in terms of the activities of transcendental consciousness.

I will not enlarge on Husserl's procedures or scrutinize these activities more closely, although it would truly be necessary to go into the details of Husserl's constitutive analysis in order to show how the world is constituted in transcendental subjectivity without being deprived of its transcendence. I will just summarize the principal results Husserl gains after he passes through the transcendental reduction, which served merely as the entrance-gate opening onto the field of transcendental consciousness.

This field proves to be a field of transcendental experience: not only is the true sense of the world's existence brought to light, but also that of the transcendental Ego in its essential relations to other transcendental Egos, and in its relation to its own self.

As regards Husserl's concept of first philosophy, I want to emphasize two issues in this experience. The first refers to Husserl's concept of constitution in its impact on his later understanding of intentionality. The second refers to some consequences concerning Husserl's claim of phenomenological presuppositionlessness and ultimate foundation; it will lead us to a more profound problematic in Husserl's first philosophy.

Husserl's intentional analysis, once it becomes constitutive analysis in the narrower sense of the term, discloses the phenomena of objects by leading them back to specific noetic activities. These are now designated as transcendental achievements; objective being in all its modalities becomes comprehensible only as being in a certain sense of being—a sense which does not reside in the being itself, but is bestowed by transcendental subjectivity. Closer examination of these sense-bestowing achievements could show furthermore that any constitution is genetic constitution. When Husserl disclosed the "horizon" as a background against which every actively constituted object stands, and when he disclosed the actuality and potentiality of consciousness as involved in mutual relationships between various acts, he was led to the decisive insight of the temporality of all constitution. That is to say, since all constitution is a matter of sense-bestowal, every actual sense-achievement is to be investigated with respect to implications of previous sense-formations. Husserl also speaks here of a "sedimented sense-history" that every constituted unity, as well as every constituting activity, possesses; it needs to be reactivated if philosophy is to offer a full and appropriate understanding of constitution and thus of being.

Hence all being turns out to be ultimately historical being. The world as a whole is to be understood as historical, and as an essentially becoming world. Correspondingly, the world-constituting subjectivity is, for reasons of principle, also historical and has to be conceived in its transcendental historicity.

Whether Husserl in fact came to terms with history in the common sense of the term, and whether he discovered a phenomenological access to mundane history, are not our questions here. What Husserl has brought to light as transcendental sense-history raises new problems for his phenomenology in respect to its own self-understanding as rigorous science. It entails new aspects in his phenomenology as first philosophy.

Throughout his life, Husserl was aware of the fact that his claim of rigorous science implied a phenomenological self-reference; phenomenology was not only to provide a certain method for solving phenomenological problems, but also the instruments for critically justifying that method. Husserl had indeed always reflected self-critically upon his own activity and had tried to get completely clear on the essence of phenomenology itself. In this respect he was trying from the start to perform phenomenology as first philosophy, in line with his definition of it in 1913.

With regard to the content and structure of his phenomenology, however, something had decisively changed in the period after *Ideas I*, when constitutive analysis was brought to full prominence. But it was precisely his "absolutely reflective insight" into the essence of his phenomenology, his first achievement of first philosophy as it was defined in 1913, that finally brought him to acknowledge that still more radical self-reflection and self-criticism were needed to make phenomenology first philosophy in the true sense. Furthermore, if he could fully realize this goal, his phenomenology as a rigorous science would be able to gain its proper dignity and value. This can be seen from the following.

If everything that can be acknowledged as being is essentially historical, if, as Husserl concluded in 1921, "history is the great fact of absolute being" (VIII, 506), then there cannot be an ultimate foundation of knowledge at all, because constitutive genetic analysis shows that any foundation which is meant to be ultimate is grounded again in passive preconstitutions, the analysis of which can in principle never be finished. This phenomenological insight is, however, in itself an absolute insight to the extent that it can be brought to absolute self-givenness.[3]

To acknowledge the genesis of all constitution has still another far-reaching consequence. Since it is transcendental genesis, it implies that there cannot be any non-historical sense-bestowing achievement thanks to which all being would gain its proper sense. And this holds true also for concepts, notions, and problems in the sciences and in philosophy as well. So Husserl finally admitted that even his own understanding of phenomenology bears in itself a heritage from the past. Husserl conceded that his idea of presuppositionlessness, as he had tried to realize it in order to establish phenomenology as a rigorous science, was quite simply a prejudice. One could also say that Hus-

---

3. In his later manuscripts, mostly still unpublished, Husserl struggled with the problem of temporal constitution, especially in regard to the self-constitution of the transcendental ego. The analysis of this constitution runs into very difficult problems, primarily because all the concepts of constitutional analysis derive from predicative forms of constitution. This fact indicates that the transcendental origins of all constitution cannot be grasped through phenomenological reflection simply. It seems that Husserl eventually came to this insight—though he never expressed it—as one of the last he was able to acquire (on this, see VI, 171).

serl, when starting his first way into transcendental phenomenology, tried to realize an idea of rigor that reflected more a radicalism in his own willing to initiate a new kind of philosophy, rather than a radical reflection on the pregiven conditions that make a new philosophy possible.

This did not mean, of course, that one had to give up the idea of a rigorous science. On the contrary, only now, and thanks to the new insights gained from his genetic-constitutive analysis, could Husserl's idea of rigor come fully into its own, if phenomenology could be established as rigorous philosophy.

III

First philosophy as mentioned in *Ideas I* is now to be considered particularly as regards the impact that the genetic-constitutive phenomenology had on phenomenological self-reflection. To get clear on the essence of phenomenology itself, as Husserl has constantly required, now means above all to take into account that there are sense-sedimentations from the past even in phenomenology, in its methods and in its goal as well. This implies that there are predecessors of phenomenology and that phenomenology rests upon presuppositions, though of a very peculiar kind. They are historical presuppositions and can be brought to light only through historical investigations. But in order to clarify the true idea of phenomenology they are to be examined as *layers of sense* preceding Husserl's phenomenology and sedimented in it, rather than as past philosophical systems in themselves. Though they certainly are, temporal systems developed in the course of time, it is not their temporality, not their specifically structured historical time, that makes them historical systems, but their contents as sediments in Husserl's own present philosophy; it is this that now matters for Husserl's establishment of first philosophy.

From this we come to understand the peculiarity of Husserlian historical investigations, as he presented them in Part One of his treatment of first philosophy in 1923, under the title *Critical History of Ideas.*[4] Husserl did not claim to contribute anything to the history of philosophy as it is commonly understood; rather he wished to call his

---

4. *Husserliana* VII contains the first half of the lectures on first philosophy Husserl offered in 1923/24; they deal with the history of philosophy. The second half of the lectures is published in *Husserliana* VIII; in this he deals with systematic aspects of phenomenology as first philosophy. In this volume Husserl, quite typically, considers the theory of phenomenological reduction as the main systematic problem in his first philosophy.

handling of the philosophical past an "archeology" of phenomenological problems (VIII, 29).

On the other hand we are now enabled to understand why Husserl, when turning to such a sense-history, resumes the topic of first philosophy[5] and gives it a more critical as well as a more substantial significance.

Only now can an ambiguity in the sense of "first" come to light in Husserl, an ambiguity that originally was mentioned by Aristotle. Husserl did not relate his considerations to those of his ancient predecessor; though explicitly adopting the term "first philosophy" from him, he found himself, for obvious and plausible reasons, closer to Descartes' *Prima Philosophia* than to Aristotle's *Metaphysics*.

Nevertheless there is a remarkable correspondence between Husserl and Aristotle in regard to the perspective on the problem of first philosophy and in regard to the structure of argumentation. I want to explain this correspondence and then conclude with Husserl's final conception of first philosophy.

First philosophy was considered by Aristotle as the search for the *arche* or the non-temporal *proton*, as it could be found in the basic concepts, forms, and categories upon which all other philosophical disciplines, such as the sciences, were dependent and on which they were based. First philosophy was also to be conceived as the philosophical science of the first principles of being (*Metaphysics* 982b9).

First philosophy in this sense was conducted by Husserl as the search for the ultimate grounds of all givenness in transcendental subjectivity. These grounds could undoubtedly no longer be sought in the way that the Aristotelian *archai* were sought. Husserl was too much a present-day philosopher, with the modern tradition of philosophy behind him, to aim at first principles in the sense followed by Aristotle, but the sort of claim to first philosophy and the structure of the argument defending it are basically the same in both cases.

There is, furthermore, still another aspect of the Aristotelian *arche* that has attracted less attention, but it turns out to be the very nucleus of Husserl's version of the problematic of first philosophy. Aristotle refers to it in the form of the principle of philosophy, *arche philosophias*. Philosophy is itself regarded as the first in that it has to take the first steps to get to the first principles; then it is a science of procedure, as a search for a philosophical way to establish first philosophy in the former sense. First philosophy in this respect is not meant to be

5. For an explication of this title, as related to the historical part of Husserl's *First Philosophy* (*Husserliana* VII), see J. Allen, "What is Husserl's First Philosophy?" *Philosophy and Phenomenological Research*, vol. 42 (1981–82), pp. 610–20.

a science of first principles, rather it is a science of first beginnings, and this implies that it is a science of its own beginning. First philosophy thereby becomes *the beginning of a philosophy* of first principles that has to be at the same time *a philosophy of the beginning* with a search for those principles.

It is in this connection that Husserl's phenomenology gains a new dimension of self-reflection. And it is in the new light of this self-reflection that the second, systematic part of Husserl's *First Philosophy* of 1923/24, under the title "Theory of the Phenomenological Reduction," actually offers a comprehensive outline of his phenomenology as a whole, and indeed in the frame of the problematic of the *arche philosophias*. To say it more precisely, the previously demanded absolute insight into phenomenology itself is no longer shaped only around methodological reflections, but is essentially focused upon the problematic of *how* to begin philosophy and *why* to begin it again at all, especially since there have been so many other "beginnings" of philosophy in the past.

Remarkably enough, Husserl's claim of presuppositionlessness as a formerly basic feature in his concept of rigorous science vanishes to the extent in which another comes into focus, the claim of *justification* (VIII, 3; I, 52). That is, if phenomenology wishes to become first philosophy, it cannot start from a certain point of departure—even if it were something indubitably given—and then just look upon itself to see how its methods work for getting certain results. Rather, the phenomenological beginning is not only to be posited, but also to be justified *as* a beginning.

Ineluctably, it is a beginning in a certain historical situation. This matter of fact made Husserl get involved in history under another peculiar aspect: if there are philosophical theories and doctrines of the past, what was it that made all of them focus on something fundamental, ultimate, or first? Obviously they do not form an arbitrary historical sequence of systems; they do have something in common. Hence Husserl, in explicating his "Critical History of Ideas" as the first part of his *First Philosophy*, writes that the substance of his historical considerations is to uncover the unity of motivation persisting through the centuries, which has lived in all philosophy insofar as it has striven to become true philosophy (VII, 142).

This unity of motivation is displayed by Husserl as the idea of science. It works as a *telos* in all scientific activities; but it is only in philosophy that this *telos* comes to its radical efficacy (*Auswirkung*, VII, 294). Because only philosophy is guided by an interest that is otherwise, in the sciences and in our everyday life, dominated by practical purposes; only in philosophy does this interest come into its own. It is the interest in truth, and indeed "only on behalf of the truth itself" (VII, 203; VIII, 103). It is the interest to find out that that which has been posited as true is really true. It is an interest in the radical justification, demonstration, and manifestation (*Ausweisung*) of all truth, and thus it is a universal interest, since any singular truth has to be seen in the horizons of further truths and can be critically justified only by penetrating into its own horizon (I, 179).

Philosophy is in principle the only science that is, and is able, to follow this interest and bring it into its proper place amidst all our other interests in life. And according to Husserl it is by phenomenological means only that philosophy can accomplish this task: phenomenology, by its very essence, provides the means for the most radical questioning as well as the most effective clarification; and this holds even in regard to the necessity of phenomenology itself. Now Husserl realizes that phenomenology was until now not at all free of hidden assumptions as long as there had been no answer to the question of the necessity of phenomenology. To put it differently, it would amount to the absolute self-foundation of phenomenology, if phenomenology could show the necessity of its own existence.

It is from these considerations that we can understand why Husserl, in characterizing his first philosophy, finally refers to *self-responsibility*, and even equates it with the "ultimate foundation" of phenomenology (VIII, 197; V, 139). This does not only mean that phenomenological research is guided by a moral principle that the phenomenologist has personally adopted when seriously doing phenomenology. Rather, it means also and especially that self-responsibility in the sense Husserl has given to it is a responsibility to make truth appear for no other purpose than for truth itself. It is a self-responsibility, because there is no other insistence beyond that of our own self that makes us responsible for bringing truth to light.

First philosophy is "first" since it is exclusively guided by the idea of truth. Phenomenology is first philosophy since it is, in the final analysis, guided by the idea of responsibility for truth: to make truth our acquisition and thus to make ourselves participate in something that goes beyond our own single life, and thereby to make it a life of human dignity.

Index of Names